Principles of Philosophical Reasoning

APQ LIBRARY OF PHILOSOPHY
Nicholas Rescher, Editor

THE PHILOSOPHY OF CHARLES S. PEIRCE
A Critical Introduction
ROBERT ALMEDER

TWO CENTURIES OF PHILOSOPHY
American Philosophy Since the Revolution
PETER CAWS (ed.)

RATIONAL BELIEF SYSTEMS
BRIAN ELLIS

THE NATURE OF PHILOSOPHY
JOHN KEKES

INTRODUCTION TO THE
PHILOSOPHY OF MATHEMATICS
HUGH LEHMAN

VALUE AND EXISTENCE
JOHN LESLIE

RECENT WORK IN PHILOSOPHY
KENNETH G. LUCEY AND TIBOR R. MACHAN (eds.)

PLATO ON BEAUTY, WISDOM,
AND THE ARTS
JULIUS MORAVCSIK AND PHILIP TEMKO (eds.)

LEIBNIZ
An Introduction to His Philosophy
NICHOLAS RESCHER

THE LOGIC OF INCONSISTENCY
A Study in Nonstandard Possible-World
Semantics and Ontology
NICHOLAS RESCHER AND ROBERT BRANDOM

THE NATURE OF KNOWLEDGE
ALAN R. WHITE

Principles of
Philosophical Reasoning

Edited by
JAMES H. FETZER

ROWMAN & ALLANHELD
PUBLISHERS

ROWMAN & ALLANHELD

Published in the United States of America in 1984
by Rowman & Allanheld
(A division of Littlefield, Adams & Company)
81 Adams Drive, Totowa, New Jersey 07512

Library of Congress Cataloging in Publication Data
Main entry under title:

Principles of philosophical reasoning.

   (APQ library of philosophy)
   Bibliography: p.
   Includes indexes.
   1. Reasoning—Addresses, essays, lectures.
I. Fetzer, James H., 1940–   II. Series.
BC177.P74 1984   160   83-15985
ISBN 0-8476-7158-5

83 84 85 / 10 9 8 7 6 5 4 3 2 1

Printed in the United States of America

To
Carl G. Hempel

Contents

Preface   ix

Prologue

1   Philosophical Reasoning   3
    James H. Fetzer

Part One   **Philosophical Principles**

2   Questioning as a Philosophical Method   25
    Jaakko Hintikka
3   Classical Logic: Traditional and Modern   44
    James Cargile
4   The Verifiability Principle   71
    George Schlesinger
5   Infinite Regress Arguments   93
    David H. Sanford
6   Ockham's Razor   118
    J. J. C. Smart

Part Two   **Philosophy and Science**

7   Scientific and Philosophical Argument   131
    Henry E. Kyburg, Jr.
8   The Method of Counterexample   151
    George Schlesinger
9   Explanation in Philosophy and in Science   172
    Paul Humphreys
10   Transcendental and Dialectical Thinking   190
    Douglas C. Berggren

11   Philosophical Refutations   227
         Hector-Neri Castaneda

Epilogue

12   The Argument from Ordinary Language   261
         Michael Scriven

References   278
Index of Names   286
Index of Subjects   288
Contributors   293

Preface

The purpose of this anthology is to present a collection of original articles devoted to exploring the existence and character of distinctively philosophical principles of inference and patterns of argument in an endeavor to better understand the theoretical structure of philosophical reasoning. Part One consists of five investigations concerning modes of reasoning that might be viewed as potential candidates within such a context, including the Socratic method (of questions and answers), deductive reasoning, inductive reasoning, infinite regress arguments, and appeals to Ockham's Razor. Part Two consists of five additional investigations concerning relations between modes of reasoning as they occur in science and in philosophy, including the exchange of language frameworks, the method of counterexample, explanation in philosophy and in science, transcendental, dialectical and scientific reasoning, and theoretical reasoning, in general. The collection begins with a critical introduction and ends with an attempt to evaluate the philosophical significance of appeals to ordinary language by a comparison with scientific methodology.

The conception of this project originated with George Schlesinger, who suggested that we co-edit an anthology with this specific theme. We agreed to work together but, during our deliberations, arrived at the decision that George would be a double contributor, while I would become the book's editor. In that capacity, I have assumed responsibility for the organization and the contents of this collection, at least to the extent to which its contributors have been responsive to editorial invitations. I am grateful to the one who met every deadline and fulfilled every obligation as well as to the many who did not: but for them, we would have no anthology at all. I have exercised the editor's prerogative by dedicating this book to Carl G. Hempel, whose work has served as a paradigm of lucid and penetrating philosophical analysis for five decades and whose influence has been as enormous as it has been deserved. Perhaps only those of us fortunate enough to have been his students are fully aware of his gifts as a teacher; yet, by his work and by his example, we have all learned from him. There are some debts, alas, that can never be repaid.

J.H.F.

Prologue

1 Philosophical Reasoning

James H. Fetzer

The issue under consideration here concerns the existence and character of distinctively philosophical principles of inference and patterns of argument, if, indeed, there are any at all. It is entirely possible, of course, that 'modes of reasoning' might exist that involve neither 'principles of inference' nor 'patterns of argument' as these notions are ordinarily understood. Should this be the case, then there could be 'modes of philosophical reasoning' that involve neither "philosophical principles of inference" nor "philosophical patterns of argument." Moreover, assuming the difference between syntax, semantics, and pragmatics, relative to a language framework L, it might be the case that, even if there were no distinctively philosophical 'principles of inference' or 'patterns of argument,' from either a syntactical or a semantical point of view, nevertheless, there could be "distinctively philosophical" objectives, aims, or goals, in which case what is distinctive about philosophy might be a function of content rather than of reasoning.

Within the present context, therefore, the purpose of this introduction is, first, to attempt to elucidate the basic characteristics of 'principles of inference' and of 'patterns of argument,' in general, and, second, to attempt to identify at least some of the crucial

Special thanks to David Smillie, James Moseley, and Douglas Berggren for stimulating my thinking on various aspects of these important questions.

issues that are examined, in particular, in the papers that follow. The place to begin, no doubt, is the distinction between 'the context of discovery' and 'the context of justification,' where "the context of discovery" refers to creative thinking in which 'reasons' do not matter. Methods of discovery are usually viewed as sources of thoughts and ideas, including, but not restricted to, imagination and conjecture, while procedures of justification are typically viewed as standards for assessing the preferability or the acceptability of various theories and hypotheses, especially those appropriate to inductive and to deductive modes of reasoning. Indeed, imagination and conjecture would seem to be 'modes of reasoning' involving neither principles of inference nor patterns of argument at all.

Another important distinction, of course, is that between normative and descriptive conceptions, where "descriptive" accounts of reasoning describe 'modes of reasoning' that actually are employed by thinking things, whereas "normative" accounts prescribe those that should be relied upon by thinking things— two classes whose members by no means invariably coincide. Even if experimental psychology were completely successful in describing and classifying those 'modes of reasoning' upon which we actually rely, this would not establish that these are the most effective, the most reliable, or the most efficient to secure a specified objective, aim, or goal. The distinguishing feature of creative thinking itself, within science and without, perhaps, is that it need not satisfy normative constraints: as Carl G. Hempel, for example, has often emphasized, while hypotheses and theories can be *accepted* into the body of scientific knowledge only if they pass critical scrutiny, they can be freely invented and *proposed* (cf. Hempel 1966, p. 16).

Although experimental psychology, in principle, cannot bridge the abyss between descriptive and normative conceptions, it can contribute to a causal account of creative thinking by investigating the kinds of conditions under which various types of creative thinking tend to occur. Causal explanations within the context of the psychology of discovery (as a descriptive domain) appear to be a theoretical possibility, therefore, even if they lack the potential to apply within the context of a logic of discovery (as a normative domain). Yet Sir Karl Popper has raised significant difficulties for the prediction of innovative thinking—even within the context of the psychology of discovery—which deserve careful consideration

(Popper 1982, pp. 64–67, and elsewhere). Indeed, if Popper's arguments are correct, then the psychology of discovery might provide a fruitful source of counterexamples to the symmetry of explanation and prediction—even in its qualified form, according to which every adequate explanation is potentially a prediction, though not conversely.

Yet another distinction ought to be drawn between those 'modes of reasoning' that apply to reasons, grounds, or evidence in the form of *sentences* and those that do not. Thus, perceptual inference, involving the description of findings of more-or-less immediate experience, requires the employment of some language framework L, yet, like creative thinking, appears to be subject to a causal as opposed to a logical analysis. The acquisition, utilization, and alteration of a language framework, after all, seem to involve the acquisition, utilization, and alteration of a (perhaps immensely complex) set of linguistic dispositions, where the process of acquiring, of exercising, and of modifying these linguistic dispositions is undoubtedly subject to psychological investigation. There then appear to be at least two different kinds of dispositions involved here: namely, those whose exercise results in descriptions of more-or-less immediate experience in the characteristic form of singular sentences, and those whose exercise involves the application of 'principles of inference.'

The distinction under consideration, in other words, is intended to mark a difference between 'principles of inference' as modes of reasoning that apply to sets of sentences as "premises," relative to other sentences as their "conclusions," and other modes of reasoning which, although perhaps involving linguistic dispositions, yield "conclusions" in the form of sentences *without* applying to sets of sentences as their "premises." Nothing said here is supposed to imply or presuppose whether inductive or deductive inference is, for example, from singular premises to general conclusions or from general premises to singular conclusions, respectively, formulations that almost invariably fail to capture the fundamental properties of inductive and of deductive reasoning as 'patterns of argument' that apply directly to sentential premises. Nevertheless, although inductive and deductive reasoning both involve 'principles of inference' from sentential premises to sentential conclusions, they may be differentiated on the basis of (at least) three fundamental features.

In the case of deductive reasoning, the principal pragmatic desideratum to be fulfilled is that deductive principles of inference are supposed to be *truth-preserving*, in the sense that the patterns of argument that they permit are such that, when applied to true premises, only true conclusions can be obtained. Thus, (successful) deductive arguments are (i) demonstrative, i.e., when their premises are true, their conclusions cannot be false; (ii) nonampliative, i.e., there is no information (or content) in their conclusions that is not already (implicitly or explicitly) contained in their premises; and (iii) additive, i.e., the addition of further information in the form of additional premises can neither strengthen nor weaken arguments such as these, which are already "maximally strong." Their nonampliative character, of course, may be invoked to explain their demonstrative character, insofar as the truth of their premises guarantees the truth of any conclusions that merely recapitulate some or all of the content of those true premises.

In the case of inductive reasoning, the principal pragmatic disideratum to be fulfilled is that inductive principles of inference are supposed to be *knowledge-expanding*, in the sense that those patterns of argument which they permit are such that, when applied to true premises, informative conclusions can be obtained. Thus, (successful) inductive arguments are (i) ampliative, i.e., there is information (or content) in their conclusions that is not already (implicitly or explicitly) contained in their premises; (ii) nonde-monstrative, i.e., their conclusions can be false, even when their premises are true; and (iii) nonadditive, i.e., the addition of further evidence in the form of additional premises can either strengthen or weaken arguments such as these. Thus, their ampliative character may be invoked to explain their nondemonstrative character, insofar as the truth of their premises cannot guarantee the truth of conclusions whose content goes beyond that of those premises, since this additional content may be false even when those premises are true.

In Chapter 2, Jaakko Hintikka suggests that 'questioning' is important not only within philosophy but also as a process for information acquisition generally. The method of questions-and-answers, of course, represents a mode of inquiry employed by parents, teachers, and philosophers since well before the time of Socrates. The questions that are actually asked and the answers that are actually given (by children, students, and all the rest) are

themselves subject to descriptive inquiries and to statistical sum-
maries. Yet, as he remarks, we are not likely to understand how
answers to questions can yield information until we know what
counts as an answer—i.e., as a full, intended, and conclusive
answer—to a given question. The issue Hintikka explores is not
the descriptive one of what answers are actually accepted, but
rather the normative one of what answers should be accepted, as
full, intended and complete answers, to a given question, while
elaborating the view that "deductive logic is likely to yield the
best clues to effective questioning."

Since Hintikka proposes an analysis of information by relying
on reference to the elimination of certain alternative situations,
courses of events, or states of affairs (as "possible worlds"), no
doubt some theoreticians may believe that his remedy is worse
than the malady it is intended to cure; but "possible worlds" as
possible ways the world might have been or might yet be are
virtually inescapable, even for those firmly committed to completely
extensional or truth-functional language frameworks: accommodating the truth-value "false" as well as the truth-value "true"
already involves distinguishing between the way things are and
the way(s) things might be. Thus, it may be more intriguing to
consider the extent to which Hintikka can sustain the thesis of
the primacy of deduction in questioning, not with respect to
presuppositions, of course, but rather in relation to "non-trivial
reasoning"—involving the introduction of new entities, for example—since it is not entirely obvious how nonampliative reasoning
can be knowledge-expanding, nonetheless.

It should come as no surprise, however, that an adequate analysis
of issues of this kind inevitably involves matters of logical form,
which tend to fall within the domain of deductive inquiries. Those
who are inclined to believe that these issues are "cut and dry"
should benefit from close study of James Cargile's consideration
of alternative interpretations of "classical logic" in Chapter 3, which
is entertained as that of first-order predicate calculi with identity.
He proposes the definition of "deductive logic" as the study of
formal proof (or as the analysis of formal validity), while pointing
out that what makes a sentence form or an argument form a 'logical
form' is not a purely formal question. The distinction that he
draws between "traditional" and "modern" conceptions, moreover,
has to do with their relative degrees of emphasis upon semantical

and syntactical properties, respectively, where Cargile claims that the traditional construction enjoys certain advantages over the modern.

During his examination of (at least) four distinct approaches to understanding "the laws of logic," such as theorems of the form, '$(x)(Fx \lor \sim Fx)$', Cargile suggests that each approach offers a different analysis: the model-theoretic approach, for example, tells us that every thing within the domain of x is a member of, say, the class of mortals or not; the property approach, by comparison, tells us that every thing x either has the property of being mortal or does not; the linguistic-translational approach tells us that this symbolizes, perhaps, "Everyone is either mortal or not mortal"; and the linguistic-substitutional approach tells us that the form, "_____ is mortal $\lor$ _____ is not mortal" yields a logical truth for all uniform interpretations of expressions of the right sort. Yet none of these claims is a logical law. Cargile himself ultimately endorses the position that the laws of logic are best viewed as "generalizations about propositions," in the sense that they convey such claims as, that every proposition is either true or false, that no proposition is both true and false, and so forth, the defense of which itself involves difficult problems about propositions and their individuation.

If the theoretical foundations of deductive reasoning are not completely settled, the situation with respect to inductive reasoning appears to be much worse. The principal difficulty, of course, is distinguishing inductive reasoning from inferential fallacies, for innumerable fallacious arguments seem capable of satisfying the conditions of being (i) ampliative, (ii) nondemonstrative, and (iii) nonadditive. Even if the corresponding conditions are sufficient to identify (acceptable) deductive principles of inference, (i), (ii), and (iii) are not sufficient to identify (acceptable) principles of inductive inference. If we adopt standard terminology for deductive arguments possessing the demonstrative property as "valid" arguments, where those that are both valid and have true premises are also "sound," then inductive arguments possessing the ampliative property may be referred to as "proper" and those that are both proper and have true premises as "correct"; yet there is no generally accepted account of the conditions for an argument to be proper.

In order to appreciate George Schlesinger's first contribution to this volume (Chapter 4), therefore, it is essential to distinguish between "verifiability" as a deductive conception and as an inductive conception; for while a hypothesis or a theory *h* is usually regarded as 'verifiable' relative to some logically consistent, finite set of evidence sentences *e* just in case *e* entails *h*, as a deductive relation (of "conclusive confirmation," let us say), this paper is concerned with the inductive relation (of "partial verification," let us say) that obtains when *e* confirms *h*, even though *e* does not entail *h*. Thus, Schlesinger's primary concern is with conditions of adequacy that ought to be fulfilled by acceptable principles of inductive inference; in particular, he proposes the condition that, if hypothesis *h* stands in the relation *R* to evidence *e*, while an alternative hypothesis ~*h* also stands in the relation *R* to *e*, then *e* cannot confirm *h* by virtue of standing in the relation *R* to *e:* no acceptable principle of inductive inference may violate this requirement.

To illustrate the significance of his principle, Schlesinger applies it to the hypothetico-deductive conception of scientific inference and to Ayer's empiricist criterion of sentential meaningfulness. According to hypothetico-deductive conceptions of scientific inference, for example, any hypothesis *h* is confirmed by an observation sentence *e* when *h* together with independently established auxiliary hypotheses entail *e*, provided that *e* is not entailed by those individual hypothesis alone. Schlesinger thus considers the "auxiliary hypothesis" obtained by forming the material conditional, *h* ⊃ *e*, where *h* and this auxiliary hypothesis together entail *e*, yet *e* is not entailed by either *h* or *h* ⊃ *e* alone. However, as he points out, this conception, which fails to fulfill his condition of adequacy, can be satisfied by any number of alternative hypotheses h^1, h^2, . . . , so long as *e* itself is well-confirmed, since the corresponding material conditionals $h^1 ⊃ e$, $h^2 ⊃ e$, . . . , must be too.

Similar considerations obtain for Ayer's empiricist criterion of sentential meaningfulness, of course, according to which a sentence *S* is meaningful if *S* together with other hypotheses entails observation sentences *O* that are not entailed by those auxiliary hypotheses alone. The appropriate inference to draw may or may not be beyond debate, however, since these arguments might be variously regarded as (a) undermining hypothetico-deductivism and Ayer's criterion, (b) objections to reliance upon extensional language within this context, or, perhaps, (c) inviting revised versions of these conceptions employing more adequate constructions (which

seems to be Schlesinger's view). Among the important issues
involved here are (i) whether this principle applies to contrary
hypotheses, h^1, h^2, . . . , in general, or to the formal contradictory
$\sim h$ of a given hypothesis h, exclusively, and (ii) whether this
principle presupposes the converse consequence condition (if e
confirms h, then e confirms any hypothesis entailing h) as well as
the special consequence condition (if e confirms h, then e confirms
any hypothesis h entails), which ought to be pursued in relation
to Hempel and Oppenheim (1945) and Hempel (1965b).

Some types of arguments, of course, are unsatisfactory less for
formal reasons than for informal reasons, such as failure to fulfill
their intended informative function. No doubt, to define "x knows
that p" by means of the definiens "x knows that q and q entails
p" would be no more acceptable than to explain the origin of
human life by conjuring up colonies of ancient astronauts from
distant galaxies. These are uncomplicated examples of reasoning
involving regresses, several sophisticated versions of which are
investigated in Chapter 5 by David Sanford, who distinguishes
between "negative" and "positive" kinds: negative regress arguments, in effect, are cited as grounds counting against a conclusion,
while positive regress arguments are offered as grounds favoring
a conclusion instead. Thus, Sanford examines Mellor's reformulation
of McTaggart's argument against the reality of time, which, he
contends, fails to distinguish an infinite series of increasingly
complex 'descriptions' of tensed facts from an infinite series of
increasingly complex tensed facts.

Aquinas's attempt to prove the existence of God as the unmoved
mover (as the uncaused cause, and so on) and Aristotle's effort to
prove the existence of ends that are desired for their own sake are
examples of positive regress arguments. Sanford undertakes the
appraisal of Aristotle's argument, which, he suggests, depends upon
the elimination of infinite series of desires and of closed loops of
desires. As an illustration of a closed loop of desires, he offers the
case of John, who wants to make more money in order to buy
expensive suits in order to wear them to the bank in order to
impress bankers in order to obtain more loans in order to invest
in certain schemes in order to make more money. While it is not
entirely clear that this 'closed loop' might not be better viewed
as an 'open spiral' (since John wants *more* money to buy *new*
suits to impress *other* bankers, and so forth), an interpretation of

this sort leads to an infinite series of desires: either way, therefore, Sanford seems to have shown that regress arguments are difficult to defend.

The principle of simplicity, of parsimony, or of economy (as it is variously known) has proven surprisingly hard to define. In Chapter 6, J.J.C. Smart begins by distinguishing the "ontic" formulation, which applies directly to the way things are, from its "epistemic" versions, which apply instead to the way we think things are; for, as Mill asked, how could we know that nature itself satisfies such a principle? As Smart sees it, the literal version of Ockham's (or "Occam's") Principle ("It is in vain to do by many what can be done by fewer") should be displaced by the version that, other things being equal, we should prefer simpler to complex theories. Ultimately, however, Smart remains doubtful that the assumption that simpler theories are more likely to be true than are their complex alternatives can be sustained: quantum mechanics and general relativity, after all, are neither easily understood nor easily applied. It is tempting to conclude that Ockham's Razor, like the principle of induction, lies beyond justification.

Smart concedes that he himself has sometimes misapplied considerations of simplicity ("Entities must not be multiplied beyond necessity") in arguments favoring the elimination of mental states by brain states; for, when properly unpacked, his position assumed what it was intended to prove: if it is not necessary to postulate nonphysical mental entities, they should not be postulated; it is not necessary to postulate nonphysical mental entities; therefore, they should not be postulated. Perhaps what is critical about simplicity after all, Smart suggests, is a function of plausibility; perhaps "plausibility in the light of total science is the best touchstone of metaphysical truth" and philosophical arguments play an ancillary role. Or (to advance another view) perhaps the underlying desideratum is really 'elegance' rather than 'simplicity,' in the sense of deriving maximal sets of consequences from minimal sets of assumptions in order to maximize, say, explanatory power (in science) or theoretical significance (in philosophy).

These reflections tend to support the possibility that the same 'principles of reasoning' might apply in science and in philosophy alike, which Henry E. Kyburg, Jr. endorses in his analysis of these questions in Chapter 7. He contends there are three basic forms of argument, two of which—deductive inference and statistical inference—involve transformations within a given language framework, while the third involves the replacement of one framework Lⁱ by another Lʲ. Kyburg focuses his attention upon the exchange of one language for another, especially since, when languages are regarded as representing relations of meaning, "then the choice between alternative languages is simultaneously a choice between systems of *a priori* truths." He argues that this issue ought to be resolved by adopting the principle of preferring some language L whose accepted sentences yield the largest number of predictively significant observational consequences, while suggesting that the choice between 'phenomenalistic' and 'realistic' language frameworks can be evaluated on this basis.

Among the fascinating features of Kyburg's presentation is his critique of "the classical line" in philosophical reasoning: namely, the tendency to attempt to derive necessary conclusions from 'clear and distinct' intuitions by means of deductive arguments. This approach almost always precipitates a controversy between conflicting intuitions, generating endless disputes. In Kyburg's view, even the persuasive force of 'counterexamples' to philosophical theses is a function of their intuitive appeal. Intuitive approaches in philosophy, however, are no more likely to yield philosophical benefits than intuitive approaches in science would be likely to yield scientific progress. Indeed, the shortcomings of appeals to intuition appear to be rooted in their similarities to the exercise of imagination and of other methods of discovery that lack a normative dimension: perhaps, as he recommends, the function of counterexamples should be construed as that of representing classes of cases that, as with moral principles and specific instances, require adjudication.

The role of counterexamples in science and in philosophy, no doubt, is enormously different, since scientific counterexamples arise in the form of observations and experiments that stand in conflict with hypotheses and theories. Thus the intersubjective reliability of agreements upon the results of perceptual inference generally outweighs the informative content provided by incompatible generalizations as a function of proper inductive reasoning, even though the "experiential findings" to which inductive principles apply are by no means guaranteed to be true. Nevertheless, in spite of its apparent infirmities, perhaps no technique is more frequently utilized in philosophical controversy than is the counterexample technique, as Schlesinger emphasizes in his second contribution to this volume (Chapter 8), which is an attempt to diagnose the theoretical significance of this widely employed method. Thus, Schlesinger especially castigates the familiar tendency to salvage positions from philosophical refutation by minor adjustments to effect *ad hoc* rescues.

As illustrations of his contentions, Schlesinger discusses four cases: Hempel's analysis of explanation, Harman's definition of "knowledge," Plantinga's conception of induction, and Pollock's interpretation of subjunctive conditionals. He argues, for example, that alleged counterexamples to Hempel's analysis of explanation have failed to appreciate an underlying desideratum: namely, that "explanations" cannot explain the occurrence of event E if there are "counterparts" explaining the occurrence of $\sim E$ equally well, as would be the case relative to an explanans consisting of any true generalization T, any instance it entails I, and the events E and $\sim E$ alike, when T and $I \supset E$ "explains" E, yet T and $I \supset \sim E$ "explains" $\sim E$ in a parallel way. If Schlesinger is on the right track—and no explanation occurs if there is a contrary counterpart, in his sense—then if contrary counterparts invariably exist (relative to a specific explication of explanation), then there are no explanations (relative to that specific explication).

There is room for potential dissent over whether or not Schlesinger has captured the crucial aspects of each of these examples: "An act of explanation," he says, "essentially consists in pointing out the unique conditions that exist which unequivocally require that E (the explanandum-sentence) be true"; for it could be maintained (a) that explanations are intended to explain why their explanandum-events occur; (b) that explanations are not required to establish the truth of their explananda; and, (c) that probabilistic explanations, in any case, could not possibly satisfy such a conception. In his investigation of philosophical explanations in relation to scientific realism, for example, Humphreys suggests that (explanation-seeking) why-questions characteristically arise only when (reason-seeking) why-questions have already been answered, since explanations are only sought when a questioner has reason to believe that the explanandum-sentences (describing the events to be explained) are true, perhaps by means of prior perceptual inferences. Nevertheless, few are likely to disagree with Schlesinger's principal point: namely, that counterexamples should be recognized as symptoms of what may well be more deeply rooted maladies, which are the source of these difficulties.

In Chapter 9, Paul Humphreys attempts to ascertain the extent to which "philosophical" and "scientific" explanations might satisfy the same adequacy conditions, taking Hempel's original criteria as his point of departure. A crucial problem he encounters, therefore, is locating suitable substitutes for "covering laws" (in scientific explanations) to serve as general premises (in philosophical explanations), a function that, he claims, can be fulfilled, at least in principle, by "methodological inference principles." Humphreys offers the conception of philosophical explanations as explanations in which at least one of the explanatory premises has philosophical content, which is unlikely to be illuminating without an independent account of "philosophical content." He explores the logical structure of several kinds of philosophical exchange, including an analysis of the role of impossibility theorems within this context. And he observes that "philosophical methods," in general, should "be free, as far as it is possible, from presuppositions which automatically exclude particular philosophical positions," a consideration that motivates his exploration of the extent to which the condition of truth for "explanations" entails commitments to realism as opposed to instrumentalism.

Not the least valuable feature of Humphreys's discussion is his analysis of appeals to the principle of the common cause, which serves as a paradigm for consideration of philosophical explanations that postulate new entities within the framework of "inference to the best explanation." According to the common cause principle, if a collection of phenomena occurs with a frequency higher than would occur merely by chance (and there is no direct causal connection between them), "then their joint occurrence *must* be explained by appeal to a common cause." A difficulty that he does not consider is how the conditions required for its application are ascertainable, in principle; that is, when *does* a certain class of phenomena "occur with a frequency higher than would occur merely by chance"? Nevertheless, he argues (i) that this principle is weaker than the principle of sufficient reason; (ii) that it is also weaker than the principle of universal causation; (iii) that it does not claim to apply to explanations in abstract domains; (iv) that it can be used to support different types of explanations; and (v) that it does not entail the explainability of every actual regularity.

Indeed, this last point is an important one, since realists would be committed to explanatory circularities or to explanatory regresses, if there could never be "unexplained explainers." Douglas C. Berggren's contribution (Chapter 10), which is also concerned with relations between scientific and philosophical patterns of argument, has three primary aspects: first, an analysis of (Kantian) "transcendental" and of (Hegelian) "dialectical" reasoning; second, an account of (what he refers to as) archaeological, teleological, and semiological kinds of explanation (within a transcendental framework); and third, a consideration of several alternative principles of identity. According to Berggren's reconstructions, transcendental reasoning is committed to the discovery of the essential presuppositions of scientific and nonscientific modes of thinking, while dialectical reasoning attempts to demonstrate "how apparently unavoidable conflicts not only can, but must, be mitigated." Thus, it would be interesting to explore the extent to which transcendental reasoning involves the application of deductive principles of inference as well as whether dialectical reasoning might arise from the need to satisfy "total evidence" requirements within these philosophical contexts.

In Berggren's account, there are three rather different varieties of explanation: archaeological explanations, for example, explain the occurrence of inert events as the result of certain antecedent conditions that are sufficient for their occurrence (as manifestations of causal necessities); teleological explanations, however, explain the occurrence of intentional actions as necessary in order to realize desired ends (as manifestations of instrumental necessities); while semiological explanations, by comparison, explain the occurrences to which they apply as "mere signifieds," made possible by their linguistic and cultural contexts (as manifestations of conventional necessities). Thus, it is worthwhile to consider the possibility that these varied types of explanation might be subsumable under a more general analysis, such as Hempel's covering-law account, for example, and still have to satisfy the same conditions, in spite of their initial appearance of enormous diversity. But Berggren's blend of continental and analytical approaches is intriguing.

The three principles of identity that he considers are the following: everything is what it is (a) and not something else (Plato); (b) only by virtue of being other than what it is not (Hegel); and (c) only by virtue of being other than itself (Derrida). Without attempting an evaluation of these principles, it would be beneficial to compare this discussion with Cargile's discussion of standard principles of identity within first-order predicate calculi. The principles of the identity of indiscernibles and of the indiscernibility of identicals, of course, are logically equivalent to the second-order principle, $(x)(y)[(x = y) \equiv (F)(Fx \equiv Fy)]$, which, however, should be displaced by the principle, $(x)(y)[(x = y) \equiv (t)(F)(Fxt \equiv Fyt)]$, insofar as things may gain or lose properties while still remaining the same things—with the understanding that proper names denote distinctively different members of presupposed reference classes, where things cease to be members of such a class when they no longer instantiate some reference property. Issues of identity, moreover, are important to several of the papers presented here, including Hintikka's analysis of the logic of questions and answers.

It would be wrong to imply that principles of identity such as these are altogether uncontroversial. Cargile himself, for example, suggests that such principles involve the choice between "chronologizing" properties and denying identity across time. The "chronologization of properties," however, may be more adequately viewed as the "chronologization of predications" in order to avoid the blunder of embracing infinitely many properties (for each ordinary property) rather than infinitely many instances (of each such property) without sacrificing identity across time and without violating Ockham's Principle. Castaneda, by comparison, raises a host of problems of another kind about identity in the form of "the paradox of reference," which reflects the importance of intentional elements in the analysis of identity relations. An individual named or described by the name or description 'x' might be identical with the individual named or described by the name or description 'y,' and yet others—or even that individual himself— might be unaware that this is so, in which case someone could believe, for example, that 'Fxt' and '$\sim Fyt$' were both true, where it appears as though something is true of x that is not also true of y, contrary to the assumption of their identity and the principles offered above.

In his discussion of "the paradox of reference" in Chapter 11, Hector-Neri Castaneda indicates (at least) six alternative approaches toward its resolution, while elaborating in some detail the account that he recommends, namely, *guise theory*, according to which a distinction should be drawn between "sameness" and strict identity, where the latter but not the former satisfies $(x)(y)[(x = y) \equiv (F)(Fx \equiv Fy)]$, or its chronologized counterpart. This distinction largely depends upon differentiating between "epistemic sameness" (which is a function of belief) and "worldly sameness" (which is a function of truth). It might be maintained that "the paradox of reference" is really an illusion, on grounds such as that, even if someone z believed 'Fxt' and '$\sim Fyt$' (when $x = y$, of which z is unaware), it would not mean that something were true of x that were not also true of y; for any (unwittingly false) belief that z has about x at t is also an (unwittingly false) belief that z has about y at t. And, while this account (almost certainly) is not one that he would be willing to accept, it is also (almost certainly) not one that he would claim to refute: in Castaneda's view, philosophical theories may be more (or less) adequate than their alternatives, yet, in general, they are incapable of refutation.

According to his conception of philosophy, the primary objective that has dominated its history is to understand the structure of the world and of experience; nevertheless, we are not entitled to assume that one theory ("the master theory") has to emerge as the asymptotic limit of our collective efforts. As a consequence, the development of successively more and more comprehensive theories is the method most likely to contribute toward philosophical advances. Appeals to Ockham's Razor are comparatively unimportant, since its application to theories is complex and since we have no reason to believe the world is simple. Counterexamples are comparatively unimportant too, except in expanding our evidential resources, because philosophical theories characteristically cannot be proven to be false. Criticism of philosophical theories ought to be comprehensive and wholistic, because arguments ($p \supset q$ and p entails q) are otherwise subject to piecemeal complaints (q does not follow from $p \supset q$ and q also does not follow from p). Ultimately, language serves as our guide in the construction of philosophical theories, since our conception of the world and of experience is given by "the structure of all the semantico-syntactic contrasts of our language."

Castaneda's rejection of refutation as philosophically insignificant stands in marked contrast to Popper's conception of "conjectures and refutations" (or of "trial and error") as the fundamental method of inquires within science and without. It should be emphasized, therefore, that the negative significance of *successful* attempts at refutation falls within the domain of deductive methodology, while the positive significance of *unsuccessful* attempts at refutation falls within the domain of inductive methodology (cf. Fetzer 1981, p. 176). Thus, while Popper would agree to the crucial importance of developing more and more comprehensive theories, part of his rationale is that their successively greater and greater content renders them increasingly vulnerable to refutation. Moreover, while Popper's approach suggests that inductive and deductive reasoning are the primary methods of inquiry (apart from imagination and conjecture), it is much less obvious that Castaneda entertains precisely the same conception.

Michael Scriven's contribution (Chapter 12) is devoted to the question of whether there is some type of appeal to (or argument from) ordinary language that not only avoids the assumption that "what everybody says is so must be so," on the one hand, but also the paradigm case presupposition that ordinary usage is "one about which we cannot be mistaken." He suggests that, while serious investigations of what words mean must begin by separating correct from incorrect usage (by ascertaining cases in which those words properly apply as well as those in which they do not), nevertheless, those who appeal to ordinary language are characteristically proposing *working definitions* for specific concepts, which is highly analogous to proposing *working hypotheses* for scientific phenomena. Thus, even though arguments from ordinary language are occasionally at fault for committing certain sorts of fallacious appeals (by their denial of linguistic arbitrariness, by their reduction of philosophy to triviality, and so on), these are not features which no appeal to ordinary language could do without and still serve its purpose.

In lieu of the old "paradox of analysis" according to which either we already know what we are talking about (in fitting meanings to words), in which case philosophy is trivial, or else we do not know what we are talking about (in fitting meanings to words), in which case philosophy is impossible, Scriven offers a new dilemma confronting "solutions by definition" according to which either we define an old word by means of a new word (but why should we bother?), generating the problem of irrelevance, or else we redefine that old word by a specific proposal (but which should we adopt?), generating the problem of imperfection. And, even though some may quarrel with one or more of Scriven's own examples (he contends, for instance, that there are not two senses of probability, only one), it is difficult to disagree with his claim that, although it is hazardous rather than trivial to propose a redefinition of existing terms, it can be a worthwhile undertaking, nevertheless—not in the simplification of complex concepts but for the benefit of the development of theories.

It is reasonable to suppose, of course, that different activities have different aims, objectives, and goals: empirical science, for example, aims at the discovery of laws of nature, in general, while physics, chemistry and so forth focus upon discovering the laws of physics, of chemistry, and so on, as features of the physical world. The philosophy of science, by comparison, aims instead at the discovery of a theoretical and conceptual framework that might provide an adequate understanding of empirical science as an activity that is able to fulfill its intended role. From such a point of view, the philosophy of science is a "higher order" (or a "meta-level") activity, which takes empirical science as its own object of inquiry, and similar considerations obtain for the philosophy of religion, the philosophy of language, and all the rest. Inquiries of this kind may serve (at least) three functions: first, ascertaining whether or not a certain aim, objective, or goal is attainable at all (a matter of *exoneration*); second, ascertaining the principles and procedures by which it can be attained (a matter of *vindication*); and, third, ascertaining those instances in which it has been attained (a matter of *validation*). These kinds of inquiries thus constitute special types of justificatory activities (Fetzer 1981, ch. 7).

A structural engineer, of course, could be described as engaging in the profession of ascertaining whether or not particular structures can be built, of ascertaining the principles and procedures by means of which those structures can be built, and even of ascertaining instances in which such structures have been built. In order to secure the appropriate conception, therefore, the "higher order" (or the "meta-level") aspect of philosophical investigations needs to be emphsized; for, in their most characteristic respects, philosophical investigations are focused upon particular *linguistic contexts*, where crucial notions may be either ambiguous or vague or otherwise insufficiently well defined to serve their intended roles. For distinctively philosophical investigations are (implicitly or explicitly) directed toward the discovery of theoretical and conceptual frameworks adequate for understanding an activity or a domain, especially through the formulation of proposals concerning the most adequate use of language to achieve this specific goal. Thus, a structural engineer would be engaged in a philosophical investigation if, say, he were concerned with the development of a theoretical and conceptual framework adequate for understanding how engineering can fulfill its intended role.

Once these conceptual and theoretical foundations have been laid, then an activity or a domain ceases to be an area of active philosophical interest but instead tends to become amenable to routines. The construction of proofs within the predicate calculus is generally not a philosophically interesting activity, by virtue of having been reduced to a matter of routines; yet, particular aspects of the deductive domain, especially concerning its foundations, continue to invite philosophical investigation. Cargile's aim, for example, is to discern the properties that should be displayed for a form to qualify as a "logical form." Hintikka's goal, analogously, is to discover requirements that ought to be satisfied for an "answer" to qualify as full, intended, and complete. Schlesinger's objective is to explore the criteria that should be met for evidence *e* to "confirm" a hypothesis *h*. And similarly for the rest. These inquiries advance (implicit or explicit) proposals regarding the most adequate theoretical and conceptual frameworks to adopt within their domain, where these recommendations have the character of "explications" in a sense that Hempel has refined; for theory construction and concept formation are so closely related as to be inextricably interwined (Hempel 1952, pt. II).

The criteria by which a proposed explication may be assessed, moreover, are essentially intersubjective. An adequate explication must satisfy conditions of *syntactical determinacy*, i.e., the logical form of the characteristic contexts within which the explicated term is correctly used must be made explicit; of *definitional relevance*, i.e., there must exist some nontrivial context of usage within which the term explicated actually occurs in that language; and of *theoretical significance*, i.e., the purported explication must further our understanding of the corresponding activity or domain. Thus, if these reflections are well founded, then the principal difference between the ordinary language approach reflected by Scriven and the explicative approach represented by Hempel perhaps consists in a difference in degrees of emphasis on the relevance criterion and on the significance criterion, respectively. Hence, from this perspective, philosophy itself is properly regarded as a normative approach toward understanding both language and the world.

The fact that these authors approach these problems from such a point of view, no doubt, can be dismissed as inductive evidence for an ampliative conclusion, which may be false, nevertheless. And, indeed, this objection must be right, since even if almost all who call themselves "philosophers" were preoccupied with descriptive inquiries instead, that in itself would not be enough to demonstrate that this account is wrong: philosophical recommendations, as Castaneda recognizes, are almost impossible to refute. Moreover, philosophy can no more properly be viewed as what the members of a presumptive *community of philosophers* do than science can be adequately defined as what the members of the presumptive *community of scientists* do: insofar as the possibility of "malpractice" remains, the principles and procedures by which a discipline is defined cannot be adequately ascertained by empirical methods alone (Fetzer 1981, ch. 1). That the conception of philosophy advocated here might be received as "hopelessly old-fashioned" by those who embrace historical and relative constructions, of course, I acknowledge willingly but without apology. For 'philosophy' is not what the philosophers do; on the contrary, the 'philosophers' are those who do philosophy.

PART ONE

Philosophical
Principles

2 Questioning as a Philosophical Method

Jaakko Hintikka

1. Questioning as a General Knowledge-Seeking Method

Questioning is not only an important philosophical method; it offers a useful model for many different types of knowledge-seeking. For the time being, I shall in fact treat questioning as a process of information-gathering in general. Only later, once the structure of information-seeking by questioning has been discussed, can we see how variants of this method are particularly adept to serve the purposes of philosophical thinking.

The best known historical paradigm of questioning as a philosophical method is the Socratic *elenchus*.[1] It is of interest to see how several aspects of this celebrated technique can be understood and put into a perspective on the basis of my analysis of questioning as a philosophical method.

Before doing so, we nevertheless have to look at the logical structure of question-answer sequences. Here the first question that is likely to come up is probably going to be the skeptical one: What's so new about the idea of questioning, anyway, as a knowledge-seeking method? It is one of the first ideas likely to occur to anyone interested in philosophical or scientific or hermeneutical method, and it has in fact occurred to a number of philosophers, such as Plato, Francis Bacon, Kant, Collingwood, Gadamer, and Laudan.[2] Moreover, a large number of different treatments of the logic of questions are on the market.[3] It is surely not realistic to expect new insights to ensue from this old idea—or so it seems.

2. The Logical Structure of Questions.

What is new and promising about the approach I am proposing is that it is based on an adequate analysis of the crucial question-answer relationship.[4] Before we know what counts as an answer (intended, full, conclusive answer) to a given question, we cannot hope to understand how answers to questions one asks can yield information, for we don't really know what an answer to a given question is likely to be. Surprisingly, this crucial question-answer relationship is not analyzed satisfactorily in the earlier discussions of the logic of questions, in spite of the fact that the right analysis follows naturally from the basic idea of considering questions in informational terms. The line of thought—I shall call it, in analogy to Kant's "transcendental deductions," a "model-theoretical deduction"—which yields the right analysis is important enough to be sketched here.[5] It relies on the idea that having information (knowing something) amounts to being able to eliminate certain alternative situations or courses of events ("possible worlds").[6] This is the true gist in the often-repeated idea of "information as elimination of uncertainty."[7] What it means is that a person's, say b's, knowledge state in a "world" w_0 is characterized by reference to the set of all those "worlds" w_1 that are compatible with what b knows in w_0 (and by implication to the set of worlds that are excluded by b's knowledge). These will be called the epistemic b-alternatives to w_0. Then it will be the case that a sentence of the form

(1) b knows that p

is true in w_0 if and only if it is true that p in all the epistemic b-alternatives to w_0.

Furthermore, a wh-question like

(2)   Who killed Roger Ackroyd?

is to be analysed for my purposes as a request for a certain item of information. What information? Obviously, the information the questioner has when she or he can truly say

(3)   I know who killed Roger Ackroyd.

In general, a specification of the informational state that the questioner requests to be brought about is called the *desideratum* of the question in question. Thus (3) is the desideratum of (2).

Now (3) is naturally, not to say inevitably, analyzed as

(4)   ($\exists x$) I know that (x killed Roger Ackroyd)

where "x" ranges over persons. For what more could it conceivably mean to know *who* did it than to know *of some particular person x* that *x* did it? In model-theoretical terms, (4) means that there is some individual x such that, in each world compatible with everything I know, x killed Roger Ackroyd. This is, of course, but saying that I have enough information to rule out x's not having done it.

3. Question-Answer Relation Analyzed.

What is now going to count as a conclusive answer to (2)? Let's suppose someone tries to answer the question (2) by saying "*d.*" (I am making no assumptions concerning the logical or grammatical nature of this response, as long as it makes (5) below grammatically acceptable. It may be a proper name, definite description, indefinite description, or what not.) This reply is a conclusive answer if and only if it provides the questioner with the information that was requested. For the sake of argument, I shall assume that the reply is true, honest, and backed up by sufficient information. What information does it then bring to the questioner? Clearly, the information that enables him or her to say, truly,

(5)   I know that d killed Roger Ackroyd.

This is the state of knowledge (information), actually brought about by the reply "*d*". But it is not necessarily that state of information requested by the speaker, for this requested state is expressed by another proposition, viz. (4). Hence the reply "*d*" is a conclusive answer, i.e., it provides the requested information, *if and only if* (5) *implies* (4).[8]

But when does this implication hold? First, why should it ever fail? The model-theoretical perspective provides an instant answer. What (5) says that the term "*d*" picks out, from each world compatible with what I know, an individual who in that world killed Roger Ackroyd. The reason why this does not imply knowing who did it is that those several references of "*d*" need not be the same person. We may put it as follows: my knowing that someone or other killed Roger Ackroyd means having enough information to rule out all courses of events under which someone or other did not kill him. But in order to know who did it, I need further information: I have to have enough information to guarantee that the killer of Roger Ackroyd is *one and the same person* in all the worlds my knowledge has not yet eliminated.

Thus the extra premise one needs to infer (4) from (5) will have to say that the term d picks out the same individual from all the worlds compatible with what I know, i.e., that there exists some one individual x such that in all those worlds $d = x$. But, according to our observation concerning (1), something is true in all the worlds my knowledge does not rule out if and only if I know that it is true. Hence the extra premise needed to restore the implication from (5) to (4) is

(6) $(\exists x)$ I know that $(d = x)$.

This, then, is the criterion of conclusive answerhood. The reply "d" to (1) is a conclusive answer if and only if it satisfies (6).

What is remarkable about this result is not the particular condition (6). Indeed, it is precisely the condition one would expect. By the same token as the near synonymy of (3) and (4), (6) can be expressed more colloquially by

(7) I know who d is.

And this is obviously a necessary and sufficient condition for the reply "d" to satisfy the questioner. For if the questioner does not know who d is, this reply does not enable him or her to know who it was who killed Roger Ackroyd. Instead, it would prompt the further question, "But who is d?" or some equivalent response.[9]

What is remarkable about the criterion (6) of conclusive answers to (1) is, first of all, that it is generalizable.[10] Even though the technical details of some of the generalizations are messy, the leading idea is clear in all cases.

Even more remarkable is the fact that the aptness of my criterion of conclusive answerhood can be proved. The intuitive model-theoretical argument outlined above can be transformed into a formal argument, which relies on these principles of epistemic logic that codify my model-theoretical assumptions sketched above. Likewise, the generalizations of my criterion likewise can be proved to be correct in the strictest sense of the word in most of the relevant cases.[11]

In view of the crucial importance of the question-answer relationship (criterion of conclusive answerhood) for any study of knowledge-seeking by questioning, a couple of further remarks are in order. The analysis of the question-answer relationship I have offered is an inevitable consequence of a certain way of conceptualizing knowledge (information). Hence those critics have been barking up the wrong tree who have tried to criticize it by reference to the surface phenomena of language, including unanalyzed and ill-understood "intuitions" that the critics profess to have about the logical implications between different natural-language sentences.[12] The only relevant criticism would be to develop an alternative model-theoretical framework for (an alternative way of conceptualizing) information and knowledge, and an alternative way of codifying the idea that a question is a request of information. There is no need for me to respond to self-appointed critics who have not done this.

4. Further Problems

The outline account given above leads to further problems in virtually all directions. Here is a sample:

(i) Besides being a request for a certain item of information, a question implies certain restraints as to how this request is to be fulfilled. We need an account of these restraints.[13]

(ii) It is not enough to use logicians' time-honored models as implementations of the idea of alternative states of altering or courses of events. For if we do so, we are led to the paradoxical conclusion that everyone always knows all the logical conclusions of everything he or she knows. What is the appropriate generalization we need here?[14]

(iii) There is another way of taking a question like (1), viz. to take the requested state of knowledge to be expressible by

(8) (x) $(x$ killed Roger Ackroyd $\supset$ $(\exists z)$ $(z = x$ & I know that $(z$ killed Roger Ackroyd$)))$.

In other words, the speaker wants to be aware of the identity, not just of one person who killed Roger Ackroyd, but of all of them. How are the two representations (4) and (8) related to each other?[15]

(iv) What are the precise conditions on conclusive answers to more complicated questions? How are such complex questions to be analyzed in the first place?[16]

(v) Many perfectly respectable responses to a question don't satisfy my condition of conclusive answerhood, but nevertheless contribute partial information towards a conclusive answer. How are such *partial answers* to be defined? How can we measure their distance from a conclusive answer?[17]

(vi) Such representations as (4) or (8) assume that quantifiers and epistemic operators (e.g., "I know that") are informationally dependent on each other transitively, so that they can be represented in a linear fashion. Can this assumption fail? What happens if it does?[18]

5. Strategic Aspects of Questioning—Presuppositions of Questions

Such questions can easily be multiplied.

It would be a serious mistake to take these new problems, and others like it, to constitute evidence against my approach. Here it is in order to anticipate the self-awareness that our discussion of knowledge-seeking by questioning can engender. One of the most important advantages, perhaps the most important advantage, of the questioning model is that by its means we can discuss and evaluate, not just someone's state of knowledge at a given time (vis-à-vis the evidence one has at the time) but also entire strategies of knowledge-seeking.[19] Then the value of an answer A to a question Q of mine (or the value of conclusion I draw from such an answer A) cannot be measured in the sole terms of the knowledge (theory) this answer A yields. Rather, we must also consider the opportunities for further questions and answers that are opened by the original answer A. The basic reason for this is that questions cannot be asked in a vacuum. A question can only be asked after its presupposition has been established. Hence one may need answers to earlier "smaller" questions in order to be able to ask the crucial questions whose answers are likely to yield the information really desired.

Here we can also see the usefulness of game-theoretical conceptualizations. From game theory we know that utilities cannot be assigned to individual moves. Utilities, which in my information-seeking games depend essentially on the information (knowledge) sought, can only be assigned to entire strategies.

Likewise, we can see here the importance of another feature of my analysis of questions and answers, viz. the role of presuppositions. In the example above, the presupposition of (2) is

(9) (∃x) (x killed Roger Ackroyd),

that is

(10) Someone killed Roger Ackroyd.

Obviously, (2) can be sensibly asked only if (10) is true. Once again, my definition is generalizable beyond our particular example. In general the presupposition of a wh-question is obtained by omitting the outmost epistemic operator or operators "I know that" from the desderatum of the question. The presupposition of a wh-question minus the quantifier is called the *matrix* of the question

6. Significance of New Problems

Self-applied to the knowledge-seeking that is involved in my approach to questions, answers, and question-answer sequences, these observations imply that the approach should not be judged on the basis of the theory it has reached at one time. Even less should the open questions my approach prompts be counted against it. On the contrary, the ability of an approach to lead to interesting problems is a strong reason in its favor. These problems are evidence for its power to give rise to new questions whose answers are likely to essentially increase our knowledge of the subject matter.

This illustrates neatly how my general theory of knowledge-seeking by questioning can enhance our self-awareness of our own philosophical enterprise and its methods.

7. Meno Answered

The nature of the question-answer relation and of the presuppositions of questions deserves a few comments. Part of the philosophical relevance of my observations on these two subjects—especially on the former—can be expressed by saying that they provide a solution to Meno's puzzle.[20] On the basis of what we have found, it is in fact easy to see how Meno's paradox comes about. Applied to *what is* questions, my criterion of answerhood yields the following result: Suppose Socrates asks the definitory question

(11)   What is d?

The desideratum of (11) is

(12)   I know what d is.

Then a reply, say "b," is a conclusive answer only if Socrates (i.e., the questioner) can truly say,

(13) $(\exists x)$ I know that $(b = x)$,

in other words, can truly say,

(14)   I know what b is.

Thus it looks as if the question (11) can be answered conclusively only if the questioner already knows an answer. No wonder poor Meno was perplexed by this paradoxical-looking circularity.

The solution to Meno's problem lies in the fallaciousness of the word "already" in my formulation of the problem just given. The right conclusion to draw from my criterion of conclusive answerhood is not that the questioner must already know what the answer (in our example, the term "b") stands for prior to the reply, but rather that it is part of the task of that reply to provide the collateral information that enables the questioner to say, truly, (13) ($= (14)$). The right conclusion here is thus that an adequate response to a wh-question will have to serve two different functions. To put the point in the form of a paradox, it is not enough for a reply to provide (what is usually taken to be) an answer to the question (viz. a true substitution-instance of its matrix). It must also give to the questioner enough supplementary information to bring it about that the conclusiveness condition is satisfied, i.e., that the questioner knows what the reply term refers to *after* the reply has been given. This double function of replies to wh-questions is the true moral of Meno's paradox. It represents an important insight into the role of replies (answers) in discourse.

Speaking more generally, by spelling out the presuppositions for asking different kinds of questions as well as the conditions that conclusive answers to them have to satisfy, we can show just what a questioner has to know before he or she can ask a question and receive an answer to it, and thereby solve Meno's problem in its most general form.

All this highlights in turn a general truth about questions and answers. They are very much a discourse phenomena, and their theory must be developed as an integral part of the logic and semantics of discourse, as distinguished from the logic and semantics of (isolated) sentences.

8. Different Sources of Information

One feature of the conceptualizations expounded above is that they are independent of the specific nature of the answerer (source of information). For this reason, the theory of knowledge-seeking by questioning that is based on these conceptualizations is applicable to several different kinds of information-gathering. In order to see one of them, we may borrow a page from Kant's *Critique of Pure Reason* and think of the experimental inquiry of the physical sciences as a series of questions a scientist puts to nature.[21] (The page in question is B xiii.)[22] In this application, we can once again see the crucial role of the question-answer relationship. For Kant's emphasis is on the way in which a scientist can actively guide the course of investigation by choosing correctly the questions put to nature. The mechanism of this control is of course precisely the question-answer relationship. A question *Q* predetermines its answers in that they have to be answers to this particular *Q*. I shall not pursue this application here, however.

Another interesting application along related lines is to construe observations—be they scientific, clinical, or pretheoretical—as answers to questions put to one's environment.[23] This point is vividly illustrated in Sherlock Holmes's famed "deductions," which I have interpreted as so many questions put to a suitable source of information. (They will be discussed below.) Not only does Sherlock occasionally call his "Science of Deduction and Analysis" also a science of *observation* and deduction.[24] He repeatedly speaks of the same conclusion as being obtained, now by deduction or "train of reasoning," now by observation or perception. Upon meeting Dr. Watson, Sherlock Holmes says: "You have been in Afganistan, I *perceive*" (emphasis added). Yet he later describes a long train of thought (cf. below) he needed to reach that "conclusion."[25] On another occasion, Sherlock is surprised that Watson "actually [was] not able to *see* [emphasis added] that that man was a sergeant of Marines," even though Dr. Watson had just referred to this conclusion as a deduction ("How in the world did you deduce that?") and even though Sherlock himself has to use no fewer than thirteen lines to explain the different steps of his train of thought.[26]

Less anecdotally, assimilating observations to knowledge-seeking questions offers a natural framework for discussing some of the hottest problems in the contemporary philosophy of science, such as the concept-ladenness and theory-ladenness of observations.[27] For instance, if an observation is construed as a question, then the information it yields depends on the concepts in terms of which the question is formulated. Likewise, the observation, being a question, depends on the antecedent availability of its presupposition, which ultimately depends on the theory one is presupposing. We are obviously dealing with an extremely promising line of investigation here.

9. Activating Tacit Knowledge

The applications I am primarily interested in here are nevertheless in a still different direction. The source of information need not be outside the questioner. It may be addressed to the questioner's own memory or to whatever other sources of "tacit knowledge" he or she may possess. Then the questioning process becomes a process of activating tacit knowledge.[28] It seems to me that there is an especially dire need here of satisfactory semantical and logical analysis, for the process of bringing the relevant items of tacit information to bear on one's reasoning is practically never dealt with by philosophers and methodologists. Likewise, it seems to me that psychologists could profit from a better conceptual framework in dealing with this subject matter. Thus it is an extremely important subject in several respects.[29] In earlier papers, I have argued that much that passes as "inference" or "deduction" in nonphilosophical jargon really consists in sequences of implicit questions and answers.[30] In many of the most striking cases, such questions are answered on the basis of information that the questioner already has available to himself or herself but which the question serves to call attention to. It is precisely this quality of Sherlock Holmes's "deductions" that so frequently made them look "elementary" once they were spelled out. How did Sherlock know that the good Dr. Watson had been to Afganistan when he was introduced to him? Here is a paraphrase of Holmes's "train of reasoning":[31]

> What is the profession of this gentleman? He is of a medical type, but with the air of a military man. Clearly an army doctor,

then. Where has he been recently? In the tropics, for his face is dark, although it is not the natural tint of his skin, for his wrists are fair. But where in the tropics? He has undergone hardship and sickness, as his haggard face tells clearly. His left hand has been injured, for he holds it in a stiff and unnatural manner. Now where in the tropics could an English army doctor have recently seen so much hardship and got his arm wounded? Clearly in Afganistan.

Apart from the observations that the famous detective is using, he is relying on perfectly commonplace knowledge about sun tan, medical clues to one's past, and recent military history.

Actualization of tacit information is also the gist in philosophers' appeals, so prevalent in our days, to what are known as "intuitions."[32] I have argued elsewhere that it is a serious mistake to construe them as the data that philosophical theory or explanation has to account for. If they are to have a legitimate role in philosophical reasoning, they must have some other role in philosophical argumentation. But what is that role? We don't find a satisfactory answer in the literature.

10. Analogy Between Interrogation and Deduction

On my model, what does guide the choice of questions that activate tacit knowledge? My answer is: largely the same strategic considerations as govern the choice of the best lines of questioning in general. But what are those strategic principles? It is hard to be specific, but a couple of relevant observations can nevertheless be made. The presuppositions of questions must be among the conclusions a questioner has reached. The crucial questions are typically wh-questions, and their presuppositions are existential sentences. (Cf. (9) above.) The decisive strategic consideration therefore is: Which of the available existential sentences should I use as presuppositions of wh-questions? An answer to such a question will instantiate the matrix of the question, which is an existential sentence. Hence the strategic choice just mentioned is nearly analogous to the choice faced by a deductive strategist. For it has been shown that the crucial consideration in the quest of optimal strategies is the choice of the existential formulas to be instantiated at each stage of the deduction, which is here assumed to be roughly a natural-deduction or *tableaux*-type procedure.[33] In other words, the principles that govern the choice of optimal questioning strategies are extremely closely related to the choice of the principles that govern one's quest of the best deductive methods. In short, deductive logic is likely to yield the best clues to effective questioning. No wonder Sherlock Holmes called his art of investigation, which I have interpreted as a questioning method, "The Science of Deduction." The same road can be traveled in the opposite direction. Because of the parallelism between deduction and questioning, suitable questions can trigger the right deductive conclusions by the answerer, and may thus serve inversely as heuristic guides to the right deductive strategies.[34]

Hence a philosophical inquirer should discard the misleading positivistic generalization model and think of his or her task, not as a series of generalizations from the data offered by "intuitions," but on the model of Sherlock Holmes's "Science of Deduction and Analysis." In so far as my questioning model is applicable, i.e., insofar as Kant is right, such generalization from random data plays a much smaller role in science itself than philosophers seem to imagine these days, let alone in philosophical inquiry.

Another symptom of the insufficiency of the generalization model is that it does not offer any clues as to how our intuitions (the data) have to be changed if they prove unsatisfactory.

Here, then, we can see one of the main services that my questioning model can perform when thought of as a paradigm of philosophical method. It can guide a philosopher in activating the tacit knowledge that constitutes the raw materials of a philosopher's inquiry. In particular, it shows that important guidelines for this task are forthcoming from our familiar deductive logic. Successful thinking is colloquially referred to as "thinking logically." Philosophers might be well advised to take this idea more seriously than they are currently doing.

11. Trivial vs. Nontrivial Reasoning

Part of the force of the near analogy between questioning and deduction that I have argued for is brought out by the question: What characterizes nontrivial (synthetic) reasoning? I have argued on earlier occasions for an answer to this question applied to deductive reasoning.[35] (It has turned out that this answer was not only anticipated but strongly emphasized by C. S. Peirce, even though no one had understood his idea in the interim.)[36] Very briefly, and omitting all sorts of technicalities, the idea is that a logical inference is trivial ("corollarial," Peirce would have said) if it does not involve the introduction of any new entities into the argument. An inference is nontrivial ("theorematic," Peirce calls it) if it depends on the introduction of a new object into the purview of the reasoning. The more numerous such auxiliary objects are that a reasoner has to bring in, the more highly nontrivial is the reasoning. Historically, the paradigm case of such introductions of new objects into an argument have been the so-called auxiliary constructions of elementary geometry, a paradigm reflected by Peirce's choice of his terms.

The partial analogy between interrogation and deduction explained above allows us to generalize the trivial-nontrivial distinction to empirical reasoning relying on questioning over and above deductive reasoning in contemporary philosophers' narrow sense of the term. The extension is neatly illustrated by an example I have used before, viz. "the curious incident of the dog in the night-time" in Conan Doyle.[37] The famous racing horse *Silver Blaze* has been stolen from its stable in the middle of the night and its trainer, the stablemaster, has been found killed out in the heath. Everybody is puzzled till Sherlock Holmes directs our attention "to the curious incident of the dog in the night-time." "The dog did nothing in the night-time." "That was the curious incident." What Sherlock is doing here is in the first place to ask a few well-chosen questions. Was there a watchdog in the stable during the fateful night? Yes, we know that. Did the dog bark at the horse-thief? No, it did not. ("That was the curious incident.") Now who is it that a trained watchdog is not likely to bark at in the night-time? Its master, the trainer, of course. Each question and its answer may be "elementary," as Sherlock would say, but what makes the entire line of thought nontrivial is that Holmes brings, for the first time in the story, a new factor to bear on the solution of the mystery, viz. the dog. This introduction of a new object into the argument parallels an "auxiliary construction" by a geometer. It doesn't merely add a psychological twist to the tale; it is what logically speaking enables Holmes to carry out his "deduction."

The most famous deduction in the philosophical literature to be conducted in the form of a question-answer dialogue is Socrates's conversation with the slave-boy in Plato's *Meno*.[38] It illustrates forcefully the same power of auxiliary constructions (more generally, auxiliary individuals, in logicians' sense of individual) to facilitate nontrivial conclusions. In the *Meno*, Socrates extends the slave-boy's purview by introducing three new squares adjoining the original one. (See *Meno* 84 d.) The original one is here:

The completed one looks like this:

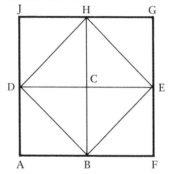

(The lines BE, EH, and HD are likewise introduced by Socrates in so many words in 84 e–85 a.) Once all these constructions have been carried out the conclusion is obvious: the square of BD can be seen to equal twice the square of AB. This argument depends crucially on the "auxiliary constructions" Socrates is allowed to carry out.

If the role and nature of such auxiliary constructions is not understood and appreciated, the power of philosophical questioning methods to yield nontrivial conclusions will be an intriguing puzzle. It is a small wonder, it seems to me, that this puzzle should have provoked Plato to hypothesize in his doctrine of *anamnesis*, i.e., of a memory-like knowledge of those unexpected conclusions.[39] It would also be interesting to try to consider theories of innate ideas in the same light.

12. Thinking as Unspoken Discourse

One way of bringing out the crucial general significance of a suitable questioning model for the conceptual analysis of human thinking in general is the following: Time and again in the course of Western thought, philosophers have proposed to consider *thinking* on the model of *speaking*. Plato describes "thinking as discourse, and judgment as a statement pronounced, not aloud to someone else but silently to oneself."[40] Likewise C. S. Peirce asserts that "all thinking is dialogical in form. Your self of one instant appeals to your deeper self for his assent,"[41] and again, "One's thoughts are what he is 'saying to himself,' that is, saying to the other self that is just coming into life in the flow of time."[42] One reason why this idea is so suggestive is that, if it is right, the extensive and powerful logic that has been developed for the study of spoken or written *sentences* may be expected to help us to understand the nature of *reasoning* and *thinking*.

Yet this suggestive idea has never led to major insights into the nature of thinking or reasoning. Why? In our days, Peter Geach has made an interesting effort to use the idea and construe the concept of thinking or "judging," as Geach calls it, "as an analogical extension of the concept *saying*."[43] In spite of Geach's famous ingenuity, the results are rather meager. We can now see why, more generally, the suggestive idea of thinking as internal saying has not proved as useful so far as one might have hoped. The answer is implicit in Plato's and Peirce's formulations. They don't just compare thinking with saying, but with *discourse*—a discourse between several different selves. Hence it is not any old logic that can be hoped to be useful for understanding reasoning through the Plato-Peirce analogy; only a genuine logic of discourse as distinguished from logic done on the sentence level will do. We could call the latter "sentential logic" in contrast to discourse logic if the term had not been pre-empted. What is striking about most of the usual logical conceptualizations and theories is that they move on the sentence level. They don't take into account differences between different speakers, for instance differences between what they know. Furthermore, most of the conceptualizations concerning the logic of questions in earlier literature have likewise been sentential.

Characteristically, Geach, too, tries to use the analogy between thinking and saying to examine, not different types of inferences one can make in one's thinking, but the various kinds of judgments one can make, such as "judgments of identification," "judgments about sensible particulars," ets. In other words, his conceptualizations remain predominantly on the sentence level.

Now questions and answers offer the simplest example of a discourse phenomenon that cannot be reduced to sentence-level phenomena. Indeed, there would not be any point in asking a question if the speaker and the hearer knew the same things or if epistemic differences between them did not matter. In view of the importance of the respective epistemic states of the parties in a question-answer dialogue, it is not surprising that my criterion of conclusive answerhood (cf. (16) above) is formulated in terms of what the questioner knows (i.e., knows after he or she has received a reply). If there is anything remarkable in my criterion, it lies in the fact that there is no need to refer to the other features of the dialogical situation.

Hence my theory of questions, answers, and question-answer dialogues offers a handy paradigm case for the study of characteristically discourse phenomena. According to what we have found, this implies that it also promises, via the Plato-Peirce analogy between discourse and thinking, to serve as an analogical model for at least some instructive sample cases of reasoning (thinking). In brief, it offers us the best hope that I can see of vindicating the Plato-Peirce analogy, at least in the case of selected sample problems. Only in terms of a dynamic theory like my theory of question-answer interaction can one hope to bring logical theorizing to bear on the study of reasoning and thinking in the way Plato and Peirce expected.

Several of the developments outlined, mentioned, or anticipated above receive their natural places in this overall perspective. It was for instance mentioned earlier that the process of calling the right items of tacit information to active duty can be approached as if it were a questioning procedure. This characteristically thinking process can in other words be handled by means of an analogy with explicit discourse. Likewise, the deep connections between actual deductive strategies in logic and the skills of a Sherlock Holmes-type practical cogitator uncovered above bear witness to the viability of the same analogy. In the last analysis, it is perhaps the capacity of the questioning model to throw light on the nature of thinking more generally that makes it so useful a part of a philosopher's methodology. For a philosopher's last but not least task is to enhance our awareness of our own thinking. In philosophy only an examined thought is worth thinking.

Acknowledgment: the work on this paper was made possible by NSF Grant #BNS 8119033 (PI: Jaakko Hintikka).

Notes

1. For a recent survey, with references to literature, see Santas 1979, especially ch. 2. Of the earlier literature, cf. Robinson 1953.
2. For Kant, see *Critique of Pure Reason* B xii–xiii; for R.G. Collingwood, see *An Essay on Metaphysics*, Oxford: Clarendon Press, 1940; for Hans-Georg Gadamer, see *Truth and Method*, New York: Continuum, 1975; for Larry Laudan, see his *Progress and Its Problems*, Berkeley: University of California Press, 1977, *Science and Hypothesis*, Dordrecht: D. Reidel, 1981a, and "A Problem-Solving Approach to Scientific Progress," in Ian Hacking, ed., *Scientific Revolutions*, Oxford: Oxford University Press, 1981.
3. See the bibliography in my monograph *The Semantics of Questions and the Questions of Semantics*, Amsterdam: North-Holland, 1976. The best known ones are probably Belnap and Steele 1976; Harrah 1963; Katz 1968; Åqvist 1971.
4. For this analysis, see *The Semantics of Questions* (note 3 above), chs. 2–3, and below, sec. 3.
5. The similarity between Kant's "transcendental deductions" (and "transcendental expositions") and my argument is perhaps not accidental. See my paper "The Paradox of Transcendental Knowledge" (forthcoming).
6. As I have repeatedly pointed out before, the fashionable term "possible world" is highly misleading, and has in fact misled several philosophers. The alternatives considered in the actual applications of my model-theoretic semantics need not be any more comprehensive scenarios than those involved in most applications of probability calculus.
7. What this adage thus amounts to is to assert the *propositional* character of information and knowledge. For a proposition can be characterized in terms of the class of worlds it excludes, which is precisely the "uncertainty" eliminated by coming to know it.
8. This question is of course tantamount to a special case of the question as to when existential generalization is valid in epistemic contexts. I have discussed this problem in *Knowledge and Belief*, Itheca, N.Y.: Cornell University Press, 1962; *Models for Modalities*, Dordrecht: D. Reidel, 1969; *The Intentions of Intentionality*, Dordrecht: D. Reidel, 1975; and in "New Foundations for a Logic of Questions and Answers," forthcoming.
9. In actual discourse, the likely response is something like, "But what is he like?" The reasons for this are explained in my *The Semantics of Questions*, note 3 above, pp. 45–46, 50–54.
10. Cf. here *The Semantics of Questions* (note 3 above) and "New Foundations for a Theory of Questions and Answers" (forthcoming b).
11. One version of the formal argument is in effect given in my book, *Models for Modalities*, Dordrecht: D. Reidel, 1969a, pp. 121–27. (In saying this, I am

relying on the observation made in note 8 above.) The methodological situation is discussed briefly in my paper, "Questions With Outside Quantifiers," in R. Schneider, K. Tuite, and R. Chametzky, eds., *Papers From the Parasession on Nondeclaratives*, Chicago: Chicago Linguistics Society, 1982, pp. 83–92.

12. These critics are typically victims of a widespread failure by philosophers of language and linguists to understand what a genuine theory or theoretical explanation is in language theory.

13. They have not been discussed satisfactorily in the literature. One main feature here is the relativity of the request to the truth of the presupposition of the question; cf. *The Semantics of Questions* (note 3 above), pp. 28–29.

14. An answer is provided by Veikko Rantala, "Urn Models," *Journal of Philosophical Logic*, 4 (1975): 455–74; and Jaakko Hintikka, "Impossible Possible Worlds Vindicated," ibid., pp. 475–84. Both are reprinted in Saarinen 1979. The philosophical implications of this answer are studied in my book, *Logic, Language-Games and Information*, Oxford: Clarendon Press, 1973.

15. See *The Semantics of Question* (note 3 above), chs. 4–5.

16. The most explicit generalization is found in my "New Foundations for a Theory of Questions and Answers" (forthcoming b).

17. See chapter 3 of *The Semantics of Questions* (note 3 above).

18. See "Questions With Outside Quantifiers" (note 11 above) for a somewhat surprising answer.

19. For the whole subject of questioning strategies, see Jaakko Hintikka, "Rules, Utilities, and Strategies in Dialogical Games," in Hintikka and Vaina 1983.

20. Plato, *Meno* 80 d–e.

21. This is part and parcel of Kant's "Copernican Revolution" in philosophy, which means focusing on what *we* do and what conceptual tools *we* use in acquiring the knowledge we have or can have.

22. Cf. my essays on Kant, collected partly in *Knowledge and the Known*, Dordrecht: D. Reidel, 1975a.

23. Cf. here Hintikka and Hintikka, 1982.

24. Arthur Conan Doyle, "A Study in Scarlet," in Baring-Gould 1967, vol. 1, pp. 143–234, especially pp. 159–60.

25. Ibid., pp. 150, 160.

26. Ibid., pp. 164.

27. The classical, albeit not necessarily definitive, statement of this view on observation is found in Hanson 1958, especially ch. 1. How neatly the theory-ladenness of observations fits into the model of knowledge-seeking by questioning was already pointed out in Hintikka and Hintikka 1982.

28. Cf. here Jaakko Hintikka, "The Logic of Information-Seeking Dialogues: A Model," in W. Essler and W. Becker, eds., *Konzepte der Dialektik*, Frankfurt a.M.: Vittorio Klostermann, 1981, pp. 212–31.

29. An indication of the problem situation is found by comparing philosophers' accounts of deductive inference with their accounts of inductive (and other non-deductive) inference. In the latter field, one of the prime problems is the reliance of certain promising accounts, especially the so-called Bayesian one, on what is known as *the requirement of total evidence*. What it means is that the total body of evidence one has at one's disposal is referred to essentially in the account. Of course, that is not only not what one actually does in a scientific inference, but it is arguably impossible to do. Now an analogous problem of total evidence (totality of premises at one's disposal) haunts what philosophers say of people's actual deductive inferences. They have nothing to say of how the deducer selects the appropriate premises from the totality of potentially available premises. In so far

as an account is attempted of what people actually do when arguing deductively, the current accounts are hence subject to the same objection to reliance on total evidence as their nondeductive cousins.

30. See the papers referred to in notes 19, 23, and 28 above.

31. The paraphrase is very close to the original. Essentially all that I have done is to use the interrogative mode more often that Doyle. See "A Study in Scarlet" (note 24 above), pp. 160–62.

32. Cf. here my paper, "Intuitions and the Philosophical Method", *Revue Internationale de Philosophie* 35 (1981b): 127–46.

33. These procedures go back to Beth 1955, pp. 309–42. It is reprinted, with further references to the literature, in Jaakko Hintikka, ed., *The Philosophy of Mathematics*, Oxford: Oxford University Press, 1969. Beth's original paper remains, in spite of several inaccuracies, the freshest exposition of this technique. The *tableaux* method is closely related to Hintikka's slightly earlier method of model sets, which goes back to Hintikka 1955, pp. 11–55. A brief exposition of it is found in chapter 1 of Jaakko Hintikka, *Logic, Language-Games and Information*, Oxford: Clarendon Press, 1973. A textbook using the Beth-Hintikka techniques is Jeffrey 1967.

34. In other words, we can in this way understand better the role of questioning in education. See here my paper, "A Dialogical Method of Teaching," *Synthese* 51 (1982a): 39–59.

35. See my *Logic, Language-Games and Information*, Oxford: Clarendon Press, 1973; and "Surface Information vs. Depth Information," in Jaakko Hintikka 1969.

36. See my paper, "C. S. Peirce's 'First Real Discovery' and Its Contemporary Relevance," *The Monist* 63 (1980): 304–15, with references to Peirce.

37. Arthur Conan Doyle, "Silver Blaze", in Baring-Gould 1967, pp. 261–81; see here p. 277.

38. Plato, *Meno* 82–83.

39. Plato, *Meno* 81 e.

40. Plato, *Theaetetus* 190 a; cf. *Sophist* 263 e.

41. C. S. Peirce, *Collected Papers*, vol. 2, sec. 26.

42. Ibid., vol. 6, sec. 338.

43. Peter Geach 1957, p. 75.

3 Classical Logic: Traditional And Modern

James Cargile

It is common nowadays to mean by "classical logic," the first order predicate calculus with equality. This system is a major cultural object of contemporary American philosophy. Most "Introductions to Logic" are introductions to it in one version or another. There are logically significant differences in various formulations. some will have finitely many axioms with a rule of substitution, some infinitely many axioms presented schematically, some no axioms and extra rules of inference, some will count open sentences (ones with free variables—variables not bound by quantifiers) as well-formed formulae, others will not. However, the syntactic rules of the various formulations are similar enough for purposes of this discussion to allow setting aside their differences. Our purpose is to enquire as to why this system is "classical," and to compare it with the earlier traditional "laws of classical logic."

One difference between possible formulations worth special comment is that while it is usual to assume an infinite supply of names, n-place predicate letters for every *n* and variables, it is also possible to have only finitely many of these. The rules of syntax will *allow* infinitely many well-formed formulae in either case, but the latter approach is consistent with skepticism about the infinite. The former, fairly standard treatment of predicate calculus accepts infinite sets. The traditional laws of classical logic do not entail such a commitment. My basis for saying the modern predicate calculus is called "classical logic" is merely my recalling this term to have often been so applied. That is no basis for following up the question whether the classical version of this system is committed to infinite sets. But let us suppose that the *cultural object* is not so committed.

Whether a string of symbols is a well-formed formula of predicate calculus is a question reducible to geometry (or mechanical drawing, or some such). This might seem false, in view of formulae written free hand on black boards, but these are representations of pieces in a game in which pieces are definable by their shapes and the moves consist in spatial arrangements of shapes. It is of course not shape or spatial arrangement that makes a version of predicate calculus using Polish notation and some more usual version both versions of the same system. But shape and rules of spatial arrangement are all that is necessary to produce a thing that then by virtue of other considerations qualifies as a version of predicate calculus. A version of predicate calculus could be presented entirely in spoken discourse, and the sounds "Eee-eks-eff-eks" could play the role of the well-formed formula *(Ex)Fx* with no requirement of a right-to-left spatial understanding of the sounds.* But there would still be considerations of order that were spatial in the broad sense. We should distinguish between considerations about the role of a form or the function of a thing of certain form, which may be played by something of a different form, and form proper, which is a spatial notion, involving order and arrangement.

I will say that the predicate calculus allows a *geometric* notion of form (whether "topological" or some other would be a better term is beyond the level of exactness aimed at here). By contrast, a *restricted* notion of form or *form plus restrictions*, starts from a blank form in the geometric sense that is accompanied by nonformal restrictions on what may be substituted into the form. Thus we might get a "subject-predicate" form by requiring that what goes in one blank be an expression that qualifies as a subject, or a "conditional" form where what goes in one blank qualifies as antecedent, and so on.

---

*Throughout this essay I adopt the convention of being *completely* casual about whether to use quotes.

On the other hand, we may say that a statement is functionally subject-predicate or conditional, meaning that it accomplishes the function of singling out a subject and attributing a predicate, or of presenting one proposition as conditional on another. These functions are not tied to any specific form. Besides geometric and restricted form, there is the *translational* notion of form, according to which a statement or sentence is of a certain form if its translation is of that form in a more proper sense.

The mechanical clarity of form in predicate calculus makes possible a mechanical notion of formal proof. A rule of inference amounts to a rule that "allows" putting down marks of one kind of shape after marks of another kind of shape in a game called "constructing a proof." Any *theorem* of predicate calculus can be "derived" or "proven" in this formal way in a finite number of steps with no consideration as to its content or meaning.

It can be proved that with respect to these mechanical proof procedures, the system is consistent—no formal "contradiction" can be proved in it, and the question whether one formula or set of formulae is derivable from another by these formal procedures is quite precise. Specifically, the usual axioms can be shown to be independent of each other.

The predicate calculus is not syntactically *complete*, since non-theorems can be added to the system as axioms without the resulting system being syntactically inconsistent. But it is famous for being "semantically" complete, and this is a virtue that could not have been claimed in any precise way for traditional classical logic. This completeness amounts to the fact that, for any syntactically consistent class of formulae of the calculus, there is an "interpretation" that makes every member of the class "true." This can be proven by Henkin's ingenious method so that the "truth" of a formula such as *Fa* consists merely in the fact that the name *a* is paired with itself and the predicate *F* is paired with a class of names *n* such that *Fn* is syntactically provable in a certain ingeniously chosen maximal consistent extension (another syntactic notion) of the predicate calculus, and the name *a* happens to be a member of that class.

These proofs of completeness, consistency, and independence do not involve having formulae of the calculus represent statements. You might say that the ingenious interpretation of a formula in the Henkin completeness proof makes the formula express a claim, but you certainly don't have to see it this way. The proof of syntactic consistency only shows that no formula and its "negation" are provable, where a "negation" is a certain mark that has certain rules laid out to determine its role in a game of putting down patterns of marks.

I propose to define logic as the science that studies formal proof. An alternative is to say it is concerned with formal validity. But, as these terms are defined in the modern "classical" logic, validity is not a fully formal notion. An argument is said to be valid (in the standard definition for the standard predicate calculus) if there is no interpretation that makes the premises true and the conclusion false. This may be a fact about a form, but the interpretation of a form involves nonformal considerations about what various symbols are "assigned" or "denote," etc. On the other hand, rules of inference just say that in the proof game, if you have something of such-and-such shape, you may follow it with something of such-and-such shape, etc. A prominent feature of the logician's skill is in playing such games well and knowing lots about them.

It might seem that this conception would make logic hard to practice with respect to a natural language and that it would be hard to distinguish between logic and transformational grammar.

Well, there is a similarity between a grammatical rule such as "if *A* and *B* are well-formed formulae, then so is *A* & *B*" and a rule of inference such as "from *A* & *B* you may infer *A*." In the predicate calculus, there is the difference that well-formedness is a decidable property detectable by a mechanical routine, while theoremhood is not. But in my opinion, the distinction between logic and grammar depends on nonformal considerations about the forms studied. In English, formal rules of proof will require forms with restrictions, such as "from *A* & *B* infer *A* where the first *A* and the second are replaced with one sentence that expresses the same proposition at each occurrence." (That may not be adequate, but as an example, perhaps it will do.) Conjunctive simplification will be logical rather than merely grammatical because it tells us how to go from truth to truth, or something like that. A precise distinction between logic and grammar won't be attempted here, but the distinction surely is not purely formal. Logic is the study of *forms* of "inference," purely formal forms of inference, where what makes these forms logical ones is not a purely formal matter.

With this rough account of logic, if we look at the traditional laws of logic as embedded in a natural language in something like the way axioms or theorems are in the predicate calculus, the traditional version may look pretty deficient. Even if we grant that the notion of form will not be "geometric" but rather "form with restrictions," there is not, in the tradition, anything like a complete account of formal derivability.

Without such an account, questions of completeness and independence for the traditional laws are obscure. It is not clear what it would be to state a few laws from which "all others" follow or what it would be to settle such a question as whether the law of excluded middle is "included in" the law of noncontradiction, as it often has been.

For example, consider this typical presentation of a law by Leibniz:

> I assume that every judgment (i.e., affirmation or negation) is either true or false and that if the affirmation is true the negation is false, and if the negation is true the affirmation is false; that what is denied to be true—truly, of course—is false, and what is denied to be false is true; that what is denied to be affirmed, or affirmed to be denied, is to be denied; and what is affirmed to be affirmed and denied to be denied is to be affirmed. Similarly, that it is false that what is false should be true or that what is true should be false, that it is true that what is true is true, and what is false, false. All these are usually included in one designation, *the principle of contradiction.* (From his Encyclopedia entry "On the General Characteristic," Loemker, p. 225)

One might feel that a number of things are run together here, but first we must ask what the ground rules are for determining whether two things have been run together or are genuinely equivalent. And this is part of determining what classical logic, as opposed to some other system, is. Various factions would want to distinguish excluded middle from noncontradiction or even from bivalence. It is alright to have a theory, which counts them as the same, as long as you have some criterion for what it is to be the same.

However, the mere fact that these questions about consistency, completeness, and independence cannot be precisely answered for the traditional logic does not mean the modern system is preferable. The easier precision may be achieved by leaving out concepts that are important in spite of being less clear. What we have for predicate calculus are not so much precise proofs of consistency, completeness and independence as precise proofs of precise versions of these concepts, where there may be much of importance left in the originals. The precision at the level of syntax does not yet give us a system of logic in the full sense. The forms need to be made into *logical* forms rather than mere ink shapes.

The traditional laws, though, do not represent the traditional *logic* very clearly. They are in terms of things, properties, and propositions rather than of sentence forms. They traditionally represent very general *metaphysical* laws rather than laws governing a formal game of proof that is based on the forms of sentences, even the looser "form plus restrictions" kind of form. There were truly formal laws in traditional logic, but the three main laws often cited as "laws of thought" are not examples of these. These laws were presented either as laws about propositions or as laws about things and their properties.

1. *Noncontradiction*: (a) in terms of things and properties: no thing both has a property and does not have (lacks) that same property; and (b) in terms of propositions: no proposition is both true and not true (nontruth, *in a proposition*, = falsity).

2. *Excluded Middle*: (a) For every thing and every property, the thing either has the property or lacks it; and (b) every proposition is either true or not true (= false).

3.1 *Identity*: (a) Every thing is identical with itself; and (b) every proposition entails and is entailed by itself.

A slight "conceptual" element has already crept into the above formulations, but they are good representatives of a long standing tradition. One needed supplement is an explicit assumption about negation:

Neg: (a) every property *F*, has a negation, which is the property of not having the property *F*; and (b) every proposition has a negation, which is another proposition, that has a different truth value from the original.

This assumption is not usually separated in traditional formulations. It does not follow from 1–3.1, but if we add the assumption that there are only two truth values, 1(b) and 2(b) follow from *Neg*. (This requires interpreting "has a different truth value" to mean "has no truth value in common with.") Also, if we assume that truth is a property, then 1(b) and 2(b) follow from 1(a) and 2(a). From *Neg* it follows that the negation of the negation of a proposition always has the same truth value as the original.

Of course, to *identify* a proposition or property with its double negation would be a further assumption.

Falsity is to truth as negation is to something, which has sometimes misleadingly been called "affirmation." This is misleading because to assert a negation is just as much to affirm some proposition as any other assertion is. But the following assumption shows some connection between affirming or asserting and truth.

Redundancy: To predicate truth of a proposition is the same as asserting it. To predicate falsity is the same as asserting its negation.

This assumption is plausible with respect to propositions. In modern terms, the claim is that the assertion that the proposition that *p* is true is logically equivalent to the proposition that *p*. This is not true for sentences. The assertion that the sentence *S* is true is not logically equivalent to the sentence *S*. Even saying that may sound confused! Better, we can say that uniformly substituting a sentence in the blanks of " '_____' is true if _____" does not yield logical truths.

(To digress, this latter fact is important and often overlooked. It was a valuable observation of G.E. Moore's, that such a sentence as, "The sentence, 'At least one person is a King of France' expresses the proposition that as least one person is a King of France," does not express a necessary truth. Since that sentence is in a good sense analytic or "semantically valid," or "true by virtue of facts about language," it serves to show that analyticity is not equivalent to necessity. It is often claimed that some necessary truths are not analytic. But this shows that analyticity does not even guarantee necessity. For that matter, the fact that a sentence is a logical truth does not make it necessarily a logical truth or necessarily true. But that, interpreted in such-and-such way, it is a logical truth, will be necessarily true, and this is usually behind calling a sentence a logical truth.)

Another assumption often taken for granted traditionally involves other compounds besides the one-place compounder, negation. Thus it is assumed that for every two propositions (not necessarily distinct), their conjunction is a proposition and the conjunction of two properties is a property. If the things conjoined are distinct, the result is distinct from both of them; if otherwise, it is not. These assumptions could be extended to cover all connectives, and for the truth functional connectives, there would be available rules for calculating the truth of compound propositions from the values for the components.

Whether the proposition is something distinct from sentences and also from properties is a matter of disagreement. Three facts about propositions are particularly relevant here. First, propositions such as that two and two is four were true long before there were people. Second, when an argument is logically valid in the traditional sense, it is impossible for its premises to be true and the conclusion false. That is, there are necessary connections between propositions. Third, propositions are what we believe when we believe truly or falsely, and it seems possible for people to believe or assert the same proposition even if they speak no common language.

These points have seemed to count against identifying propositions with sentences or with mental items such as images. Historically, philosophers who do treat propositions as sentences, or especially those who treat them as mental constructions (as the empiricists did) tend either to reject some of these assumptions or to reject some of the traditional laws of logic or to question the necessary truth of the laws, or to question whether the laws have any "content." The mentalism of traditional empiricism has been out of fashion for some time, but even when the proposition or Fregean "thought" is treated as a nonmental abstract entity that is the object of belief, this brings in a mentalistic note that is unsatisfactory to many materialistically inclined philosophers. These philosophers sometimes hold that "belief" is a very imprecise and unscientific term. If the notion of belief isn't good enough for modern psychology, they say, it shouldn't be coming in at such a fundamental level as logic. Dispositions to utter sentences in various ways are all right for these thinkers, but belief strikes them as unscientific.

I cannot address here the question whether propositions can be identified with sentences or classes of sentences, and belief be exchanged for various dispositions with respect to sentences. Still, insofar as propositions are not sentences, belief is important in their individuation. We have two distinct propositions p and q whenever an agent may believe truly or falsely that p without believing truly or falsely that q, and something similar applies for properties.

It may be objected that some propositions could not be believed by anyone. For example, it may be held that only you can grasp the proposition expressed by "I do not exist" as applied to you, and you could not believe this proposition. Or it may be held that no one can believe "I have a body and it is not the case that I have a body" and so on. These are disputable claims, but they can be avoided by modifying the assumption so that either a proposition is believable or its negation is. (Of course "I exist" is still open to Kantian-empiricist objections that it lacks "content," is purely "formal," etc.)

This leaves the objection that some propositions are too complex to be believed. For persons, this is probably true, but since we are talking about possible minds, those who believe in the existence of such propositions will probable not deny the possibility of higher minds. Those who believe there are infinite propositions (such as infinitely long conjunctions) should not reject the possibility of infinite minds.

It is true that the individuation of beliefs can be very imprecise and problematic. It is popular nowadays to speak of the "web of belief" and point out that to believe in something new will involve a very complex number of changes in one's system of beliefs. Close attention to this point may have been brought about in some philosophers by reflecting on the semantics for predicate calculus. Interpreting one formula involves interpreting at least one predicate that occurs in infinitely many other formulae, so that an account of truth for one formula needs to fit in systematically with the rest of the formulae of the calculus. Actual believing is not bound by such perfect systematic accuracy, but our ordinary ascriptions of belief usually presuppose attributing at least a rough grasp of at least a roughly systematic language so that coming to believe, say, "I have a brother in Cleveland" will involve a changed attitude to quite a range of sentences (besides any changes in nonlinguistic behavior).

This recognition of the web of belief is very fine, but it would be a mistake to think that since beliefs never come in units like propositions are traditionally conceived to be, that it follows that this traditional conception is unsound. For me to come to believe the proposition that I have a brother in Cleveland would necessarily involve my believing lots of other propositions I don't now believe. But its one thing for it to be necessary for there to be several propositions believed when you come to believe that p and quite another for there to be several propositions that are necessarily believed when you come to believe that *p*. It may be necessary that if I come to believe that *p*, then I come to believe something else, where *q* would do for the something else; and yet it is nonetheless *possible* for me to believe that *p* without believing that *q*, so that the propositions can be individuated, and the beliefs of them individuated in terms of them, by appeal to these possibilities.

Of course, the webster would most likely reject this discussion in terms of propositions and possibilities out of hand. The idea is that there is no bad problem about the individuation of sentences, and we can recognize that crediting someone with understanding and accepting one sentence will usually involve crediting him with understanding and accepting a great number of other sentences, without thereby undercutting our method of telling one sentence from another. But with propositions taken as distinct from sentences, our individuation criteria are tied up with our acceptance criteria in a way that makes the traditional pretense of individuating propositions unsound. In spite of the great value of recognizing the web of belief, this conclusion is not warranted.

This is not to deny that the individuation of propositions and beliefs is not much less clear than it is for sentences. That the sentence "The King of France is wise" is distinct from the sentence "At least one person is a King of France, at most one person is a King of France, and any King of France is wise" is obvious, but whether the propositions they express (in an appropriate context, etc.) are identical is a difficult question. And testing by asking whether we can imagine believing one proposition without believing the other will not appeal to the webster's sense of scientific accuracy. This is not the place to discuss this further. That a proposition is something such that either it or its negation is a possible object of belief won't be assumed here. But it is part of the traditional notion of a proposition as it occurs in the traditional laws of logic.

To say that a proposition is not the case is the same as saying it is false, as in "The proposition that all men are male is not the case," which is more briefly "That all men are male is not the case." But this latter is ambiguous since it may be taken as a mere reordering of "It is not the case that all men are male" and this may be treated as of the form "It is not the case that *p*" where the "*p*" represents* the proposition rather than the "That *p*."

---

*Remember our convention about quotes!

Alternately, it could be read as "It is not the case—that *p*," where we have the attribution of falsity as before.

In the one case, we designate a proposition ("that all men are male") and attribute falsity (= not being the case). In the other, we attach to a sentence that expresses a proposition ("all men are male") a grammatical operator ("It is not the case that"). In both cases, the same proposition is expressed by the final grammatical result. But the analysis in terms of the grammatical operator yields a concept of grammatical negation that is distinct from the grammatical predication of falsity (or of not-being-the-case).

In this way we arrive at a concept of an operation of negation that is distinct from the act of predicating falsity. The result of these acts is the same when the object is a proposition. To predicate falsity of a proposition is the same as asserting its negation. The acts may be different, but the same proposition (the negation of the original) is asserted in each act. But we can predicate falsity of anything, for example, of the Washington Monument. We can say of it, that is, that it is a proposition and not true, though of course this is to make a false claim. But we cannot negate the Washington Monument (except perhaps in some irrelevant meaning of "negate"). For negation is an operation performed in its grammatical aspect by starting with a sentence that expresses the thing to be negated and then performing the grammatical operation of negation upon it. And there is no sentence that expresses the Washington Monument. On the other hand, to predicate falsity we only need to designate the Monument, and that we are equipped to do.

Such a form as "For every *p*, either it is the case that *p* or it is not the case that *p*" ("either *p* or not-*p*") is not standard English. But that is unimportant. Anyway, its instances are not designators of propositions ("that all men are male"), but rather expressors of propositions ("all men are male"). The form may perhaps be taken to express a generalization about propositions. But the means by which this is accomplished is not the one used in natural language. The traditional laws of classical logic are generalizations about propositions in that they express the claims that every proposition satisfies a certain condition, such as being either true or false, or not being both true and false. It makes no difference if we describe these conditions instead as either being the case or not being the case, or not both being the case and not being the case. But if the variable does not take designators as values, but rather takes expressors as instances, then what is the condition that form can be taken to attribute to every proposition? The answer depends on how we interpret the form. We can interpret it in such a way that it does not express a general claim about propositions. But then it may not express a general claim at all. Our law may be a general claim about the form rather than a general claim expressed by the form.

Of course interpreting the traditional classical laws as about properties and propositions does not simply render them fully determinate. Quite a variety of views about these things are compatible with the classical laws. There can be disagreement not only over what properties exist but over what they are like.

For example, consider the "Sorites Paradox," in which a vague predicate like "is a tadpole" seems to express a property for which excluded middle does not hold. One answer (which I favor) is that everything is either a tadpole or not but we may not be able to decide every case satisfactorily. Knowing is one thing and being is another. But it can also be said that there is no such property as being a tadpole, only a parametric family of properties, "n percent tadpole" for values of n from zero to one hundred. While I do not believe this really helps, it is a view of properties that is just as compatible with the classical laws as the more natural view.

For another example, we need a law which appears in predicate calculus with equality that is not usually mentioned with the traditional laws.

3.2 *The Indiscernability of Identicals*: if the thing that is a is identical with the thing that is b, then for every property, if a has the property, so does b.

This law was not traditionally stated, probably because it was assumed to "follow" from Noncontradiction. If you deny 3.2, then there would be a thing a that was F and yet the very same thing b would not be F, so the very same thing would be both F and not-F, violating Noncontradiction. I have seen "derivations" like this accepted by contemporary philosophers, and there is in fact something to it, but that can't be considered further here.

This law (3.2) has the consequence that a thing that is a at time t cannot be identical with a thing that is b at time t' unless every property of a is a property of b. So those who want to say that I, for example, am the same thing now as when I a moment earlier had no pen in hand, must say that there is no property of having a pen in hand, but only, having a pen in hand as of a certain time, a property I then always have. In other words, the classical laws including 3.2, require a choice between "chronologizing" many properties or else denying cross time identity for many cases where it is usually assumed to hold. This is a metaphysically significant issue about properties where the classical laws do not determine an answer.

This indeterminacy might seem to mean that, strictly speaking, our "laws" 1–3 do not express definite propositions until we interpret them specifically to resolve the many questions as to what we mean by "properties" and "propositions." However, I think this difficulty can be set aside by following (a little way) the view (uncongenial as its setting is) that the reference of many general terms is determined by our actually encountering a kind of thing— that is, specific instances of the kind—and naming the kind ostensively, without knowing much about the kind, as the kind of thing that this thing we have encountered is. We encounter properties all the time, and in the classical laws, we express knowledge about them, however unclear the other facts of their nature may be to us.

A different source of ambiguity in the classical laws concerns the modality of the claims. Is it that nothing does both have and lack a property or that nothing could? Still another interpretation makes the law express *a priori* knowledge: We (lucky ones with proper education) know for certain that nothing could both have and lack a property and that everything has or lacks a given property.

This is important in connection with denials of the classical laws. It is one thing to say there are propositions that are neither true nor false, another to say there could be, and yet another to say that you (and all of those guys bragging about their "education") don't know there are no such propositions.

These modal ambiguities need to be resolved (unlike the earlier mentioned questions as to exactly what properties are like). But then they can be resolved easily enough.

The amount of interpretation needed in order for the predicate calculus to make statements and express concepts, especially to express logical laws, rather than mere syntactic theorems, is quite another matter. Four ways of "interpreting" formulae will be discussed here.

On the "model-theoretic" account, we specify a domain of objects and each name of the calculus is made to stand for an object in the domain. Each n-place predicate letter "F" is made to stand for a class of n-tuples of the domain. An atomic formula $F^n(a_1, \ldots a_n)$ will be true if the n-tuple named by $(a_1 \ldots a_n)$ is in the class of n-tuples named by F^n, and false otherwise.

Let the domain be the integers, and a be 3 and F be the prime numbers between 4 and 10. It is clear that Fa is false, but what *Fa says* is far from clear. It doesn't seem that it says that 3 is a prime number between 4 and 10, any more than it says that 3 is a nontrivial factor of 35 or that 3 is either 5 or 7. No one way of specifying the members of the set assigned to F is essential to the model-theoretic interpretation of Fa. But in my opinion, if someone tells you that a thing is a member of a set of things which set he identifies to you as the set of things that have a certain property, he has told you that the thing has that property. The model theoretic "semantics" doesn't come out as very explicit about what interpreted formulae say. It only gives truth conditions.

An alternative account may be called "The Property Interpretation," according to which F^n stands for an n-ary relation, or property (when n = 1). Names go as before, and $F^n(a_1 \ldots a_n)$ is true if the n-tuple named by $(a_1 \ldots a_n)$ are in the relation named by F^n. On this account, what is said by, say Fa, when F stands for being a prime between 4 and 10 and a for 3, is much clearer, except for the name a. We know what is predicated, but how we identify the subject is problematic. Is it 3, or the prime number before 4, or what? In natural language, the way we designate the object is always a feature of the thought that is behind what we assert. Whether it is always a feature of what we assert is to some extent open to arbitration. When I say "That is a marble," my *thought* is not individuated merely by the predicate and the reference of "that" but we could arbitrarily count *assertions* so as to ignore that part of the thought that secured the reference and focus only on the reference. At any rate, if we wish to consider the way we determine the reference as part of what is said, Russell's theory of descriptions is the way to do this in the language of Predicate Calculus and in natural language as well.

But then what *is* said with Fa? Russell got into trouble with that—trying to interpret logically proper names. The truth is that

Fa doesn't express a complete thought on this interpretation—it represents a predication, where the means of determining the referent of the predication is left out. On the model theoretic interpretation, even the connotation or sense of the predicate is left out as well. But "left out" is very vague. Perhaps it's a little clearer to say that *Fa* itself doesn't say anything about being a prime number in the model theoretic version of our foregoing example, while it does in the property interpretation.

Another account is "translational" or "linguistic." The names stand for names in a real language such as English, and the predicate letters stand for predicates (as opposed to sets or properties). So *Fa* might symbolize "Hamlet is a prince."

If we then went on to give an account of the truth of "Hamlet is a prince" in terms of "correspondence," we might have a problem with lack of a proper correspondent for "Hamlet." And even with "Charles is a prince," we might wonder why we shouldn't just "eliminate the middle man" and use a model theoretic or property interpretation. Well, the "middle man" would be handy for telling us what *Fa* says on this interpretation, namely that Charles is a prince. On this account, the calculus would be serving just as a test for "formal" logical relations between natural language sentences. It seems that a definition for truth or falsity would not be needed. Without a truth definition, the model-theoretic or property interpretations would give us, not statements, but ordered pairs of sets (or properties) and things, leaving a question as to the point of the exercise. But translationally, we get the statements with or without an account of truth. Here, to be "classical" is to graft on a requirement that all our symbolized statements have truth values in the right way.

Turning to the question of extending the definition of truth from the case of atomic sentences to the ever more complex formulae constructible in the calculus, the translational approach divides into one way that interprets compounds by translating them into natural language connectives and quantifiers, ("The Full Translational" style) and alternately, interpreting quantifiers so that $(Ex)A$ says that there is a name such that uniformly substituting it for x in A yields a true sentence ("Translation for atomic sentences plus substitutional quantification").

The apparatus for forming compounds in predicate calculus is based on truth-functional connectives, ones such that the truth value of a compound proposition can be calculated from the truth values of the components and the truth tables for the connectives. Such connectives can be safely translated into English only with accompanying defeaters of misleading implictions. When combined with quantifiers this can be especially difficult. For example, the formulae $(x)(Ey)(Fx \rightarrow Gy)$ and $(x)(Fx \rightarrow (Ey)Gy)$ are provably equivalent and thus should be interpreted as always having the same truth value. But the most straightforward English readings are clearly nonequivalent. For example: (1) "For all x there is a y such that if x tells a dirty joke, y is offended" may be false in a situation where (2) "For all x, if x tells a dirty joke, then there is a y such that y is offended" is true. This example can be better symbolized by insisting on a formalization that introduces a quantifier for the dirty jokes, since the problem arises because the English (1) implies there is a y who is offended by every joke told by x while (2) is content merely with every joke told by x being offensive to some y, not necessarily the same y on each occasion. But to match up compounds in predicate calculus with English compounds by a general recursive procedure would be very likely to give rise to mistranslations of this sort.

Thus the full translational approach is likely to be unreliable. The substitutional approach would involve only getting names and atomic predicates from natural language and then providing its own quantifiers and connectives. However, on this approach, it wouldn't be possible to satisfactorily represent such a statement as that there is at least one thing that has never been named or otherwise made the object of an identifying reference. The full translational approach could take in this statement but has the other drawback just noted.

Of course these drawbacks don't mean the interpretations don't yield statements, only that the verdict on the logical relations between the statements given by the calculus may be incompatible with our intuitions about the actual relations between sentences. If we give up trying to represent those relations, the problems disappear, but the point of the exercise becomes questionable.

There is no hope for trying to capture all the logical powers of English sentences by translating them into predicate calculus, at least not with one translation per sentence. It's enough to observe that singular subject predicate or relational sentences in English (atomic sentences) can be inconsistent with each other, while in predicate calculus, all atomic formulae are mutually consistent. Logical Atomism was an attempt to get around this with an idea of the real language behind the misleading grammar. But that is hopeless. "John is a bachelor" is inconsistent with "John is married." If you say that the former is "really" the compound "John is male and not married, etc.," you will still have to admit "John is male" is also compound. Admittedly, a properly trained modern philosopher can describe cases in which a male bears children (that's in mythology) and perhaps has no sex organs or even female sex organs (on the side)—but there's a limit to this dodging logical consequences! The search for an "atomic predicate" in natural language is a wild goose chase because, for every property F, a thing's having that property entails some thing's (the original or some other) having some distinct property G such that neither F nor G is a component of the other.

Though I will drop these two "linguistic" styles of interpretation, the one with substitutional interpretation of quantifiers makes for an easy account of how to recursively define truth for formulae of the calculus, relative to an interpretation. For the property or model theoretic accounts, this is harder when moving from quantifiers attached to atomic open sentences to quantifiers attached to compounds, unless you follow a substitutional reading of quantifiers. That reading allows easy statement of a recursive rule such as "$(Ex)A$ is true if uniformly substituting a name for x throughout A yields a true sentence." The motivation for an "objectual" reading of quantifiers is that there may be unnamed things, so that while Fa_i isn't true for any name a_i, $(Ex)Fx$ may still be true. This description makes the motivation rather incoherent, since it calls for wanting $(Ex)Fx$ to come out true before it is even interpreted, as a motive for interpreting it a certain way. But the motive is to be able to *express* the claim that there are unnamed things.

The practice of mathematicians would seem to allow something like "Consider the class of unnamed things, select a member at random, call it a, etc." Or there is the mathematician's joke about proving that every integer has an interesting property, by *reductio*. If there were integers with no interesting properties, there would be one that was the least such, and that's an interesting property.

These practices make it easy for mathematicians to talk about "assigning" elements of the domain to variables, by way of giving a recursive truth definition for the predicate calculus. But this is not necessary, and a truly "objectual" interpretation can be given by showing how to read (*Ex*)*A* as a way of saying that something satisfies condition *A* where *A* may be nonatomic just as we can with (*Ex*)*Fx* where *F* is an atomic predicate. This is done in Quine's essay "Variables Explained Away."

One additional law often listed among the traditional laws of classical logic is:

4. *The Dictum de Omni et Nullo*: This was an attempt to summarize syllogistic logic in one principle. Rather than going into that thicket, I will just cite instances of this law.

(a) If *all* *A*s are *B*s and all *B*s are *C*s, then *all* *A*s are *C*s.
(b) If *no* *A*s are *B*s and all *C*s are *B*s, then *no* *A*s are *C*s.
(c) If *this* *A* is a *B* and all *B*s are *C*s, then *this* *A* is a *C*.

This transfer of "all" or "no" from premise to conclusion is, I assume, the source of the name for this law, which I will discuss without stating. (I will also refrain from discussing the point that syllogistic logic seems to leave out the logic of relations. There is some treatment of multiple quantification and relation in traditional logic. How much can't be pursued here.)

This law makes another step toward completeness in traditional logic, though it is far from being adequate for that. It concerns the *instantiation* of generalizations, and it appears significantly different from instantiation in predicate calculus because in the latter, instantiation is an immediate inference, while in traditional logic it is syllogistic. If we let condition *F* be that of not being able to square the circle, then from (*x*)*Fx*, *Fa* follows in predicate calculus directly. Here "follows" applies even regardless of the interpretation of "*F*" and "*a*." It is a rule of syntax that *Fa* can be "derived" immediately from (*x*)*Fx*. But in the language (natural language) of traditional logic, "Hermann Potzreebie is not able to square the circle" follows from "Every thing is a thing not able to square the circle" only if we add the premise "Hermann Potzreebie is a thing."

It may be objected that "Herman Potzreebie is a thing" is peculiar and ambiguous. This is true. It is *formally* required, and formal considerations don't always determine meaning at all precisely. One way it could be interpreted, though, is as follows: "*a* is *F*" follows from "Everything is *F*" only if we add the assumption "*a* exists."

This resembles the procedure in some systems of logic that are put forward as *alternatives* to the standard "classical" predicate calculus. That is, the formal requirement of traditional classical logic resembles the formal requirement in a modern departure from "classical logic." In "classical" predicate calculus, *Fa* follows from (*x*)*Fx* and entails (*Ex*)*Fx*. Alternatives either reject the first on the grounds that (*x*)*Fx* may be true but *Fa* not (because *a* doesn't denote) or reject the second on the grounds that *Fa* may be true without *a* denoting even though (*Ex*)*Fx* is false. The motivation for these two rejections is incompatible, but the remedy they call for is the same. The first alternate requires the premise (*Ex*)(*x* = *a*) be added to allow the inference from (*x*)*Fx* to *Fa*, the second requires the same premise to allow the inference from *Fa* to (*Ex*)*Fx*.

However, the model-theoretic or property interpretation of predicate calculus includes what amounts to the blanket assumption of the required extra premise, since they require that an interpretation has the names have referents. And the linguistic interpretation can only allow a nonreferring subject-predicate interpretation of *Fa* (such as "Hamlet is a prince") to be true if it also allows a "nonexistential" interpretation of the "existential" quantifier, which amounts to interpreting "Hamlet is a thing" or "There is such a thing as Hamlet" to be true even though "Hamlet" in "Hamlet is a prince" doesn't refer to anything. There is a confusing variety of ways in which this underdetermining requirement could be met. One is the substitutional interpretation according to which (*Ex*)(*x* = *a*) only claims that there is a name that can be put for "*x*" in (*x* = *a*) to yield a truth. And on this account, (*Ex*)*Fx* follows from *Fa* even if there exists no thing that satisfies condition *F* and *Fa* is counted true (because it symbolizes a sentence such as "Hamlet is a prince," which plays a certain language role, etc.)

It is these alternative systems that actually diverge from the traditional interpretation of logical rules. Either the objectual or the linguistic interpretation justifies the move from *Fa* to (*Ex*)*Fx*, the former by supplying the assumption that *a* exists, the latter by taking the existential bite out of the conclusion. To justify rejecting the move requires finding *Fa* true and (*Ex*)*Fx* false. And this is done by linguistically interpreting *Fa* ("Everybody knows that Pegasus was a flying horse") while objectually interpreting (*Ex*)*Fx* ("There are no flying horses"). To consistently follow the linguistic style would either get the conclusion that the alternative system wants to reject, or would involve the perilous ("Everybody knows there are no flying horses") translational approach for compounds described earlier.

Now, how does the predicate calculus express laws of logic? Any acceptable way of interpreting formulae of the calculus will make such a theorem as $(x)(Fx \lor {\sim}Fx)$ true in every interpretation, which is known as being "valid." But in what sense is that formula a law of classical logic, beyond being a theorem in a system called "classical logic"? On some model theoretic interpretation, it will tell us, say, that every member of the domain of people is a member of the class of mortals or not. Or rather, it will "tell" us some skeletal version of that. On the property account it could be that every thing either has the property of being mortal or doesn't. On the linguistic translational account it would symbolize something like "Everyone is either mortal or not mortal." On the linguistic-substitutional account it would be that the blank form "_____ is mortal $\lor$ _____ is not mortal" yields a truth for all uniform substitutions of the right sort of expression. None of these is a logical law. They are at best *instances* of a law.

A departure from the "first order" predicate calculus to a "higher order" would allow $(F)(x)(Fx \lor {\sim}Fx)$ (quantifying the predicate variable), which could be read on a property interpretation as like our classical law (2). But a similar thought can be expressed in terms of regular restricted predicate calculus in two ways. Internally, a formula such as $(x)(y)(Px \to (yIx \lor {\sim}yIx))$ can be used to say that for all x and y if x is a property, then either y is an instance of x or y isn't an instance of x. Externally, in explaining the status of $(x)(Fx \lor {\sim}Fx)$ we can go beyond saying it is valid, true in every interpretation, and explain why, because any set (or property) you pick for F will be such that for any domain, any element of the domain will either belong to the set or not (have the property or not).

To do this is not required and would not be in the spirit of linguistic interpretations. Correspondingly, philosophers have disagreed as to whether the laws of classical logic should be viewed as very general necessary truths about things, properties, and propositions or rather as truths about language owing their generality to, say, our adopting certain rules of interpretation. These alternatives are not incompatible. It might be held, for example, that our natural recognition of these general necessary truths is behind our having the relevant language rules. But those who grant *only* the language rules will be leaving out the necessity. It is not necessarily true that every substitution instance of the form (*Fx* ∨ ~*Fx*) is true.

Unless, that is, we so qualify the "form" and the licensed "substitutions" that the result is not merely linguistic anymore. We can say that if the name "*a*" names something and *F* represents some property then the sentence "*Fa* ∨ ~*Fa*" when interpreted as a disjunction, will be true, and be saying something necessarily true that is about names and sentences. But it is primarily about things and properties.

This "external interpreting" of predicate calculus gives a logical theory in which the calculus with its syntax and even its semantics is only a part. That is, the logical theory is something beyond the interpreted calculus. It may be the traditional classical logic!— with many of its obscurities creeping back in. From an external point of view, our endorsement of excluded middle as an item of *a priori* knowledge can be expressed with reference to (*Fa* ∨ ~*Fa*) just as well as with reference to (*x*)(*Fx* ∨ ~*Fx*). The sharp differences between the roles of these formulae in the calculus does not preclude either one being equally good as reference point for expressing the thought that for every thing and every property, the thing either has or lacks the property. This thought of traditional logic is not more sharply expressed within the interpreted calculus. It is expressed with reference to the calculus (if one is disposed to express it) and this can be done in a variety of ways. And at this level of expression, the function of the system may again be metaphysical and ontological with the sharp logical work—formal analysis of proof—receding into the background.

It is now time to discuss the most formidable criticism, raised both in ancient and in modern times, against the traditional classical laws, namely that they involve an unlimitedly general use of the notion of truth in a way that leads to inconsistency. The inconsistencies are known as the semantic paradoxes, and there are an unlimited number of instances of them, though the variety of novel cases is not so great. One of the simplest involves a sentence

(A)   *A* is not true,

which it seems will be classed both as true and as false by the procedures for assigning truth values that are implicit in the traditional classical logic, so that the system violates its own law against contradiction.

In my book *Paradoxes*, I set out a theory about predication which, in my opinion, solves the semantic paradoxes by showing how to assign truth values to the paradoxical sentences in a way that is not only consistent but rationally justified by the classical laws of logic. That general account cannot be given here, but one important point concerns the idea that, since *A* is a subject-predicate sentence, it will be true if the thing denoted by the subject term has the property expressed by the predicate. This is a big mistake. It is like the idea that is put forward in the property interpretation of predicate calculus, which was that *Fa* is true when the thing *a* stands for has the property *F* stands for. The trouble with this principle is that for some properties, when they are attributed, other properties are necessarily also attributed. In the case of the paradoxical sentences, this is of logical importance. When a property is attributed or predicated, the thing which performs that predication is true only if all the properties it attributes are possessed by all the things to which they are attributed. To attribute *F* to *a* may be a false performance even if *a* has the property *F*, if the predication also attributed properties not possessed by the things to which they were attributed.

For a sentence to be true is for what it says to be true. What it says is relative to the language, but the truth of what it says is not. "Gold dissolves in aqua regia" says, as a sentence of English, that gold dissolves in aqua regia. That it says this is relative to its role in English. But that what it says is true, that gold dissolves in aqua regia, is not so relative. To say a sentence is true in language L just means that what it says as a sentence of L is true *simpliciter*.

The sentence *A* attributes to *A* the property of nontruth. But it also expresses, says, asserts something as a sentence of English, which is not properly describable due to the infinite regress we get into in trying to say what it is, but which we can describe for logical purposes as whatever it is that *A* says. Whatever this proposition is, *A* says it, and thus by the law *Redundancy*, that is the same as predicating truth of it. So *A* attributes to what *A* says both the property of truth and the property of nontruth, and is thus contradictory. So *A* is not true.

How then, can we use those last words, the same words as *A*, to give the true assessment of *A*? Well, we are using a different sentence token, and even if it had been the same token (a tricky case not to be bothered with here) the meaning would be different because we are referring to another statement. Our claim that *A* is not true is not self-referring. We say that whatever it is that *A* says, it is contradictory and thus not true. But *A* says whatever it is that *A* says. That is, *A*, in a certain use of that token to say something, says what ever it is that is said by that use of that token to say something. But we are not engaged in that use of that token. So there is no basis for a presumption that that is what we are saying and thus no basis for the application of *Redundancy* to what we are saying.

What proposition it is *A* is asserting is not clear, since it involves an infinite regress in trying to spell it out. But the linguistic devices employed by *A* insure that it predicates nontruth and truth of the same thing.

This is oversimplified. *A* really performs the function of conditional predication. It says (in part) that either the sentence *A* does not express a proposition or it expresses a nontrue (= false) one. If the condition of the predication is satisfied, that is, if *A* does express a proposition, then the conditional predication of nontruth is enacted, and the evaluation proceeds as described.

The classical law *Redundancy* is just a start toward a theory of predication. The predicate calculus connot represent, so as to reflect in its syntactic proof relations, all the properties that necessarily accompany the attribution of a given property. But it can represent some fundamentally important consequences of predication. From $(x)(Fx \rightarrow Gx)$ and Fa, we get Ga. Externally understood, we see from this that when you conditionally predicate being *G* of everything that is *F*, then with respect to everything that is *F* (such as the thing *a*) you are responsible for its being *G* (*Ga*) as a condition of the truth of your conditional predication. Thus we learn that to say every *F* is *G* is to predicate being *G* of every *F*.

Now consider the claim that *some F* is a *G*, that something that has property *F* has property *G*. A standard view is that this *does not* involve attributing the property *G*. This is a very standard view that is, in my opinion, an insuperable obstacle to an adequate general answer to semantic paradoxes. The truth is that "Some *F* is a *G*" logically necessitates "Everything is such that if nothing but it is *F*, then it is *G*." This corresponds to the fact that in predicate calculus, $(Ex)(Fx$ & $Gx)$ entails $(x)[(y)((y \neq x)$ $\rightarrow \sim Fy) \rightarrow Gx]$. And this means, that by our previous law, when you assert "Some F is G," then it may happen that you thereby predicate being G of something (whether or not you know it). This will happen, for example, when only one thing is F, and G is then attributed to that thing, or when nothing is F and G is then attributed to everything.

When these laws of predication, which apply to all properties, are combined with Redundancy, which is just about the property of truth (namely that asserting a proposition is predicating truth), the resulting theory of predication sounds very radical. For example, to assert anything about anything (predicate anything of anything) is to assert something of every thing. And to assert any proposition is to assert every true proposition. These consequences merely reflect familiar facts about classical predicate logic: the first, that p is trivially equivalent to $(x)p$ (everything is such that p); the second, that a true proposition is materially implied by every proposition, plus the fact that to assert p is the same as asserting that everything materially implied by p (which of course includes p) is true. The apparent strangeness of this theory should be dispelled by properly distinguishing between asserting as being logically responsible for the truth of and asserting as it involves belief. In my technical logical sense of "assert," there is only one necessarily true assertion, or rather, all assertions of necessary truths assert all the same propositions. But the propositions are individuated in terms of possible belief, so that there are infinitely many distinct necessarily true propositions.

A more complete account of this theory about predication and its application to the variety of paradoxes can't be developed within the present context. My purpose is to compare the treatment of truth in the traditional classical logic with that in the modern predicate calculus. I believe my theory vindicates the classical laws as absolutely unrestricted general laws about truth as a property against the charge of inconsistency. This unrestricted generality is lacking in the modern system. And extensions of or alternatives to the system will diverge in other ways from the spirit of the traditional laws. The principal reason, in my opinion, is that the truth about the paradoxes (e.g., my theory) requires giving up the unrestricted generality of something that was never a vital feature of the traditional logic, but which is a key feature of the modern system, namely, purely formal rules of derivability.

This may be made a *little* clearer by considering the formula of the predicate calculus, $\sim Ta$, in an interpretation in which a names that very formula.

At the outset, there is the trouble that $\sim Ta$ is not treated as a sentence token, like the token A (which has many copies), which was the Liar Paradox case. The formula $\sim Ta$ would standardly be treated as a *type*. In my opinion, there are no such things as letter and sentence types. There is the property of being, say, a letter "a," which lots of marks have by virtue of shape and role, etc., but there is no such thing as "The letter a." To say a formula is true in an interpretation should mean that all tokens of a certain kind are true in that interpretation.

This will be ignored to facilitate further discussion. But it may be a significant source of the contrast between the way traditional logic can talk about truth and the way the predicate calculus can.

So suppose that we wish to make T represent the predicate "is true." On a model theoretic interpretation, of course, we would have to be content with the extension of the predicate. But we can't have even that. To interpret T requires assigning a set to it. If the set includes the wff $\sim Ta$, then $\sim Ta$ is false in this interpretation, since the thing a stands for is in the set T stands for, making Ta true. If the set doesn't include the wff $\sim Ta$, then $\sim Ta$ is true in this interpretation. In other words, $\sim Ta$ is in the extension of T in this interpretation if and only if $\sim Ta$ is false in the interpretation. This means that T doesn't capture the extension of the property of truth for formulae of the calculus in this interpretation ("This interpretation" being "the" interpretation with a naming $\sim Ta$).

This indicates how the model theoretic interpretation of predicate calculus manages to be "semantically consistent" with nothing to fear from semantic paradoxes. These interpretations don't allow reflecting semantic properties well enough to allow the formulation of the paradoxes.

On the property interpretation, we can having a naming $\sim Ta$ and T naming the property of being true. But then Ta is trivially false, which makes $\sim Ta$ true by the truth table. What has happened? Well, the thing a names is not true or false. Neither is a sentence as a collection of marks. It is only true as a sentence of a language. Ta is only true or false in an interpretation. In the above interpretation, call it I, Ta is false because it attributes to $\sim Ta$ a property, truth, which ~*Ta* doesn't have. ~*Ta* does have the property of truth in *I*, whatever that is.

So could we let *T* stand for the property of truth in *I*, and *a* stand for ~*Ta*? Of course, but that only gives us an interpretation *I'* which represents about *I* what we have already been saying about it. Could we make an interpretation, say *I**, such that in it, *T* stood for truth in *I**? Well, truth in *I** for *Ta* would mean *T*'s naming a property possessed by the thing named by *a*, which is still ~*Ta*. And that property can't be truth in *I**, because the only way ~*Ta* can have that property is if ~*Ta* is not true in *I**. It is not possible for there to be such an interpretation *I** and thus there is no such property as truth in *I**.

Truth is a property of what is said. But on the set theoretic and property interpretations, it is quite unclear what is said by an interpreted formula. Truth in an interpretation is clearly defined, but its connection with truth is not so clear.

We can turn to linguistic interpretations. They do very well at making clear what is said. We can certainly arrange for ~*Ta* to come out as a *symbolization* of "The formula (sentence) *a* is not true." Then waiving the type-token problem, we can have a Liar-type paradox and my theory will give a consistent account of why what the formula, so interpreted, says, is false. But the trouble is that this truth assignment will not mesh with the syntax. Both *Ta* and ~*Ta*, and also (*Ta* ∨ ~*Ta*), will come out false. A theorem will be classed as false! Of course, on this interpretation, (*Ta* ∨ ~*Ta*) is not at all an instance of the law of excluded middle, despite its geometric form. And while something false will be "provable"—that is, the ink marks associated with a false proposition will play a theorem-role in a game of lining up marks—nothing false will be *provable*. But this is a severe restriction on the usefulness of the syntactic apparatus when dealing with such a property as truth.

Well, I would certainly admit that I have yet to answer the challenge that perhaps this feature of truth as opposed to nonsemantic properties only shows that truth is not a property, or any other of the questions that should be raised. I have been able to show very little of my account of the paradoxes, but I hope it is enough to bring out how it conflicts with a general formal account of proof. The difference between the traditional logic and the modern system with its superbly precise syntax is that the traditional logic can consistently give truth a more general role, by being less concerned about purely formal deduction. On the other hand, the formal syntax raises a problem as to how, if at all, we use it to express any concepts or to say anything at all. The more we attack this problem, the more we threaten the neatness of the syntax.

4   The Verifiability Principle

George Schlesinger

Introduction

The Principle of Verifiability may well be claimed to be a more exclusively philosophical methodological principle than most other methodological principles employed by philosophers. Typical methodological devices, like infinite regress arguments, *petitio principii* arguments, or advancing counterexamples, are designed to exhibit the falsity of particular claims or the invalidity of certain arguments. The truth of statements and the validity of arguments, of course, play a vital role in many disciplines. The Principle of Verifiability, however, is typically employed to determine whether sentences themselves that are purporting to convey statements are meaningful or not, which may well be supposed to qualify as a characteristic philosophical concern.

Although this principle has had a relatively short history, it is rich in extraordinary episodes. Its advocates, who initially hoped it might serve as a panacea capable of dissolving many of the intractable problems of philosophy, as well as their opponents, included a large number of first-rate intellects. Yet, some of the assertions they made and some of the arguments they constructed would be difficult to believe had they not been so well documented. They are therefore worth reviewing if for no other purpose than to confirm how perilously slippery is the road that leads to the elusive goal of philosophical understanding. I hope, however, to achieve something more here. I hope to show that, now that we are capable of taking a dispassionate approach to the issue at hand and of assessing it more soberly, the principle, when properly understood, can be seen as a unique tool, nevertheless, with the aid of which valuable insights may yet be obtained.

Meaning and Verifiability

The Principle of Verifiability is essentially the doctrine that a sentence is meaningful if and only if it is verifiable. It is a remarkable fact that no lengthy essays are to be found that explain the intimate connection between verifiability and meaning. There are, futhermore, no essays that explain why it should be necessary to be able to indicate the method one would use to obtain evidence to establish the credibility of what has been said in order to assign meaning to sentences used or an understanding of the statement conveyed by those sentences. The following passage is probably one of the more detailed explanations that has been advanced:

> To understand a proposition means to know what is the case if the proposition is true. One can understand it without knowing whether it is true. To become aware of the sense of proposition one has to get clear about the procedure, otherwise one cannot understand the proposition either. . . . (Waismann 1967, p. 244)

This, however, does not seem entirely compelling. There is undeniably some connection between truth and meaningfulness, since a declarative sentence without any truth value would be meaningless. But does it really follow that a person does not understand a proposition unless he is able to describe precisely the exact circumstances under which it would be true? Numerous statements made by physicists concerning the latest discoveries about subatomic particles and about black holes seem to be understood fairly clearly by intelligent persons although they may not have the slightest idea how to verify them.

I am unsure whether it is discussed in any of his published work, but I have heard Herbert Feigl, one of the founding members of the Vienna Circle, explain that the idea underlying Verificationism is the claim that 'a difference must *make* a difference.' If I understand this succinct argument correctly, it means that when faced with a sentence S we should ask ourselves, does it, or could it possibly, make any experiential difference whether S is true or is false? In other words, the crucial question to be asked is, are there any observable features of the universe that would be one way rather than another if *S* were false rather than true, or vice versa? If the answer is no, then apparently there *is* no difference whether *S* is true or false. That presumably means that *S* is devoid of meaning. Perhaps Feigl's motto is the best expression of the rationale for adopting the verificationist criterion of meaning.

The Definition of 'Verifiability in Principle'

While so little has been said about the really interesting question concerning the precise connection between observational significance, empirical meaningfulness or scientific intelligibility, and verifiability in principle, an inordinate amount has been written, for no useful purpose whatsoever, on the question of the precise definition of 'verifiability in principle.'

Let me begin by saying that assuming we are talking about 'weak verification,' which is often referred to as 'confirmation,' that is, the receiving of a certain degree of evidential support, then the following very simple definition is available:

A sentence *S* is confirm*able* in principle if circumstances can coherently be described under which *S* would be confirm*ed*.

This seems to be a fairly unassailable criterion of confirmability. Admittedly, we may be far from having a confirmation theory and be unable to articulate in detail the precise conditions under which a given *S* is confirmed by certain evidence. But that should in no way affect our assessment of the viability of the idea of Verificationism. Clearly, in spite of the fact that no one has given a full account of the necessary and sufficient conditions under which a hypothesis is confirmed, not a single person would doubt that 'confirmation' is a central notion crucial in determining the degree of credibility of a given hypothesis. To the extent that we accept the notion of confirmation in practice, we seem to be committed to accepting confirmability in principle—and to be able to see an intimate link between the two. There seem to be no more grounds for viewing the concept of meaningfulness that is based on possible confirmation as vague or obscure than there are for regarding the concept of credibility based on actual confirmation as vague or obscure.

This really is all I need to say on this topic; however, I cannot ignore one of the liveliest disputes of this century that endured for several decades. This dispute was generated by philosophers who have, for whatever reason, decided that, in the context of a defense of the verificationist theory of meaning, it is essential to fully articulate the required relationship between a hypothesis and the evidence supporting it (even though, with regard to the question of the credibility of empirical statements, this was commonly known not yet to have been done). In the 1930s, A. J. Ayer put forward the following suggestion:

> A sentence S has empirical significance (or is empirically meaningful) if there are subsidiary hypotheses that, together with the sentence, entail some observation sentence O not entailed by the subsidiary hypotheses alone.

Way back in 1939, of course, Isaiah Berlin complained that Ayer's suggestion is completely useless, since, if accepted, every sentence is meaningful. The reason is very simple. Let S be any sentence whatsoever and O some observation sentence: then, by Modus Ponens, S together with $S \supset O$ entails O while the subsidiary hypothesis $S \supset O$ on its own does not entail O. Hence, S must be regarded as meaningful by Ayer's criterion (Berlin 1939, pp. 225–28).

Let me invite attention to several remarkable points. First of all, Berlin's objection is devoid all foundation since it involves a very elementary error. However, this has not inhibited others who have dealt with the topic from regarding his argument as completely devastating. When I say "others," I include the defenders of verificationism among them. Even Ayer himself was convinced that Berlin's clever argument had destroyed his criterion and went on to construct a more elaborate one immune to that attack. Against this, however, Church raised an even more ingenious objection that was based on exactly the same error as before. Skipping a few decades, we find, as recently as 1980, an authoritative book in the philosophy of science by Clark Glymour, entitled *Theory and Evidence*, citing with full approval Berlin's attack on Ayer's original proposal (p. 33).

I shall try to explain as carefully as I can the fundamental mistake that has been universally overlooked in the context of the debate under review. I begin by describing a very basic principle that should be a part of any *reasonable* theory of confirmation. This principle is almost trivial and would appear compelling even to persons who are quite ignorant about science and scientific method, who have never heard of any rules of confirmation and who have no idea what observations may serve as evidence for what hypotheses. Suppose such a person were told that some reason exists to regard a hypothesis *h* as confirmed by certain evidence *e* because *h* is related to *e* in such and such a way, but that exactly the same reason also existed to regard ~*h* as confirmed by *e* because precisely the same relation obtained between ~*h* and *e*. Surely common sense alone would tell him that under such circumstances *e* does not support *h* more than ~*h*, nor ~*h* more than *h*, and hence the end result must be that *e* provides zero support for *h* as well as for ~*h*. Thus, I believe, no one should wish to deny the following principle, which is a concise formulation of what has just been said:

(P) If hypothesis *h* has the relation *R* to *e*, but, ~h too has *R* to *e*, then *e* cannot confirm *h* by virtue of *h* having the relation *R* to *e*.

Even if *R* should happen to be the paradigm of some confirmatory relation in general, in the particular case where ~*h* has *R* to *e* no less than *h* has *R* to *e*, then *e* is completely symmetrically related to *h* and ~*h* and, therefore, cannot confirm one to a greater degree than the other. If we provide *h* with *n* units of support and similarly ~*h* with *n* units of support, surely the total amount of support either receives is the same, i.e., zero. Thus, it may be claimed to be an adequacy condition for confirmation theory that any acceptable principle of confirmation ought to satisfy the condition (P).

In order to provide a simple illustration of its intended effect, let us consider a confirmation rule that would be an exact parallel to Ayer's confirmability principle:

(HD) A hypothesis *H* is confirmed if together with an auxiliary hypothesis *established as credible* it entails a *true* observation sentence *O*, not entailed by the subsidiary hypothesis alone.

This is, in fact, a fairly well-known rule widely held by philosophers and represents the Hypothetico-Deductive rule of confirmation. It is obvious that (HD) could be objected to (and indeed it has been objected to) as being useless (Glymour 1980, p. 33), since on its basis any hypothesis whatsoever could be confirmed. For let us pick an arbitrary hypothesis H and any highly confirmed true sentence O; then clearly

(1) $H \ \& \ (H \supset O) \rightarrow O$

where $H \supset O$ is true since its consequent is true, yet it does not on its own entail O. Consequently, we are forced to admit that if we adopted (HD) then any H would be confirmed by any highly confirmed true O by virtue of (1).

This, of course, is a blunder. Like any other rule of confirmation, (HD) should be subject to the restriction expressed by (P). For to regard H as confirmed by O because of (1) would be a clear violation of (P), since it is also the case that

(1′) $\sim H \ \& \ (\sim H \supset O) \rightarrow O$

It is thus clear that H and $\sim H$ are related to O by the same relation from the fact that merely by substituting $\sim H$ for H in (1) we obtain its mirror image (1′), and conversely.

It is worth adding that this is so only as long as H is an arbitrary proposition; in some specific instances where H stands for some special proposition, (P) does not apply. Consider for example:

H_1 = The temperature at the center of the sun is 0°C.
O_1 = A bolometer of type B placed in a specific location has its indicator in position p.

Assuming the truth of fairly well-established radiation laws, the magnitude of the distance from the sun to the earth, that rate of fall of temperature along the sun's radius, and the properties of B, we can establish the truth of $H_1 \supset O_1$. Then we apply

(1*) $H_1 \ \& \ (H_1 \supset O_1) \rightarrow O_1$

and observe O_1 to be the case; consequently, we conclude that H_1 has been confirmed. In part, this is a somewhat rough summary of the actual way scientists have determined the temperature at the center of the sun. Now it may appear for a moment that here too we have a violation of (P) since it is also the case that,

(1*′) $\sim H_1 \ \& \ (\sim H_1 \supset O_1) \rightarrow O_1$

The answer however is that (1*′) is *not* the perfect image of (1*); that is, H_1 and $\sim H_1$ are not really identically related to O_1. In the case of (1*′) the only reason why $(\sim H_1 \supset O_1)$ is true is because

O_1 is given as true. It is different in the case of (1*). As we have explained, there is a set of well-established laws that support the truth of ($H_1 \supset O_1$), which was therefore credible even before O_1 had been observed. There is thus no complete symmetry between (1*) and (1*′); in other words, the confirmation obtained for H_1 through (1*′) is unique and is not cancelled by a mirror-image confirmation of its contradictory through adherence to condition (P).

The only difference between Ayer's criterion and (HD) is that the latter refers to actually *established* observation sentences, while "*O*" in Ayer's criterion stands for a *possible* observation sentence. Since it is obvious that a sentence is confirmable if and only if circumstances are describable under which it would actually be confirmed, Principle (P) applies to Ayer's criterion no less than to any rule of actual confirmation. Given this result, however, Berlin's objection falls apart, since his example of S & ($S \supset O$), where S is just any sentence, is clearly in violation of (P).

As noted above, Ayer himself was substantially shaken by the (entirely unfounded) charge that his criterion conferred empirical significance indiscriminately upon every sentence; as a result, he hastened to construct a more elaborate criterion. After the new criterion had also been attacked, it was amended, and so on. At a certain point, the conclusion was reached that this process was going to lead nowhere. Consequently, Carnap tried a new approach, namely, abandoning the effort to construct a criterion for the meaningfulness of whole sentences and focusing upon individual words instead. He proposed a test by passing which individual words may gain admission into a system of empirical theory and become terms of its language. When a word becomes a legitimate term of a language, its significance relative to other components of the same language is thereby established. As to sentences themselves, any syntactically well-formed sentence in which every term is significant—by virtue of having passed Carnap's test—is to be regarded as meaningful.

I shall not spend much time on discussing Carnap's suggestion in general, but only roughly on why it did not succeed: a sentence may be constructed strictly according to the rules of syntax and may employ nothing but significant terms, yet fail to make sense. Hence, it remains essential to have a test for the meaningfulness of whole sentences.

The regrettable failure of philosophers to pay attention to one of the most elementary and compelling principles of confirmation has led to the eventual abandonment of hope for the construction of a viable Principle of Verifiability. The following, for example, is one of many descriptions of the decline and fall of Verificationism:

> Verificationism has seen better days. Attempts to give an account of *sentential meaningfulness* in terms of a sentence's relation to observation sentences and to use this account to purge philosophy of meaningless metaphysics are hardly the fashion in recent literature. Increasingly, subtle attempts to specify the relation that must obtain between a sentence and an observation sentence if the sentence is to be verifiable fell upon increasingly subtle counter-examples. Gradually the program's supporters have lost the faith. (Stich et al. 1973, p. 84)

I would like to emphasize that while, as we have seen, a simple and perfectly viable principle of this type is readily available, this by no means implies the meaninglessness of all metaphysics. Metaphysical hypotheses are, as a rule, defended by arguing that certain experiences are best accounted for by them or that those experiences may be looked upon as empirical evidence for that metaphysical hypotheses by virtue of which they are not only meaningful but credible as well.

Objections to Verificationism

It should be mentioned that other attacks have also been made on Verificationism. None of them have been successful to any degree. Let us consider four.

(1) According to Verificationism the factual meaningfulness of sentences is essentially tied to observation sentences. It is thus supposed that we recognize observation statements when we see them and know how to distinguish them from what are, by contrast, theoretical statements. But, in view of the theory-ladenness of all discourse and various other facts, many philosophers have denied that such a distinction can be drawn. R. Swinburne is among those who state that the notion of an 'observation statement' is ambiguous enough to be unhelpful in distinguishing between all that is factually meaningful and all that is devoid of meaning. He says:

> So although men may be agreed *by and then* about which statements are observation statements, I see no reason to suppose that the

degree of consensus is vastly greater here than over which statements are factually meaningful. And if that is so, the confirmationist principle is not going to be of great help in clearing up the latter. (Swinburne 1973, p. 73).

The simple reply to this is, first of all, that 'confirmability in principle' and meaningfulness are in the same boat as 'confirmed in practice' and credibility, and if the latter need not be abandoned because of the ambiguities surrounding the notion of an observation statement, neither need the former. But, of course, the latter notion is in no trouble, for whatever difficulties there may be in distinguishing between observation statements and statements that are not, at any time there is some set of statements that is generally regarded as having been established as credible, irrespective whether they are or are not to be called "observation statements." Thus, a sentence is meaningful if a situation can be described in which it is supported by statements that have been established as true.

(2) In the article just quoted, Swinburne makes another interesting criticism calculated to demolish Verificationism. He claims that it may be easily demonstrated that there is an indefinite number of propositions that share a certain form and are so constructed that they cannot be verified under any circumstances, yet which are undeniably meaningful. One such example is:

p_1:   Among possible claims about the prehuman past which the best evidence ever to be obtained by man makes highly improbable, some are nevertheless true.

Everyone will be convinced that p_1 is meaningful. For let q be a particular highly improbable claim about the prehuman past. Then if we properly understand what 'highly improbable' means, we know that it is different from 'false.' It therefore makes sense to say that q is highly improbable but not false. But if that makes sense, then surely p_1, which claims merely that there is at least one proposition that is like q, must also make sense.

Now as to the claim that p_1 is in principle unconfirmable, what would amount to confirmation that p_1 is true? That p_1 is true would be supported if we confirmed Q, where Q asserts that q (which is a claim about the prehuman past), although highly improbable, is nevertheless true. This, however, seems impossible. Q, after all, is a conjunction of two statements a and b where:

    a: *q* is highly improbable by the best evidence ever to be obtained by man.
    b: *q* is true.

Q is true if both its conjuncts are true. If, however, we should confirm *a* to be true, that would amount to the disconfirmation that *b* is true and vice versa. It is thus not possible that there should be evidence that *Q* is true and therefore no evidence that p_1 is true. On the other hand, that p_1 cannot be disconfirmed follows simply from the fact that it is an existential statement and that such statements, in general, cannot be falsified.

The grievous error in Swinburne's argument, however, is that he has assumed for no good reason that the only way in which to confirm p_1 is to actually get hold of some *q* that can be demonstrated at one and the same time to be both highly improbable and true. But, of course, p_1 may not only be confirmed but also may be rendered firmly credible, even if we have not the slightest idea of what *q* may be like, simply by showing that p_1 follows by the rules of either deductive or inductive logic from other established propositions. Thus, it is a well-known fact that in many lotteries conducted throughout the world, each of the large number of tickets involved has only an exceedingly small chance of winning the main prize, yet it is certain even before the drawing takes place that one of them is going to win it. This provides us with practical situations in which, with respect of any ticket *t*, the best evidence supports the contention that, proposition of the form, although '*t* is going to win,' are highly improbable, for each lottery one such proposition is inevitably true. We may therefore regard this as inductive evidence that p_1 is true.

In addition, of course, we may also argue from the very nature of the notion of 'probability' that p_1 is very likely to be true. After all, p_1 is true if any one of $Q_1, Q_2 \ldots Q_n$ is true, where *n* is an exceedingly large number (in view of the fact that there are so many statements about prehistoric times that are likely to be false). Suppose the probability that Q_1 is true is *m* and so on. Then the probability that p_1 is true is equal to the probability that $Q_1 \lor Q_2 \ldots Q_n$ is true. This, in view of the enormous size of *n*, is very high even though *m* itself is very small.

    (3) The following objection differs considerably from the previous ones; it goes so far as to imply that the principle may be regarded as meaningless on the basis of the very tenets that logical

positivists insist upon. This objection was raised way back at an early stage of Verificationism, but there are still people today who believe the objection to provide a very effective weapon against the principle. It has been agreed among empiricists that there are two kinds of cognitively meaningful statements:

(i) Synthetic *a posteriori* statements in which the predicate is not contained in the subject and it is essential to make some observation in order to ascertain their truth value.

(ii) Analytic *a priori* statements the truth of which can be ascertained prior to any observation through understanding the words constituting the sentence conveying the statement.

Thus, the verification principle, itself which verificationists naturally take to be meaningful, must fall into one of these two categories. It should seem quite obvious that it is not synthetic *a posteriori*, since correctness of the principle cannot be observed under any describable circumstances. It might have been synthetic *a posteriori* if the principle had been arrived at after having observed that people in general fail to understand unverifiable statements. In fact, however, the whole point of the verification principle has been to use it to disqualify sentences that sound quite intelligible. Unquestionably, 'devoid of cognitive meaningfulness' is a broader notion than 'unintelligible' and the principle therefore cannot be claimed to be based on the observation of what in practice people do or do not comprehend.

We might be inclined, therefore, to hold that the principle is analytic *a priori*, i.e., that it expresses a convention of our language. Some philosophers firmly reject this view, since upon examining ordinary language we clearly do not find such a convention. A statement like 'All bachelors are unmarried men' is a paradigm of an analytic *a priori* statement, for any speaker of the English language will tell you that the sentence expresses the truth by virtue of the meaning of the words it contains. But this is certainly not so in the case of the verification principle. There is also another basic difference between the two: there is no good reason why we should not readily accept the convention that 'bachelor' and 'unmarried man' are synonymous. No one would be motivated to insist that some other word rather than 'bachelor' should be synonymous with 'unmarried man'! However the acceptance of implications of the verification principle does place upon us a considerable commitment. Thus, if the connection between meaningfulness and Verifiability is not forced upon us by experience but, instead, only by convention, we may well want to refuse to accept the convention and its far reaching restrictive implications.

> If the convention is without foundations, if it is arbitrary, then why should we take it seriously? The positivists who considered these questions either abandoned positivism or found a third category for statements, the category of recommendations. If the verification principle is a recommendation then on positivist grounds it is not meaningful. It is a sign that the positivist feels good about certain kinds of speech and uncomfortable about others. How positivists feel about different things decides nothing about the intelligibility of expressions. (Edgar 1980, p. 122)

I believe, however, that the positivist can easily defend his thesis by maintaining that his principle is analytically true. It is unquestionably true that not all analytic sentences are like 'All bachelors are unmarried men,' where the meanings of the terms involved is entirely transparent to all speakers of the language. Some meanings have to be established through what Carnap called 'philosophical explication.'

For example, we read in the philosophical literature that '*S* knows that *p*' means '*p* is true and *S* believes that *p* and *S* is appropriately justified in his belief'! If this is an adequate definition of the concept of knowledge, it amounts to the assertion of an analytic truth. Yet upon being asked what '*S* knows *p*' means, very few speakers of the language will give us the conjunction of the above three statements. Even an accepted authority like Webster says that 'know' means: (i) To have knowledge; (ii) To be or become cognizant. No mention is made of 'truth,' 'belief,' or 'justification.' Thus it is one thing to give the meaning of a term by a dictionary based on a knowledge of the language and another to explicate meaning by a philosopher. There is, of course, a basic difference between lexical and explicative definitions. The former offers a definition of a *word* in terms of *other words*. Explicative definition, by contrast, is an attempt to provide the meaning of a given *concept* with the aid of *different concepts*. Both types of definitions, however, if accepted are to be treated as necessary truth.

(4) The following objection is likely to look to most people as the best of all the objections that have been made. Suppose there exists a unique person SP, a Super-Predictor, who is capable— without employing any method but by saying whatever first comes

to his mind—unfailingly to predict the future. Let us assume it as an undisputed fact that in millions and millions of past occasions SP's predictions have turned out to be true and that there have been no occasions on which he was wrong. Now let

S = The event e has happened

where e is described as an event that has not the slightest effect on anything and is therefore undetectable directly or indirectly by any sort of observation. We would be inclined to treat S as a paradigm of a sentence that is logically unconfirmable, since we would contradict S if we offered a description of circumstances under which S might be confirmed. Now, as I have said, we are supposing that SP is a contemporary of ours who has made thousands upon thousands of correct predictions and never an incorrect one, and thus we have a very solid basis for giving full credence to anything he says. Let us then suppose that he asserts that S is true. There seems to be no reason to deny that in such a case S would have to be regared as strongly verified by virtue of the fact that it has been asserted by a unique person who has proven himself, beyond reasonable doubt, to speak nothing but the truth.

If we were to accept this argument, however, then it is quite clear that the verification principle would have become completely useless. Few will want to deny that it is logically possible that such an SP could exist. It is also very easy to imagine that SP could claim S to be true, no matter what sentence S stands for. It then follows that there are no meaningless sentences at all, since every sentence would be verifiable in principle. We could always coherently describe a situation in which SP claims S to be true.

In truth, of course, this objection is entirely unfounded. Suppose it were asked: what would happen if SP made the prediction that tomorrow it will rain and tomorrow it will not rain, or any other self-contradictory prediction? Would we have to believe him? The obvious answer is that, given our description of SP, we may be fully assured that he would never make such a prediction. Similarly, on the justified assumption of the complete reliability of SP, we may be fully confident that he would never utter a sentence and claim it to express a true proposition, when that sentence were in fact devoid of meaning and hence did not express any proposition. It would be incompatible with the strongly established claim that

SP invariably speaks the truth to assume that he would say that a sentence S made a prediction that is going to materialize when that sentence made no prediction at all. In other words, since S is a meaningless sentence, it would amount to a contradiction to maintain that SP, a perfect truth-teller, would assert S. In short, S has not been shown to be verifiable, in principle, since it has not been shown that SP could assert S. In fact, if we had somebody whom we treated until now as a perfect predictor and truth-teller, than his asserting S, like his asserting that tomorrow it will and it will not rain, would amount to conclusive evidence that, contrary to our belief, he was not a perfect truth-teller, after all.

It may well be asked: how could we know that S is meaningless because unverifiable? The only way, of course, is by looking at S and figuring out that S is incapable of being verified in the standard way that we normally call 'verification.' It goes without saying that we cannot attempt to try to find out by way of observing whether or not S is something SP would assert. It is only *after* we have established (in the normal way) whether or not a given sentence is verifiable that we are in a position to determine whether or not S is the kind of sentence that SP might assert. Of course, the same goes for the task of distinguishing between consistent and inconsistent sentences. It is only through the application of deductive logic that we can do this. Once we have determined that a given sentence is self-contradictory, we may well say that a genuine perfect truth-teller would never assert it. But, of course, no one would entertain the absurd thought that we might test the logical coherence of a statement by asking ourselves whether SP would assert it. In the same way, it is clear that no amount of investigation of the nature of such a splendid luminary as SP could yield any clue at all concerning the question whether a given sentence is verifiable in principle. It is only through an examination of the scope of standard, mundane scientific methods that the empirical meaningfulness of sentences that lack actual confirmation can be established.

There is also a deeper point. I cited Feigl's view that the basis of Verificationism is not that meaningfulness is linked to the method of establishing truth of falsity, but rather that anything of substance must have some concrete manifestation. Suppose it is claimed that a state of affairs denoted by 'Σ' obtains in the universe. If Σ is a genuine state of affairs, then the world must be different from what it would have been without Σ. That is, the physical element *S* of Σ could not be entirely identical with what they would have been had they not given rise to Σ. The verificationist insists on being able to behold these manifestations, at least in principle, before he is prepared to grant meaningfulness to the claim that Σ obtains. But SP vouching for the truth of that claim cannot amount to each a manifestation; for that is not an observable display by the relevant entities of characteristics they themselves possess.

Misuses of Verificationism

In the rest of this article, I propose to discuss the possible application of the Verifiability Principle. In this section, we shall look at some remarkable views that have been expressed in this connection and that are way off target concerning the genuine usefulness of this principle.

(1) M. Schlick, the major founder of the Vienna Circle where the principle originated, explained that a sentence stating the temperature at the center of the sun is, for example, meaningful, since it is conceivable that a physicist and his instruments could penetrate unscorched into the innermost part of the sun. Only sentences that are logically impossible to verify are thus devoid of meaning. Examples illustrating this are provided by Schlick:

> Take some examples. The sentences, 'My friend died the day after tomorrow'; 'The lady wore a dark red dress which was bright green'; 'The campanile is 100 feet and 150 feet high'; 'The child was naked but wore a long nightgown'; obviously violate the rules which in ordinary English govern the use of words occurring in the sentences. They do not describe any facts at all; they are meaningless, because they represent logical impossibilities. (Schlick 1936, p. 154)

This is very puzzling. It is clear to begin with, that none of the quoted sentences is in fact unverifiable logically, physically, or in any other sense. For example, we could take an ordinary meter rod, apply it to the campanile and as a result we should be able to observe very distinctly that its height is either not 100 feet high or not 150 feet high. Hence, we could conclusively verify that at least one of the conjuncts of the sentence is false. It therefore follows that the conjunction, 'The campanile is 100 feet and 150 feet high,' can directly and decisively be discovered to be false.

But since a meaningless sentence is one that fails to express any proposition while our sentence expresses a false proposition, it cannot be meaningless.

Should it be the case, for whatever reason, that Schlick holds that contradictions are in fact meaningless, we do not need the Verifiability Principle to see that each one of these sentences is contradictory: that fact is obvious to all who understand the language. At any rate, is Schlick trying to convey to us that recognition of the vacuity of the cited sentences is a paradigm of the revolutionary achievements of the philosophical movement he has founded?

(2) Carnap, one of the greatest analytic philosophers of this century, wrote a famous article entitled, "The Elimination of Metaphysics," in which he argues vigorously and at length that, with the aid of the Verifiability Principle, it is possible to demonstrate the vacuity of all metaphysics and to show that some of the (allegedly intractable) profound problems of human existence are pseudoproblems requiring no solution, merely dissolution. Among the examples he cites to show the lack of meaning of certain terms he includes such phrases as 'The Absolute,' 'The being of being,' 'being-in-and-for-itself,' and 'the non-Ego.' Later he selects a whole passage from the work of Heidegger to illustrate the meaninglessness of metaphysics:

> What is to be investigated is being only and—*nothing* else being alone and further—*nothing*; solely being, and beyond being—*nothing*. *What about this Nothing?* . . . *Does the Nothing exist only because the Not, i.e., this Negation exist?* Or is it the other way around? *Does negation* and the Not exist only because the Nothing exists? . . . We assert: *the Nothing is prior to the Not and the Negation.* . . . We know the Nothing. . . . *Anxiety reveals the Nothing.* . . . That for which and because of which we were anxious, was 'really' nothing. Indeed: The Nothing itself—as such—was present. *What about this Nothing?—The Nothing itself Nothings.* (Carnap 1960 in Ayer 1960, p. 67)

Carnap seems to have succeeded in showing that just quoting a short passage, without parodying or disparaging Heidegger, may be sufficient to discourage one from studying him. Apart from this, however, it is impossible to discern precisely what Carnap had in mind when he cited this paragraph. Why does Carnap concentrate exclusively on the metaphysical theory of a single esoteric writer? Why does he not consider more familiar metaphysical issues discussed by many different philosophers, such as the questions whether there are any dynamic temporal properties; whether possible worlds are or are not real; or whether universals as well as particulars exist? Furthermore, contrary to what he claims, his examples are not suitable illustrations of how the Verifiability Principle can help to expose pseudostatements. Genuine cases in which we discover meaninglessness through the use of principle are interesting in this sense: we are confronted with a sentence that is not gibberish, that is well formed and seems to make good sense; but upon closer examination we realize that there is, in principle, no way in which any observation could serve as evidence for the truth or falsity of what has been said. The significant point is: that the sentence makes enough sense that we clearly understand why what normally should have been a relevant method of verification cannot be carried out for the particular sentence in question.

A rather unimportant candidate for being ruled out as devoid of factual meaning through the application of the Verifiability Principle is the assertion, 'Last night every physical object in the universe shifted eastward a hundred miles.' We seem to understand what is being said, and it certainly makes sense to claim that *A* or *B* or *C*, etc., shifted eastward, but we realize that in the peculiar case where *A and B and C and* everything else is said to have shifted we lose our usual means for measurement.

When it comes to an utterance like, 'The Nothing itself Nothings,' by contrast we are at a complete loss to describe what we cannot do, which, if we could do, would help us to establish the truth of that utterance. In brief, this sentence is meaningless not merely because of our inability to perform the required verification, but because it is unintelligible, instead.

To put it differently: if I were to read a passage in Ugaritic that I was told was written by an ancient metaphysician, surely I would not say that the passage was unintelligible to me because I did not know how to verify it, but rather because I do not understand a single word of that language.

(3) A widely discussed application of the verification principle has been to undermine religious belief. Opponents of Theism, who in the past have maintained that Theism lacks credibility, have now advanced the stronger thesis that since nothing has happened or could happen that would be relevant to the credibility of Theism,

this doctrine is unverifiable in principle and is therefore devoid of meaning. What is really extraordinary are the replies that various philosophers anxious to defend religious belief attempted to give. There is the well known but startling reply by R. M. Hare, who contends that Theism is indeed empirically meaningless and would be pointless to assert it were it the case that it intended to make any factual claims concerning the existence of anything. Enlightened Theists make no such claims: they merely recommend to us a way of life. When a Theist states 'God exists,' this is merely a peculiar way of his to urge us to be humble, charitable, and compassionate. (Hare 1964 in Flew & MacIntyre 1964, p. 96) It must be conceded, of course, that Hare has been successful in retreating into a practically impregnable position. He has little to fear that he might be forced to concede any further ground, since by now he has almost nothing left to concede.

There are other philosophers, however, who are not yet prepared to surrender everything of religious significance. For example, John Hick, a highly respected thinker, advances the suggestion that, while admittedly in this world there can be no evidence for the existence of God and therefore Theism is presumably unverifiable in the here and now, we need not exclude the possibility of eschatological verification. In other words, upon the termination of our earthly existence and our arrival in the world-to-come, we could be confronted with the Divine and thus obtain clear evidence of His existence. (Even Bertrand Russell seems to have conceded the possibility of this, as when he declared that should such a contingency arise, then instead of blaming himself for having led the life of an Atheist he would at once ask, "Sire, why did you not give better evidence of Your Existence?") It is quite remarkable that all the objections raised against Hick are based on the complaint that he has resorted to bizarre notions such as the world-to-come, which does not seem to be a well-justified criticism. After all, the survival of the soul is one of the central features of a majority of Theistic beliefs and I can see no reason why a Theist should not be allowed to employ it for any required purpose. The real difficulty in Hick's position seems to me to be that it is entirely pointless to introduce the notion of the world-to-come in this context. For what we have to ask is, what kind of experiences does he have in mind that might lead to eschatological verification? Are those experiences such that they are at least coherently describable? If they are not, then we surely must conclude that, although the world-to-come may legitimately be claimed to be a very strange world, nevertheless, even there nothing takes place that is logically impossible. Hence, in that case, the notion of the world-to-come is of no help. On the other hand, if the relevant experiences are coherently describable, then they are logically possible. But if they are logically possible, then it is in principle possible that they should be had by us in the here and now, and Theism is not unverifiable in the first place. Hence the notion of a world-to-come is superfluous for our present purposes.

Another important defender of Theism, Alvin Plantinga, feels no compunction in conceding that Theism is indeed unverifiable in principle. He vigorously argues, however, that there is no obligation on the part of a rational person to accept the Verifiability Principle, so we are free to maintain that a sentence is meaningful and capable of making an empirical claim even when it is un-verifiable. He arrives at this conclusion after demolishing the basis of the Verifiability Theory of Meaning by claiming that this criterion has not been, and cannot be, clearly stated, and thus no one knows what it amounts to.

It may not be unfair to claim that the victory Plantinga has thought he has won, in spite of the concession that Theism is completely unverifiable, is not much less a Pyrrhic victory than Hare's. After all, to a genuine Theist the most momentous feature of reality is that the universe has been created and is constantly supervised by a Divine Being. How then is it possible that the universe has no aspect whatever that points to the existence of such a Being? How is it possible that it should make no difference whether there is or is not any God? Feigl, as we have seen, succinctly described the essence of the Verifiability Principle, which is that "a difference must *make* a difference." Can one concede that by adding God to the universe or subtracting Him from the universe it makes *no* difference and still remain a traditional Theist?

But the concession that Theism is unverifiable in principle, of course, is entirely uncalled for. Recall that Hume was one of the most prominent philosophers famous for his opposition to meta-physicians, whose pronouncements, he thought, do not "contain any experimental reasoning concerning matters of fact or existence" and advised us to commit their works to the flames. Yet he took it for granted that empirical evidence is possible to support the claims of religion. It would be impossible to understand why he should have spent all those efforts in devising arguments as to why it is irrational to believe in stories concerning miraculous events, were it not that he was anxious to remove evidence that, in his opinion, would have provided a strong basis for Theism. In addition, he explicitly says in the concluding paragraph to his essay "On Miracles,"

> So that upon the whole, we may conclude that Christian religion not only was at first attended with miracles, but even at this day cannot be believed by any reasonable person without one. Mere reason is unsufficient to convince us to its veracity.

The clear implication is that a reasonable person cannot believe Theism because—and only because—Hume has successfully undermined the credibility of miracle-stories, which otherwise would amount to strong evidence supporting Theism. The reason is essentially because we would have to agree that:

$$p \ (E/T) > p \ (E/N)$$

i.e., the probability of E, say, a miraculous event like the waters of the Nile turning into blood after this was predicted by an outstanding spokesman for T (= Theism) is considerably higher than if N (= the denial of Theism) is true. It is to be further noted that Hume only denied the rationality of believing in a miracle as long as it is reported by others. There is no reason why anyone of us should *in principle* be prevented from witnessing a miracle, which would amount to a strong confirmation of Theism for ourselves.

A Constructive Use of the Verifiability Principle

My final point will be to reassure the reader that it is by no means the case that, on my liberal interpretation which does not invalidate genuine metaphysics, Verificationism is incapable of accomplishing much. The following is just one example of the important philosophical use to which the Verifiability Principle may be put.

A number of philosophers have investigated the question whether it is logically possible that there could be periods of time during which absolutely nothing changes throughout the universe. It would seem that, in the absence of any change, no detection of time would be possible and hence it could make no sense to talk about an amount of time having passed even though nothing happened. Yet in a fairly well-known article, Sydney Shoemaker has argued that this is not so. His argument has been slightly revised by Newton-Smith and recently repeated by Swinburne:

> There could be a world, divided into three regions, *A*, *B*, *C*. In *A*, physical objects vanish for a year every three years, after which objects similar to those which disappear reappear. The objects in *B* vanish for a year every four years and those of *C* for a year every five years, similar objects reappearing in the two regions after the year. These cycles of disappearance in one region can usually be observed from the other regions. The cycles of disappearance will coincide every sixty years. There would then be a period of years in which there was nothing that existed. Observers would have inductive evidence of the existence of such a period. (Swinburne 1980, p. 174)

The error of this argument is easy to see. The passage of a year during the absence of *A*, for instance, is of course measured in *B* and *C*. Consequently, the absence of *A* during which a year has passed, is measured from *B and C* and clearly not in *A* itself, which vanished. Similarly, in the twelfth year when both *A* and *B* disappear, the period of their absence measured to be a year in *C*. Thus, it is in *C*, and *C* alone, that a year has passed and nowhere else, since nothing else existed at that time. After sixty years no part of the universe remains in existence, and we cannot meaningfully talk of a year passing anywhere while *A*, *B*, and *C* are gone, since they constitute the whole of the universe.

It seems reasonable, therefore, to maintain—though of course we have no conclusive proof—that we shall not succeed in constructing a coherent story in which we could have any sort of empirical evidence for the claim that a certain amount of time has passed in the complete absence of all change. Consequently, the verification principle bids us to regard such a claim as meaningless.

It seems clear that this conclusion amounts to much more than the mere discovery that a given sentence is devoid of meaning. It has profound implications concerning the basic nature of time. There is a strong inclination to think of time as a container, in fact, the arch-container, since everything occurs *in* time. But this suggests the view that, just as in the case of other containers when emptied of their contents, we are still left with the container itself, the same should be true with time. The Verifiability Principle helps us to see that this is not so. Through the use of that principle, we are thus able to gain deeper insight into the basic nature of time.

5 Infinite Regress Arguments

David H. Sanford

Geach's remark "that often when philosophers *think* the trouble is a vicious regress, the *real* trouble arises already at the first step: if it is rightly diagnosed there, we can forget about the regress," like Passmore's discussion of infinite regress, applies to negative arguments that attempt to show that a definition, explanation, or theory is inadequate. My main example of a negative regress is D. H. Mellor's restatement of McTaggart's argument that an apparent contradiction in the *A*-series is inescapable. This argument fails to distinguish an infinite series of increasingly complex tensed facts from an infinite series of increasingly complex descriptions of tensed facts. I suggest that this example, in failing to distinguish distinct series, exhibits a difficulty present in many other negative regress arguments.

Positive regress arguments attempt to show that something with a special character exists. A series of items cannot be infinite, and also cannot loop, so it must terminate; and the final item thereby has a special character. My main example here is an argument for the existence of a desire of something for its own sake. Besides exploring various reasons for holding that series of desires are not infinite and do not loop, I consider alternative ways in which a series might terminate and alternative ways in which it might fail to terminate. While I do not conclude that positive regress arguments never succeed, I do attempt to show that more difficulties attend them than are usually noticed.

I. Negative Regress Arguments

The following, quoted in its entirety, is the shortest entry in G. E. Moore's *Commonplace Book*:

VICIOUS INFINITE SERIES
Are those only which arise from a circular definition. E.g. "is good" = "is judged to be good". (Moore 1962, p. 109)

The claim that something is good if and only if it is judged to be good, however implausible it may be, involves a circularity or regress only if it is understood as a definition. As a definition it is hopeless, as any competent philosopher should see immediately. Moore's remark that vicious infinite series are *only* those which arise from a definition is no stronger than a similar claim John Passmore makes in *Philosophical Reasoning*. After discussing Waismann's example of a mathematical infinite regress argument to show that $\sqrt{2}$ is irrational (Waismann 1968), Passmore says

> Philosophical regresses, on the contrary, demonstrate only that a supposed way of explaining something or 'making it intelligible' in fact fails to explain, not because the explanation is self-contradictory, but only because it is, in the crucial respect, of the same form as what it explains. Or again, that a proposed criterion is of no use as a criterion, because to apply it we should need already to be able to make the kind of distinction for making which it is supposed to be necessary. (Passmore 1970, p. 33)

A pungent and provocative remark about infinite regress arguments in philosophy, similar in spirit to the views of Moore and Passmore, is made by P. T. Geach in a discussion of McTaggart's argument for the unreality of time. The two central contentions of McTaggart's argument are both very controversial. Time is real, first, only if the *A*-series is real, only if there really are characteristics of being future, present, and past that events acquire or lose. But the *A*-series, second, is unreal because it involves an inescapable self-contradiction. The characteristics of being future, present, and past are incompatible. If time is real, however, every event has them all. McTaggart realizes that it is natural to respond to this supposed self-contradiction by insisting that "The characteristics are only incompatible when they are simultaneous, and there is no contradiction to this in the fact that each term has all of them successively" (McTaggart 1927, sec. 330). He argues in sections

331 and 332 that this attempt to get around the contradiction fails because it leads to a vicious infinite regress. This is the "tricky attempted proof" to which Geach refers in the following passage:

This argument is followed in McTaggart's text (332) by a tricky attempted proof that a certain way in which we might try to remove the contradiction generates an infinite vicious regress. McTaggart's critics have said much about this: I shall say nothing. Wittgenstein once remarked that often when philosophers *think* the trouble is a vicious regress, the *real* trouble arises already at the first step: if it is rightly diagnosed there, we can forget about the regress. For example, in the Third Man argument, there is *already* a contradiction in affirming simultaneously (i) that there is *just one* Form in virtue of which each object covered by the general name 'man' is to be regarded as a man, and (ii) that since this Form also, indeed primarily, is called by the name 'man', there must be a *second* Form in virtue of which 'man' applies to the first Form and to each man commonly so called; there is absolutely no need for the further elaboration of the argument, in which Plato seeks to show that by parity of reasoning we get an infinite series of Forms. So here: if McTaggart's alleged contradiction is bogus, we need not consider whether the attempt to remove it would generate a vicious regress; if it is not bogus, it suffices to show that *A*-characteristics are not objective. (Geach 1979, pp. 100–101)

Self-contradiction is the topic of McTaggart's argument, which is directed against an attempt to explain away an apparent contradiction. Neither the Theory of Forms nor the Third Man argument, in contrast, is particularly concerned with self-contradiction. Passmore does not mention self-contradiction when he discusses the Third Man, and the contradiction Geach points out can be avoided easily enough by replacing "there is *just one* Form" in (i) by "there is a Form." There are real troubles other than self-contradiction that can arise already at the first step. Although Passmore does not recommend forgetting about the regress, his treatment of Plato's argument is compatible with Geach's general point.

The infinite regress argument can then be used as an emphatic way of pointing out that if 'sharing the same property' is unintelligible, then so also is 'participating in the same form'. . . . The infinite regress argument brings home to us the fact that the intelligibility the philosopher is seeking is not to be found by going further along the path he has begun to tread; having failed to achieve it by introducing a single form into the situation, he is not going to do any better by introducing still more forms. (Passmore 1970, pp. 21–22)[1]

The real trouble arising already at the first step is that of making no progress. We should see this straight away. If we do not, we may see it after realizing that no number of steps, not even an infinite number, makes any progress toward explaining, defining, analyzing, or accounting for something.[2] Drawing attention to an infinite regress can thus have a function even though the real trouble is not due to the regress.

The argument of McTaggart's to which Geach refers has recently been restated and defended by D. H. Mellor. Mellor argues at length against McTaggart's contention that the reality of time requires the reality of the *A*-series, but he thinks that McTaggart's argument against the reality of the *A*-series is perfectly sound. Although I do not quote it here for the purpose of comparison, I believe that the original argument (McTaggart 1927, secs. 330–32) succeeds only if Mellor's paraphrase succeeds. Instead of attempting to summarize this elegant and concise paraphrase, I shall simply quote it. In Mellor's notation, the properties of being past, present, and future are represented by 'P,' 'N' (now), and 'F.'

> Then McTaggart's basic argument is that, on the one hand, the three properties P, N and F are mutually incompatible, so that for any event *e*
> $$Pe \vdash \sim Ne; \; Ne \vdash \sim Fe; \; Fe \vdash \sim Pe; \; \text{etc.} \tag{1}$$
> On the other hand, the inexorable change of tense means that every event has all three *A* series positions, i.e.
> $$Pe \; \& \; Ne \; \& \; Fe. \tag{2}$$
> But (1) and (2) cannot both be true; since if (1) is true, two of the statements in (2) must be false, so (2) as a whole must be false. But our concept of tense commits us to both (1) and (2); so it leads us inevitably into contradiction and thus cannot apply to reality. Reality therefore must be tenseless: there are no tensed facts.
>   To this the riposte is that *e* has no more than one of these incompatible properties at once, so there is no contradiction after all. Suppose for example that *e* is actually present, i.e. N*e*. Then *e* is neither past nor future, i.e. both 'P*e*' and 'F*e*' are false, as (1) requires. The truth rather is that *e will be* past and *was* future, i.e. not (2) but
> $$FPe \; \& \; Ne \; \& \; PFe, \tag{3}$$
> which is quite compatible with (1).
>   So it is. But, as McTaggart remarks, there are more complex tenses than those in (3), and not all combinations of them are so

innocuous. Specifically, there are also PP and PN, FF and FN, and
NP, NN and NF. And just as every event has all *A* series positions
if it has any of them, so it also has all these other complex tenses.
For example, whatever has any simple tense obviously also has it
now, i.e.
Pe ⊢ NPe; Ne ⊢ NNe; Fe ⊢ NFe.
Obviously also, whatever is past *was* present and *was* future, and
whatever is future *will be* present and *will be* past, so that
Pe ⊢ PNe; Pe ⊢ PFe; Fe ⊢ FNe; Fe ⊢ FPe.
Moreover, whatever is sufficiently past also *was* past, e.g. what
happened two days ago was already past yesterday; and sufficiently
future events likewise also *will be* future: which gives us PP and
FF as well as P and F.

In place then of the original three simple tenses, we have the
nine compound tenses PP, PN, PF; NP, NN, NF; FP, FN, FF. But
McTaggart's argument applies just as well to them. Because of the
way tense incessantly changes, every event that has any of these
nine tenses has to have them all; but they are not all mutually
compatible. For example, FF and PP are incompatible, since what
will be future cannot also have been past. And NP, NN and NF
are even more clearly incompatible, because they are equivalent to
the simple P, N and F.

The riposte will again be made, that events do not have these
incompatible tenses all at once. But again, saying in tensed terms
just when they do have them only generates another set of properties,
including mutually incompatible ones like PPP, NNN and FFF, all
of which every event has to have. There is, in other words, an
endless regress of ripostes and rebuttals, a regress that is vicious
because at no stage in it can all the supposed tensed facts be
consistently stated. (Mellor 1981, pp. 93–94)[3]

There are the nine double compound tenses Mellor lists, twenty-
seven triple compounds, eighty-one quadruple compounds, and so
forth. At each increase of complexity, the number of combinations
jumps from 3^n to 3^{n+1}. It may look, at first sight, as if contradictions
compound faster than they can be explained away, since each
attempt to explain away a contradiction involves an increase in
the complexity of compound tenses, and each such increase carries
in its wake still more contradictions that need explaining away. A
closer look, however, reveals that the number of new tensed facts
allegedly indicated does not increase nearly so fast as the number
of new orthographic combinations.

As Mellor says, NP, NN, and NF are equivalent to the simple
P, N, and F. That is, the compound tense expressions "NP," "NN,"
and "NF" do not refer to new tensed facts. The point can be

generalized: adding an "N" to a compound never makes it indicate a new tensed fact. PN as well as NP is equivalent to P, and FN as well as NF is equivalent to F. Five of the nine doubly compound tense expressions indicate no more than what one of the three original simple expressions indicates.

Two of the remaining doubly compound tense expression appear in Mellor's formula (3). If a tense property is a property that an event or moment can gain or lose by the passage of time, "FP" and "PF" do not indicate tensed facts. With the possible exception of events that have always been occurring, so no event occurred before they began, every event is future in the past. With the possible exception of events that will never cease to occur, so no event will occur after they are through, every event is past in the future. In no case does an event gain or lose the property of being past in the future or future in the past. "FP" and "PF" are vacuous tense expressions. Again, the point can be generalized: any expression that contains both an "F" and a "P" is a vacuous tense expression. It does not indicate a new tensed fact, no matter how complicated, because it does not indicate any tensed fact.

The explanation (3) of how an event *e* that is actually present can also be past and future—it *will be* past and *was* future—thus contains two vacuous conjuncts. An alleged contradiction can be explained away as a vacuity.[4]

Two double compound tense expressions remain, "PP" and "FF." Mellor says that whatever is sufficiently past also *was* past. How much past must something be to be sufficiently past? Mellor mentions what happened two days ago, but I assume that whatever happened two jiffys ago is past enough, where a "jiffy" can be any time increment you please, no matter how small. Whatever happened two jiffys ago was past one jiffy ago. Any past event that is insufficiently past is immediately past. I think this is a comprehensible notion. Whether "now" stands for a durationless instant or a greater or lesser temporal interval, either open or closed at the earlier end, an event *e* is immediately past if *e* is over before now and there is no temporal interval *i* such that *e* is over before *i* and *i* is over before now. So I concede that the compound expression "PP," and, for similar reasons, the compound expression "FF," do indicate tensed facts not indicated by one of the earlier simpler expressions.

So far, it looks as if each increase of complexity, although it multiplies the number of expressions by three, adds just two expressions that indicate a tensed fact not indicated before. The other new expressions either indicate the old facts or are vacuous. Seeing this should already diminish the appearance that contradictions compound faster than they can be explained away. But let us take a brief look at triply compound expressions.

Mellor says we have another set of properties, including mutually incompatible ones like PPP, NNN, and FFF. I have claimed that NNN is nothing new; it is the same as NN which is the same as N. The only possible new properties in the whole lot of twenty-seven are the other two, PPP and FFF. But the reason I gave for admitting that PP is something different from P runs into difficulties when one attempts to use it to show that PPP is something different from PP. Is something PP, but not PPP, if it is immediately past in the immediately past? This line of explanation goes through only if time is not dense. Suppose time is dense. If an event e is past, but not immediately past, then there is a temporal interval i such that e is over before i and i is over before now. If time is dense, then this interval can be divided into as many successive smaller intervals as we please. Event e is PP since it was P in i which is P. Event e is also PPP since it is P in the first half of i which is P in the second half of i which is P. Event e is also PPPP since it is P in the first third of i which is . . . , and so forth. If time is dense, no compound tense expression above the second level indicates a temporal fact not already indicated by a simpler tense expression.

If time is dense, all the supposed tensed facts can be stated using one of five expressions: PP, P, N, F, FF. (There are, of course, more than five useful verb tenses since tensed verbs can indicate temporal relations between events. See Reichenbach 1947, pp. 287–98.) The appearance of contradiction can be explained away in the manner of (3). If time is not dense, then there is no end to distinct supposed tensed facts. However many Ps are concatenated (with no Fs in the line-up to reduce the whole thing to vacuity), adding another P will indicate a still more complicated supposed tensed fact. But we should still beware of the following argument:

> At no stage can all the supposed tensed facts be stated. Therefore, at no stage can all the supposed tensed facts be consistently stated. Therefore, the endless regress of explaining away supposed contradictions is vicious.

Any supposed contradiction can still be explained away in the manner of (3).

In summary, the attempt to escape the contradictions McTaggart finds in the *A*-series does lead to an endlessly compounding series of tense-expressions. But this series does not indicate an endlessly compounding series of new contradictions to be explained away. The argument gains its apparent force by failing to distinguish a series of distinct expressions from a series of supposed tensed facts.[5] Understanding fully how arguments of a certain form succeed requires understanding how apparently similar arguments fail. Although I lack the space to consider more than one example in detail, I suggest that the failure to distinguish distinct series is a defect shared by many negative regress arguments.[6]

II. Positive Regress Arguments

The "Five Ways" of Thomas Aquinas appear in almost every current introductory philosophy anthology. Aquinas argues against the possibility of an infinite series of movers, of causes, and, in the second part of the Third Way, of necessary things that have their necessity caused by another. In no case does he argue against a definition, explanation, or theory. No one thinks that if there is a real trouble, it arises already at the first step.

Aristotle's infinite regress arguments, which serve as models for Aquinas, do not fit the descriptions quoted from Moore, Passmore, and Geach, who have in mind arguments with wholly negative conclusions: a certain philosophical account, definition, theory, or explanation will not do because it leads to an infinite regress. The negative-positive distinction is difficult to account for generally, since any assertion is equivalent to the denial of its contradictory. The distinction between positive and negative existential statements, which respectively assert and deny the existence of something, is nevertheless clear enough. Aristotle's infinite regress arguments, and the many arguments they inspire, are positive because they conclude that something of a special sort must exist. If something of this special sort did not exist, there would be an infinite regress.

There appears to be an infinite regress argument in the second conjunct of the antecedent of the following widely discussed passage from the beginning of the *Nicomachean Ethics*:

> If, then, there is some end of the things we do, which we desire for its own sake (everything else being desired for the sake of this),

and if we do not choose everything for the sake of something else (for at that rate the process would go on to infinity, so that our desire would be empty and vain), clearly this must be the good and the chief good.[7]

I shall not discuss whether Aristotle is guilty of inferring "There is some good at which every action aims" from "Every action aims at some good," how damaging this fallacy is, if it occurs, to Aristotle's main arguments for the existence of single final end of rational action, or how to construe these other arguments. I shall discuss an infinite regress argument for the weaker conclusion that not everything is desired for the sake of something else.[8] My main purpose is discussing the general structure of a kind of infinite regress argument rather than interpreting Aristotle. Aristotle's argument is about things we do, actions, done to satisfy a desire. Whether or not every action is motivated by desire, not every desire motivates an action; and I will consider an argument put in terms of desire that does not assume that the desires are motivating.[9]

The Argument in Brief

Let us say that a *series of desires* is one in which each desire except the last is for the sake of the satisfaction of the next desire. A series of desires can end in a desire for something that is desired only for its own sake.

The argument concludes that every series of desires must end in this way; for the series can neither loop around in a circle nor be infinite. Besides considering both these assumptions, I shall consider alternative ways in which a series can terminate and an alternative way in which a series might fail to terminate.

Rationality

Rationality is inherited backwards through a series of desires. Roughly speaking, if it is rational to desire Y and rational to desire X for the sake of Y, then it is rational to desire X. Let us understand "rational series of desires" to mean something different from "series of rational desires." In a rational series of desires, the desires are related to each in a rational way, whether or not the final desire is rational in itself. Even if someone is correct in thinking that he desires X for the sake of Y and even if it is rational for him to desire Y, he may be incorrect in thinking that obtaining X is an effective or rational means of obtaining Y. The assumption of rationality will be important when we come to arguments which purport to show that series of desires cannot be infinite. I shall mention briefly why I think that the notion of rational desire is more difficult than the notion of rational belief. While inconsistent beliefs cannot all be true, and inconsistent desires cannot all be satisfied, the analogy is imperfect. At least one member of a set of inconsistent beliefs must be false, and detection of such inconsistency calls for revision. Consistency of belief is a worthwhile ideal. Although at least one member of a set of inconsistent desires must be unsatisfied, it does not follow that any member of the set is in some way mistaken, inferior, unworthy, or otherwise bad. Consistency of desire is at best a two-faced ideal, and the less pleasant face looks either fanatical or moronic. The refusal to recognize conflicts between one's desires may be irrational, but once such conflicts are recognized, there are often rational ways to deal with them besides eliminating them. While many of us have some desires we wish we could get rid of, we feel that the loss of enough desires to leave the remaining desires free from conflict would diminish us as persons. A theory of rational belief will naturally refer to the pursuit of truth and the avoidance of falsity, and I do not know what parallel notions can serve a theory of rational desire.

"For the Sake of"

John wants to go jogging because he believes that jogging causally contributes to maintaining his health. That is, he wants to go jogging for the sake of his health. It is natural enough to generalize from such examples and understand *for the sake of* to be causal, or instrumental, but such an understanding is too narrow. John wants to jog a twelfth lap for the sake of jogging three miles, but jogging a twelfth lap partly constitutes John's jogging three miles rather than causes him to jog that distance. If X is desired for the sake of Y, X may be believed to be a part of Y rather than something distinct from Y which produces it.

One philosopher who distrusts the distinction between instru-mental and intrinsic goods is John Dewey. "Men shoot and throw," writes Dewey. They "do not shoot because targets exist, but they set up targets in order that throwing and shooting may be more effective and significant" (Dewey 1930, p. 226). I do not see that this casts doubt on the distinction between intrinsic and instrumental although it does suggest that, because we wrongly regard processes as valuable only for their products, we mistakenly classify either as purely intrinsic or as purely instrumental goods which are really mixed. While hitting a target may be desired for its own sake, it is also properly desired for the sake of the activity that leads to it and which, while done for the sake of hitting a target, is also desirable for its own sake.

A Possible Alternative Termination

Is it obvious that no desire can be for the sake of something that is not itself desired? The common practice of saying "I don't want it" or "I don't want to" when we mean that we do want not to have or not to do something can be misleading here. One's desires can be in conflict, and no doubt sometimes we desire something for the sake of something else that we both desire to get (keep, do, and so forth) and desire not to get. But if desires are sometimes for the sake of something that is not itself desired, I assume they are desires for something that is not an object of any kind of desire, positive or negative. They are also not merely desires for the sake of something for which the desire is not recognized or acknowledged by the subject. Clear examples are thus hard to come by, since the alternative explanation that the desire is present, but not consciously, is difficult to rule out. I still think that the possibility that a series of desires can terminate in a desire for the sake of something not itself desired, and thus terminate in a desire that is not for something desired for its own sake, should not be dismissed out of hand. Reliability accounts of epistemic justification, after all, maintain that there are justified beliefs that are neither self-justifying nor justified by any further beliefs. In the next section I shall consider another way in which a series can terminate with a member that lacks some of the properties attributed to terminating members by the infinite regress argument.

Another Alternative Termination

Desires that can be represented by a formula "S desires that p" where p quantifies over S's desires I shall, for lack of a short, accurate phrase or appropriate acronym, call *Q-desires*. All *Q*-desires are higher-order; they are desires about desires. Not all higher-order desires, however, are *Q*-desires. My desire that I not have the desire to smoke is higher-order, but its propositional content does not quantify over my desires. Certain *Q*-desires can give rise to paradox. (Suppose that someone desires that all his desires be unsatisfied, and all his *other* desires are unsatisified. Or suppose that someone desires that at least one of his desires be unsatisfied, and all his other desires are satisfied.) While treatment of such paradoxes could involve further infinite regress arguments, I am concerned here only with the relevance of *Q*-desires to infinite regress arguments similar to Aristotle's.

In the following list, the first of Professor *A*'s desires in each pair is only for the sake of the second:

- to talk to Professor *B*, to be appointed by Professor *B* to the Curriculum Committee;
- to be appointed to the Curriculum Committee, to be in a position to advocate her desires concerning curricular revision.

This series does not terminate, at least so *A* would insist, in a desire of something for its own sake. *A* wants to be in a position to advocate her desires concerning curricular revision for the sake of having her desires concerning curricular revision satisfied. There are, however, no particular desires concerning curricular revision *A* wants to satisfy. Indeed, at present *A* does not have any particular desires concerning curricular revision. (*A* also wants to own a ketch although there is no particular ketch she wants to own.)

A series of desires can end with a *Q*-desire whose object is neither desired for its own sake nor desired for the sake of any particular further desire. If we find such a case while questioning a subject about his or her desires, we can simply start our line of questioning over again with another of the subject's desires. Is its object desired for its own sake or for the sake of something else? I see no way to argue that it is logically impossible for every one of a subject's desires to be ultimately directed to the satisfaction of one or another *Q*-desire. Such a possibility does not show there to be a defect in Aristotle's argument, however, so long as any subject who realized that he or she had such a desire structure would admit that it is "empty and vain."

So far I have considered two ways a series of desires might terminate that are often ignored by those who advance the corresponding infinite regress argument. In the remaining sections, I shall consider several ways in which series might fail to terminate.

Series that Do Not Terminate because They are Infinite

Arguments with modal conclusions ought to have modal premises. An infinite regress argument that concludes that necessarily, if anything at all is desired, then something is desired for its own sake, needs the premise that an infinite series of desires is impossible. If the modal version of the argument is valid, the corresponding nonmodal version ought also to be valid. Its conclusion, that if anything at all is desired, then something is desired for its own sake, is still of interest; and it needs to assume only the nonexistence, rather than the inherent impossibility, of an infinite series of desires. The weaker assumption can be defended by an appeal to the finitude of human capacity, while attempts to defend the stronger assumption are more likely to appeal to logical properties of the relation that orders a series of desires. I will discuss these kinds of defenses in the next two sections.

Series that are in Fact Finite

How long does it take to think about something? How many things can one think about at once? Although these questions are not precise enough to have precise unarbitrary answers, we can confidently answer, no matter how episodes of thought and things thought about are individuated, that no one thinks about a thousand different things in a second. No one has unlimited time for thinking, so no one thinks about each member of an infinite set. No one thinks about infinitely many different things that one desires.

This consequence of human finitude implies that certain kinds of series of desires are always finite, but only given some additional assumptions about the series. One such assumption is easy to state: whenever one desires something, one must think or have thought about it as an object of desire. This assumption should give us pause, we who are used to the notion that unrecognized desires can influence. Motivation is only one important kind of influence. Some desires influence by causing conflicts. Some motivate only indirectly, as when we act in order to be in a position to satisfy them, although we never actually attempt to satisfy them because they conflict with stronger desires, which may or may not themselves be recognized. Most of us could learn more about the structure of our desires. Once we acknowledge a desire, the question whether we desire its object for its own sake or for the sake of something else can be disturbing. We are sometimes unsure how to answer the question. An answer we confidently accepted earlier sometimes appears to be based on ignorance or even self-deception. When we thought earlier that we desired something for its own sake, we can come to realize that we actually desired it for the sake of something else; when we thought earlier that we desired something for the sake of something else, we can come to realize that we actually desired it for its own sake; and when we thought earlier that we desired something only for the sake of *Y*, we can come to realize that we actually desired it for the sake of *Z* in addition to, or instead of, *Y*. If we can have desires of which we are unaware, the fact that we can be aware of only finitely many desires appears not to imply that no series of desires is infinite.

The question remains whether there ever is an infinite series of desires. Artificial examples of indefinitely extendable series of desires can be constructed without difficulty. Jane's desire to have a certain amount of money can turn out always to be for the sake of having a slightly larger amount of money. We can continue many numerical series indefinitely, but series of desires that trade of this capacity provide unconvincing counterexamples to the claim that actual series of desires never continue in this way. There is too much in common between the different members of the series, such as a desire to have *n* dollars, for the relation between the members to satisfy our interest in explanation. Although I shall not attempt to say generally what it is for a continuation of a series of desires to be nontrivial, I think it is not obvious that such series can ever be extended indefinitely in a nontrivial way. We may well doubt that our desire structures, even if they include much that we can recognize only through reflection and self-scrutiny, are ever of unlimited complexity.

Series that Cannot be Infinite

Negative regresses are vicious because they make no progress in providing an account. A feature that is common to some of these and to positive regresses called vicious is a supposed priority each member of the series has to its predecessor. A relevant character of each member of the series depends, in an asymmetric way, on the relevant character of its successor. Is there a certain kind of dependence which makes it impossible for a series it orders to go on without limit, which can be described generally, and which is found in many regresses called vicious? Philosophers who defend cosmological arguments for the existence of God attempt to describe special kinds of causal relations such that any series ordered by one of them must be finite. If I thought they succeed, I could attempt to generalize their results for other kinds of dependence. But I doubt that they succeed. Although I might be expected, in undertaking to write an essay on infinite regress arguments in philosophy, to attempt to say generally what makes a vicious regress vicious, I doubt that there is a general kind of dependence that is useful in explaining the viciousness of all or most vicious regresses. I think that any good reason for denying that a series of successively dependent items can be infinite has to be based on features peculiar to a series of a particular kind.

When someone desires X only for the sake of Y, there are several ways in which the desire for X might be thought to depend on the desire for Y. One kind of dependence is existential. Given that a subject desires X only for the sake of Y, if he had not desired Y, then either he would not have desired X, or he would have desired something else Z for the sake of which he would have desired X. After noting the possibility mentioned in the second disjunct of the consequent, let us ignore it and say simply that the existence of a desire not at the end of a series of desires depends on the existence of the next desire. This principle does not require that the subject be or have been aware of all the desires in a series of desires. Is there a good argument to show that no series of desires so ordered can be infinite? Arguments of the following form are suspect: If there is no final desire in a series upon which all the preceding desires depend, then none of the earlier desires would exist. Therefore, there must be a final desire, a desire which is not only for the sake of something further. Arguments of this familiar form are frequently criticised for being circular: the assumption that every desire in a series depends for its existence on a final desire is not more worthy of belief than the argument's conclusion. If arguments of the most familiar kind fail, it does not, of course, follow that a less familiar argument concerning existential dependence cannot succeed; but I am unable to produce such an argument.

Desires also exhibit a special kind of dependence. Whether a subject's acting on a desire for the sake of something is wise, rational, well-advised, and so forth, depends on whether his so acting in the circumstances is as likely to obtain it as an alternative way of acting. (It depends of course on other factors as well, for example the likelihood of the action and the alternatives also bringing about undesirable consequences. I am not proposing an exhaustive formula for assessing the wisdom of acting one way rather than another.) When an action is assessed in light of its intended consequences, the consequences need not be something desired for its own sake. One way of trying to get my furnace repaired may be preferable to another even though I desire to have a properly functioning furnace only for the sake of something else. Certain philosophers and sages advise us constantly to assess our actions in light of our ultimate goals. Even if we tend not to heed the advice, we must admit that such assessment is possible so long as our actions have ultimate goals. The question "Is acting on this desire a reasonable way of obtaining what you desire for its own sake?" could be asked much more than it actually is. But if a series of desires is infinite, the question is not answerable with respect to any of the desires in the series. One way of assessing the rationality of acting on a desire, by reference to its ultimate end, would be unavailable, since there would be no ultimate end. Also, a kind of comparison with alternative paths of action would be unavailable. However far along an infinite series of desires one consciously considers, there is always the possibility that if one were to consider still further, one would find that the further object of desire could be better obtained by some alternative course of action. While these features of desire do not show that an infinite series of desires is impossible, I think they do help support the contention that any infinite series of desires is empty and vain. An extra assumption of rationality becomes relevant at this point. The argument requires only that no rational series of desires can be infinite.

While I have not isolated a property of viciousness that is common to all regresses correctly called vicious and which belongs to any infinite series of desires, I have sketched some considerations that make the hypothesis that such series can always be continued indefinitely unattractive. Besides showing that a certain series does not go on forever, an infinite regress argument typically must also show that it cannot go around in a circle or loop.

Series that Do Not Terminate because They Loop

Given that someone loves someone else and that no series ordered by the relation "loves" is infinite, nothing follows about the existence of a first or last member. The series can perfectly well loop. John loves Mary; Mary loves Peter; Peter loves Marsha; and Marsha loves John. A series ordered by a relation which is both transitive and asymmetric cannot loop. As I say in Sanford 1975, p. 520, so long as "*R*" is interpreted in the same way throughout, any five statements of the following forms are mutually inconsistent:

(1) *Existence.* $(\exists x)\,(\exists y)\,Rxy$.
     Something exists which has relation R to something.
(2) *Asymmetry.* $(x)\,(y)\,(Rxy \supset \sim Ryx)$.
     If x has R to y, then y does not have R to x.
(3) *Transitivity.* $(x)\,(y)\,(z)\,((Rxy\ \&\ Ryz) \supset Rxz)$.
     If x has R to y which in turn has R to z, then x has R to z.
(4) *Existential Heredity.* $(x)\,(y)\,(Rxy \supset (\exists z)\,Rzx)$.
     If x has R to y, then something has R to x.
(5) *Finitude.* There are only finitely many things related by relation R.

Since the five statements are mutually inconsistent, the falsity of any one follows from the truth of the other four. The main examples in my article are arguments concerning the infinite extent or the infinite divisibility or space or time that use a premise of form (4) in support of a conclusion that is the corresponding negation of (5).[10] I claim in passing that the first two ways of Thomas Aquinas can be represented as arguing from the negation of (5) to a conclusion of form (4). Assumptions of forms (1), (2), and (3) can be so obvious, for some instances of "*R*," that they remain implicit.

Alfred MacKay thinks this scheme is useful in understanding Arrow's impossibility theorem (MacKay 1980a, 1980b). His interpretation of Arrow is controversial, and I shall not enter the controversy. One commentator says that the scheme above is supposed to account for the structure of any infinite regress argument (Riley 1982, p. 671). I do not suppose this in Sanford 1975; and although I may wish it were true, I doubt that it is. An infinite regress argument needs to rule out loops, and the transitivity of an ordering relation can be crucial in an argument to rule out looping. But a series that does not loop may be ordered by a relation that is not transitive. I do not know how to defend the claim that any argument against looping must appeal to transitivity. Even if a series is defined in terms of an ordering relation that is not transitive, however, reference to transitivity can still figure in an argument against looping. Looping is precluded so long as there is a transitive, asymmetric relation R such that any two things related by the original ordering relation are also related by R. A series of things ordered by "is exactly one inch taller than," for example, cannot loop because if one thing is exactly one inch taller than another, the first is simply taller than the second, and "is taller than" is transitive as well as asymmetric. Can a similar reason be used to show that a series of desires cannot loop?

> John, like many of his peers, is very concerned with making money. He is quick to admit that a strong desire for money motivates much of his activity, but he denies, as would most people who grasp the distinction between intrinsic and instrumental goods, that he desires money for its own sake. He holds money to be desirable only because it is useful in satisfying other desires. Any line of questioning, however, which starts with his desire for money and proceeds by repeating the question "If you do not desire that for its own sake, for the sake of what do you desire it?" eventually returns to his desire for money.

Can some appeal to transitivity and asymmetry show this unlikely story to be impossible? The assumption that "is desired for the sake of" is transitive has very strong consequences for any looping desire structure. Each desire in a loop must be for the sake of the objects of every desire in the loop. Not only will the object of every desire in the loop be desired for its own sake, but each member of any pair of desires in the loop will be for the sake of the object of the other member. Asymmetry is violated in all these cases; but it is violated anyway, in ordinary cases, whenever something is desired for its own sake. These consequences are too strong to be believed. Should we come across a character like John, we might suspect that he profoundly misunderstands his own desires in some respect. Either he desires something for its own sake without realizing it, or he desires something for the sake of something else without realizing it. We should not feel forced to hold that errors of this kind pervade the subject's desire structure so completely as the transitivity of "is desired for the sake of" would imply.

Consider the weaker assumption that "is desired for the sake of and not at all for its own sake" is transitive. According to this assumption, it is not possible that, for each of the following pairs, that John desires the first for the sake of the second and not at all for its own sake. (The loop could be lengthened by inserting details about how John plans to use his loans.)

- to make more money, to buy expensive suits;
- to buy expensive suits, to wear expensive suits to the bank;
- to wear expensive suits to the bank, to impress bankers;
- to impress bankers, to obtain more loans;
- to obtain more loans, to invest in certain schemes;
- to invest in certain schemes, to make more money.

If the relation in question is transitive, John desires to make more money for the sake of making more money and not at all for its own sake, an inconsistency. Yet it is not obvious that such a desire structure is somehow irrational or incoherent. Here is some more information about John. Although he may not realize it, one reason John wants to impress bankers is that it helps him to respect himself. And although he may again not realize it, John desires self-respect for its own sake. John's desire for self-respect is not a member of the loop. The members of the loop are nevertheless also members of a series of desires that is not a loop.

A desire can belong to more than one series of desires. A desire structure can branch both forward and backward. It branches backward when there are several desires for the sake of one thing, and forward when there is a desire for the sake of several different things. John's desire to impress bankers branches forward. Although it is a member of a looping series of desires, it is also a member of a series of desires which terminates.

Let us say that a loop of desires is *open* when it contains at least one member that branches forward and *closed* when it contains no such member. The apparent coherence of the supposition that there are open loops of desires casts doubt on the transitivity principles we have considered so far.

I shall abbreviate "*S*'s desire of *X* for the sake of *Y*" as "(*X*, *Y*)". In this notation, "(*X*, *X*)" abbreviates "*S*'s desire of *X* for its own sake." *S*'s desire for *X* branches forward if and only if for some *Y* and *Z*, there is a series of desires that contains (*X*, *Y*) but not (*X*, *Z*), and there is a series of desires that contains (*X*, *Z*) but not (*X*, *Y*). A desire of something for its own sake can be considered as a single-member closed loop of desires. If *S* desires *X* for its own sake and for the sake of something else *Y*, then *S*'s desire for *X* branches forward. There is a series of desires that contains (*X*, *X*) but not (*X*, *Y*), and there is a series of desires which contains (*X*, *Y*) but not (*X*, *X*). Single-member closed loops of desires violate no ideal of rationality, but multiple-member closed loops are suspect.

There are no multiple-member closed loops of desire if "desires for the sake of not in a forwardly branching way" is transitive. Suppose that there is a multiple-member closed loop. Any desire in the loop, by transitivity, is a desire of something for its own sake. But every member of a multiple-member loop of desires is also for the sake of something else. The supposition that the loop is closed is thus violated. Every desire in it branches forward, and a closed loop contains no forwardly branching desires. I would not argue that the transitivity of "desires for the sake of not in a forwardly branching way" holds of logical or psychological necessity. We can say, if we like, that this transitivity is an appropriate ideal of rationality and appeal to it to argue that multiple-member closed loops of desires also violate an appropriate ideal of rationality. But is the transitivity premise of this argument more obviously acceptable than its conclusion? Why not say straight away that a rational series of desires does not form a multiple-member closed loop?

Assume that no rational series of desires goes on forever, and assume that no rational series of desires forms a multiple-member closed loop. These assumptions do not imply that any desire in a rational series of desires belongs to some series of desires that terminates in a desire of something only for its own sake. Despite first appearances, they do not imply even that any desire in a rational series of desires belongs to some series of desires that contains a desire of something for its own sake, but perhaps not *only* for its own sake. Consider the following two linked, three-member, open loops of desires:

(1) (*X*, *Y*), (*Y*, *Z*), (*Z*, *X*).
(2) (*X*, *V*), (*V*, *W*), (*W*, *X*).

Both loops are open because each contains a desire for X that branches forward: X is desired both for the sake of Y and for the sake of V. Should we look for another principle of transitivity that implies that X, in the above structure, is desired for its own sake? Or, if we find no such principle of transitivity plausible, should we say that if no desire is of something for its own sake in the above structure, it is an irrational desire structure that violates some yet-to-be-formulated principle of rational desire? Or should we rather regard the structure as a prototype that can be elaborated further in developing a coherence theory of rational desire? I am unsure how to answer these questions. For the purpose of continuing the discussion, let us beg the question and assume that every desire in any rational series of desires belongs to at least one series of desires that is not a multiple-member loop, either open or closed. Then, if we still assume that no rational series of desires goes on forever, and we also assume that the possibility to be entertained in the next section is not realized, it does follow that any desire in a rational series of desires belongs to some series of desires that contains a desire of something for its own sake.

Plato and Aristotle both attach importance to the fact that some goods are desired both for their own sake and for the sake of something else. They also both think that some things are desired only for their own sake. Perhaps this view can be supported by reference to instances. I have not found a plausible way to support it with an infinite regress argument.

Positive infinite regress arguments attempt to show that a series of a certain kind terminates. Showing that such a series cannot go on forever may be the easiest part of the job, since showing that the series does not loop can be more difficult. In the next section I shall entertain the possibility that a series that neither loops nor is infinite nevertheless does not terminate.

Series that Do Not Terminate because They Trail off Gradually

Consider the following series: you, your mother, your mother's mother, your mother's mother's mother, and so forth. Everyone related to you by the ancestral of "mother of" is a member of the series. Since this ancestral relation is transitive and asymmetric, the series cannot contain loops. The supposition that the series is infinite, while not *a priori* impossible, conflicts with some of our firm beliefs about how the world works. Given that the maternal series is finite and without loops, must it therefore terminate with some motherless female ancestor of yours? Those who theorize about the evolution of sexual reproduction, for all I know, might find this conclusion acceptable; but certainly it is not a conclusion we are forced to accept from the fact that the maternal series neither loops nor continues backwards forever. We can entertain the possibility that the differentiation of the sexes was such a long, drawn out, gradual process that all the facts of your ancestry together are insufficient to determine who is the first member of your maternal series. There is no fact of the matter; any choice of an ancestor as a first member would be arbitrary.

The same sort of point can also be made with reference to characteristics that offspring appear always to inherit from parents but which reproducing organisms have not always exemplified. Must your maternal series have a first animal? A first vertebrate? A first mammal? A first primate? A first human? A first language-user? The series that ends with you and is ordered by "primate mother of" is not infinite and does not loop. For a long time all the members of your maternal series have definitely been primates. Some members of your maternal series are definitely not primates, and all of their maternal ancestors are nonprimates. From this we do not conclude that one of your primate maternal ancestors had a nonprimate mother. The characteristic of being a primate evolved gradually, over many generations. There were many generations of borderline cases of primates. (And just as we need not assume that there was a first primate, we also need not assume that there was a first borderline case of a primate.)

Once we decide that a series of things with a certain property neither loops nor is infinite, we should be cautious in inferring that there must be a first member with this property. The inference requires the additional assumption that there are no borderline cases, that any member of the series either definitely has the property or definitely does not have it. This assumption should not be made lightly. It is not generally well supported by the fact that we are unaware of any borderline cases of the relevant sort. If we have never come across a borderline case of a primate, then your maternal series contains creatures of a kind we have never come across.

A series can extend into a region so far in the past or future, or so far in space, or into a region so small, either spatially or temporally, or so huge, that we cannot be confident in applying assumptions based on our experience.[11] Series of desires do not extend spatially, and insofar as they extend temporally, they do not extend beyond our experience. Borderline cases will be located elsewhere if some kind of vagueness attaches to questions such as "Is this a desire of something for its own sake or for the sake of something further?"

There are at least two possible areas of indeterminacy. On the one hand, the vagueness of *for the sake of* may leave it indeterminate what a given desire is for the sake of. On the other hand, the vagueness of *desire* may leave it indeterminate whether someone really has a certain desire. If someone has a tendency to act so as to bring about states of affairs of a certain kind, there might be no nonarbitrary way to decide whether this tendency is properly classified as a desire. In other circumstances, there may be no way to decide, given all the relevant facts of the matter, whether the subject has the tendency.

I do not know whether to suggest that some series of desires actually fade away gradually with no definite terminating desire. We seldom submit our desire structures to the closest possible scrutiny, and I think that we are not very well acquainted with many series of desires that we see clearly to terminate. The fact that we are also not acquainted with borderline cases of a desire, or of borderline cases of a desire being for the sake of something, is not a strong reason for doubting their existence.

We can, of course, hold that some series of desires fade away gradually without holding that they all do. Series of all the possible kinds can exist together, and because of forward and backward branching, can be linked together. If some neither loop, terminate, nor go on forever, others can lead into loops and still others can definitely terminate. The mere rejection of infinite series is not sufficient to determine the structure of our desires.

III. Concluding Remark

Rather than attempt to describe and examine a large number of infinite regress arguments in philosophy, I have concentrated in this essay on two arguments, one negative and one positive. At the beginning of the essay, I represented the brief remark from Moore as overlooking the existence of positive infinite regress arguments. At this point, after seeing a number of ways in which a positive regress argument might be resisted, we can consider an alternative interpretation. Moore, rather than ignoring the existence of positive regress arguments, may mean instead to deny that they ever succeed. "Although philosophers think that infinite series of various kinds are vicious, the ones which are really vicious are those only which arise from a circular definition." I have not drawn this conclusion, but I have tried to show, by means of a single example, that more difficulties attend positive regress arguments than are usually noticed.

Notes

1. These remarks can also be applied to the infinite regress arguments D.M. Armstrong uses against various theories of universals (Armstrong 1974, 1978).
2. As Passmore puts it, the infinite regress arguments in *The Concept of Mind* show the inadequacy of certain "constitution-explanations." In attempting to explain what makes an act intelligent, for example, one makes no progress by referring to a preceding intelligent act (Ryle 1949, p. 31).
3. Permission to quote this passage from D. H. Mellor, *Real Time* (Cambridge: Cambridge University Press, 1981), pp. 93–94, is gratefully acknowledged.
4. In terms closer to McTaggart's, I made this claim before in Sanford 1968, an article which also points out significant differences between McTaggart 1908, and McTaggart 1927.
Does the discussion so far confirm Geach's claim that "if McTaggart's alleged contradiction is bogus, we need not consider whether the attempt to remove it would generate a vicious regress"? While some may already be convinced that the alleged contradiction is bogus, others, who still suspect that the attempt to remove it only results in more contradictions of the same kind, will not be convinced until they see what sort of regress is actually generated.
5. See Hart 1964, p. 309, for a convincing defense of the claim that the infinite regress arguments discussed by Timasheff 1939, p. 264, and Kelsen 1946, p. 29, fail to distinguish a vicious infinite series of laws from an acceptable unending series of cases of ever-increasing complexity. I thank Martin P. Golding for drawing my attention to these references.
6. Although I have been unsympathetic to Mellor's version of McTaggart's argument, I do not take the failure of the argument to discredit the conclusion. Other arguments for the same conclusion may well succeed. (I doubt that such arguments will involve an infinite regress.) For futher discussion of the unreality of tense, see Mellor 1981, and Sanford forthcoming.
7. I. 2, 1094ª 18–22. A less widely discussed passage in the *Metaphysics* also discusses a single final end and an infinite series together (994ᵇ 8–16).
8. Such an argument appears near the beginning of *Metaphysics* α. 2 (994ª 1–9).
9. Since motivation involves belief as well as desire, there is a reason to consider infinite regress arguments concerning justified belief in parallel with the argument concerning desire. Comparisons between the arguments could help to distinguish accidental from essential features of positive infinite regress arguments

and, because a feature neither obviously present nor obviously absent in one case may be obviously present in the other, could help to indicate possibilities that might otherwise go unnoticed. I attempted such comparisons in an earlier version of this essay before the editor informed me of the strict page limit for this volume. Some traces of these comparisons remain in the present version. I did not attempt to provide a comprehensive account of the recent literature on infinite regress arguments for epistemological foundationalism. By following the references provided by Bonjour 1978, Nathan 1980, and Williams 1981, the reader can make a good start at assembling a bibliography on the topic. Kelsik 1979 is a very full bibliography on recent epistemology.

10. I would now also mention McTaggart's argument "that there are no simple substances, and that every substance has parts within parts to infinity. Every substance is thus infinitely divisible. But this infinite divisibility is of course of a different type from the infinite divisibility generally asserted of time and space" (McTaggart 1921, sec. 180).

11. Sanford 1975 makes this point in more detail. I would now add, with respect to the argument mentioned in note 9, that one who agrees that there can be no counterexample to McTaggart's claim that every substance has parts should be cautious in inferring that every substance therefore has parts within parts to infinity.

6 Ockham's Razor

J. J. C. Smart

In the past (Smart 1959, 1963, and 1967), I have invoked Ockham's
Razor[1] in connection with the defense of physicalism, but how
Ockham's Razor really came into the matter is less clear to me
now. I was thinking of the Razor in the version *"Entia non sunt
multiplicanda praeter necessitatem."* It seems that this formula is
a seventeenth-century invention, and is nowhere to be found in
the extant writings of William of Ockham. In this and subsequent
historical remarks, I shall be generally relying on W. M. Thorburn's
very interesting paper "The Myth of Occam's Razor" (Thorburn
1918). However, Ockham did use a formula to very much the same
effect, *"Frustra fit per plura quod potest fieri per pauciora,"* that
is, it is in vain to do by many what can be done by fewer. We
can take the "many" and "fewer" here to be explanatory propositions, and in many cases these will be existential propositions.
So Ockham's Razor counsels us against an unnecessary luxuriance
of principles or laws or statements of existence. Putting it in this
way enables us to avoid a certain infelicity[2] in the post-medieval
formula. A philosopher can not multiply the fundamental entities
or sorts of entities that there are in the universe: all he can multiply
is existential hypotheses. The infelicity in the post-medieval formula
smacks of a use-mention confusion, but it is so obvious a one
that it should not mislead anyone. Despite the title of Nelson
Goodman's *Ways of Worldmaking*, we can not fill up or empty
the universe by our mere philosophical discourse. More congenial
is Goodman's earlier very witty remark that though there may be
more things in heaven and earth than there are dreamt of in our

philosophy, he is concerned that there should not be more things dreamt of in his philosophy than there are in heaven and earth (Goodman 1973, p. 34). This is very much in the spirit of the Razor.

This term "the Razor" seems to derive from Condillac who used the phrase "*Rasoir des nominaux*," and the Latin version of this "*Novaculum Nominalium*," came into vogue. The English phrase "Ockham's (or Occam's) Razor" comes from the Scottish philosopher Sir William Hamilton. Hamilton regarded this as tantamount to what he called "The Law of Parcimony" (thus spelt), according to which "Nature never works by more complex instruments than are necessary." J. S. Mill objected to this ontological formulation: how do we know this alleged fact about nature? (Mill 1979.) Indeed, he said, we know that nature often proceeds in a very complex manner to produce various effects, and we can not be confident that such effects could not have been produced in a simpler manner. According to Mill "The Law of Parcimony" is a rule of methodology, that we should not believe anything for which we have no evidence. Thus he claims that defense of the Razor requires no assumptions about the ways of nature. Even if the ways of nature were the reverse of what we now believe them to be, it would still be improper, Mill said, for us to assume a proposition about nature without our having evidence for it.

The razor suggests, reasonably enough, that if we have a choice between a theory of the form p on the one hand and one of the form $p \& q$ on the other hand, then if we have no antecedent reason to believe q, and if the explanatory force of $p \& q$ is not superior to that of p, then we should assert only p. Of course, if $p \& q$ had more explanatory force than p, this would raise the antecedent probability of q. (I am here taking it that p and q could be conjunctions of quite complex propositions.) However, in the developed sciences it is not usual for choices to be between theories of the forms p and $p \& q$ respectively.

Usually in pure science when a conjunction of propositions is needed to explain some facts, each conjunct separately will not even be a candidate for being a plausible *explanans*. However, in medicine and technology, the situation may be quite common. Thus if my lawn mower fails to start, I may consider the hypothesis that this is due *both* to a blocked carburetor *and* to a defective spark plug, but if I find that the spark plug has oiled up, I accept the simple hypothesis that this is the cause of the trouble, not that the cause is also the blocked carburetor. In pure science the choice is more likely to be between a hypothesis of the form p' & q and one of the form p, where p' is some nontrivial modification of p. The scientist does not compare the merits of p & q with that of p but rather those of p' & q with that of p. The hypothesis p' may have epistemic advantages over p sufficient to justify us in taking on the extra baggage q. The principle of Ockham's Razor, as literally construed, needs to be replaced simply by the principle that other things being equal, we should prefer more simple theories to more complex ones.

I have noted earlier that J. S. Mill cast doubt on this principle, because of the fact that nature often works in more complex ways than are necessary. Certainly we find this in natural history. The locomotive mechanism involved in walking is far more complex than is that of a vehicle on wheels. Nevertheless this consideration does not tell against the principle of simplicity. If an explorer discovers a new animal, he does not expect it to run on wheels. There is no simple or even remotely plausible explanation of how locomotion on wheels would fit into the palaeontological story of animal evolution. Motion on legs may be more complex than motion on wheels, but a theory of how animal motion on legs might have evolved may be much more simple than a theory of how animal motion on wheels might have evolved.

One thing that is needed is some theory of simplicity whereby we could show that if p is simpler than q then p has the epistemic advantages over q that it has over p & r, even though q can not be decomposed into p & r. Though a good deal of progress has been made in the theory of simplicity (for example, in Sober 1975, and 1981), I suspect that it is not possible fully to justify the idea that simple theories are objectively more likely to be true than are complex ones or even that they contain fewer arbitrary elements. For those who wish, as I do, to regard science as metaphysics, as telling us what the universe really contains and is really like, and not as a mere instrument for prediction of our experiences, the ability to justify our beliefs objectively is what is wanted from Ockham's Razor and analogous principles of parsimony. It is not that we prefer simpler theories because they are more congenial and easy for our intellects. The sort of simplicity achieved by quantum mechanics or general relativity is not a matter of easiness of comprehension or of application.

The sort of simplicity I am after is an objective simplicity, hard though it is to explicate this notion. Scientists do often seem to take simplicity as a sign of truth. Until recently, at any rate, the tests of the general theory of relativity were rather few and beset by controversy. Nevertheless the theory tended to be believed because of its beauty, a sort of simplicity, for example in its explanation of gravitation in terms of geodesics in curved space-time, which is a sort of generalization of Newton's first law of motion. Admittedly a space-time of variable curvature is less simple than a space-time of zero or constant curvature, but it is still something of the same general kind, and its postulation explains mysteries—for example, the proportionality of gravitational and inertial mass. The theory was certainly not accepted because of its practical utility: it was impossible to use it to calculate the nautical almanac, for example. Nevertheless the theory explained the approximate truth of Newton's theory, which could then be used as before to compute the nautical almanac, predict the paths of space rockets, and so on.

There is a tendency, then, for us to take simplicity, in some obscure objective sense, as a guide to metaphysical truth. Perhaps this tendency derives from earlier theological notions: we expect God to have created a beautiful universe. But what is beauty? Partly symmetry, which is a form of simplicity. Why do we love simplicity? Perhaps there is an evolutionary explanation: simplicity is merely a reflection of innate cognitive mechanisms that have proved successful during the evolution of the human species. But if this is all there is to it, we would have no reason to expect these innate mechanisms to be a good guide to theories of quantum mechanics or general relativity, which hitherto at least have had no immediate relevance to everyday practical living, still less to the needs of predators or of hunter-gatherers. The evolutionary argument is that our tastes in theories (our feelings for simplicity) must be adapted to the real world. This is no good for *justifying* (though it could *explain*) our appeal to simplicity in sophisticated twentieth-century physics. Tastes suitable for such sophisticated theories as quantum mechanics and relativity would have had no selective advantage for early humans or their ancestors. Nor is an inductive argument from the success of simple theories in the past to the success of simple theories in the future at all convincing. Such a meta-induction would be one by simple enumeration, and we have reason to think that heuristic strategies that worked in the past might well be as inapplicable to future theories (or even contemporary ones) as are the lessons of past wars for possible future nuclear wars. In such cases we indeed have good reason for thinking that the future will *not* be like the past. Furthermore, such a meta-induction may seem less cogent if we remember simple theories, such as that of Boscovich, which have been unsuccessful as compared with less simple and aesthetically pleasing theories. However, perhaps Boscovich's theory, if it is put in the wider context of physics, turns out to be less simple than it seems. As Schlesinger has argued, when we try to make a false theory accord with the facts, we encumber it more and more with *ad hoc* hypotheses and complications (Schlesinger 1963, p. 44).

I have been tempted to throw in the towel here and say that just as induction, the principle that the future will be like the past, can neither be validated nor vindicated (to use Herbert Feigl's terminology, Feigl 1950), and yet must be accepted if we are to believe anything at all about the universe, so the principle of simplicity must be accepted, even though it can not be validated or vindicated either. I think, however, that this would be too pessimistic. A vindication of induction does not now seem to be out of the question, because I think that John Clendinnen has at least got pretty close to it (Clendinnen 1982). A vindication of induction would not show that inductive policies are successful (as a validation would), but it would show why it is reasonable to use induction rather than any alternative. Clendinnen argues that any noninductive policy is irrational because it would involve arbitrary decisions and be no better than mere guessing. (Guessing can be rational, if a person's ability to guess rightly is inductively warranted, but this is not *mere* guessing.) And it is interesting that Clendinnen's argument makes the principle of simplicity part and parcel of the principle of induction. Clendinnen connects the principle of induction and the principle of simplicity together as a matter of not being arbitrary. I think that he does indeed vindicate the principle of simplicity in this way, but more is needed for my purposes in order to vindicate our preference in sophisticated science for certain more simple theories as compared with certain more complex ones. The more complex theory may not be related to the less complex one as p & q is related to p. In these cases the difference between the less complex and the more complex does not seem to be obviously reducible to a matter of arbitrariness. So I shall have to shelve this matter for the purposes of this paper and merely draw attention to the promise of Clendinnen's work.[3]

Kent E. Holsinger, in an interesting discussion paper (Holsinger 1980), has remarked that it is not often the case that two hypotheses account for the facts equally well but that one is simpler than the other. One case in which Holsinger holds that the principle of simplicity was legitimately applied is that of the issue between the Copernican heliocentric theory of planetary motion as contrasted with the geocentric theory that prevailed in Copernicus's time. However, it is a matter of debate among historians of science as to whether at the time in question the Copernican system *was* simpler.[4] Nevertheless it lended itself to transformation into Kepler's theory, and then to explanation by the laws of Newtonian mechanics, so that even if it was not more simple in what Schlesinger has called a "static" sense, it did have a greater "dynamic" simplicity (Schlesinger 1963, pp. 36ff). A system may not be simpler in the form in which it was put forward, but it may appear simpler to us in retrospect, because of the greater simplicity of later theories into which simple modifications of it were incorporated. It is hard to see how the geocentric hypothesis could have been integrated with the Newtonian theory of dynamics and of gravitation, or could have been used, as by Adams and Leverrier, to predict from anomalies in the motion of Uranus the existence and position of Neptune. It is to be expected that it is in cosmology and metaphysics, whose ties with experience are indirect and tenuous, that the true locus of simplicity, as an autonomous or nearly autonomous principle, is to be found.

Not surprisingly, therefore, a particularly good example of the principle is to be found in the writings of William of Ockham himself. Holsinger, in the aforementioned discussion note, fastens on a passage in which Ockham asserts his "*Frustra fit per plura quod potest fieri per pauciora.*" A translation of this passage from Ockham's *Summa Totius Logicae* is given and discussed in Moody 1965, pp. 49–50. Ockham seems to have believed that thought proceeds by means of "natural signs." He wanted to argue against the theory that the actual sign was some concept constructed in the mind and distinct from an "act of understanding." Ockham suggested that this act of understanding itself could be a natural sign (stand for or signify an object) just as well as could some intermediate constructed mental entity. Therefore we might as well dispense with belief in such intermediate mental entities. But even here the application of the Razor seems to have temporary usefullness only. Ockham's question was posed in terms of thought signifying objects, and modern ideas of semantics and of the mind make Ockham's question unclear. We now have quite different theories about the relationship between thought and the world. As I remarked at the outset of this essay, I myself have brandished what I referred to as Ockham's Razor. But now that I have thought more about the nature of Ockham's Razor (and considerations of simplicity in general), I begin to think that what I was brandishing was not Ockham's Razor at all. As Holsinger pointed out against M.J. Dunbar (Dunbar 1980), Ockham's Razor does not imply that we should accept simpler theories at all costs. The Razor is a method for deciding between two theories that equally account for the agreed-upon facts. I was using it to defend physicalism and to attack dualism in the philosophy of mind. The dualist would, of course, not agree that the physicalist *does* account for all the facts. The dualist thinks that he is immediately aware of nonphysical items of experience. When I brandished Ockham's Razor, or rather what I carelessly took to be Ockham's Razor, I was merely drawing attention to unpleasant complexities in the dualist theory, which made it implausible to me. The dualist would reply that if his theory is complex or implausible looking, that is just too bad, because he thinks that to deny it would be to deny obvious facts of experience. Entities should not be multiplied beyond necessity, he might agree, but according to him his nonphysical entities do not lie beyond necessity.

It begins to look as though my principle is not so much "Entities should not be multiplied beyond necessity," but rather "Entities should not be multiplied beyond what I want" (*"Entia non sunt multiplicanda praeter voluntatem meam"*???). I was in particular concerned to avoid the "multiplication of entities" that would arise from the postulation of brain processes on the one hand and associated nonphysical entities (sensations) on the other hand. The latter seemed to me to be excrescences on the face of science. In particular they would seem to imply the existence of laws connecting them to their associated brain processes, and these would be, as Feigl put it, "nomological danglers" (Feigl 1958). That is, they would stick out or dangle from the nomological net of science.

Moreover they would be laws of a most peculiar kind, since they would not relate simple or relevantly homogeneous entities. Thus, though a nonphysical sensation of blue, say, might or might not be a simple, it would have to be connected by a law to a very complex and idiosyncratic type of brain process, involving perhaps hundreds of millions of neurons, all connected together in very special ways. And yet it would have to be an ultimate law, not derivable from laws relating to simple or homogeneous entities.

I held, therefore, that it is highly implausible that there should be such nomological danglers or the entities that would hang down from them. And I still think this. But if I was using Ockham's Razor, I was misapplying it. "Entities must not be multiplied beyond necessity." If it is not necessary to postulate nonphysical mental entities, then they ought not to be postulated. (Instead, sensations should be identified with brain processes.) We might apply the principle as *modus ponens*: "If it is not necessary to postulate nonphysical sensations, then nonphysical sensations ought not to be postulated; it is not necessary; therefore we ought not to postulate nonphysical sensations." But to apply the principle in this way, we would need to possess ourselves of the minor premise, which in the present case is the very point at issue. Was I not therefore thinking in terms of an affirmation of the consequent, and hence of an invalid argument? In other words my considerations about the horrors of nomological danglers suggest that we should not hold that sensations are nonphysical. One may be tempted to use the Ockhamist principle to deduce "It is not necessary to hold that there are nonphysical sensations." But if one did so, one would be affirming the consequent.

It therefore looks as though these considerations about the horrors of nomological danglers are heuristic only. The vital *philosophical* argument comes when we argue that it is *not* necessary to believe that sensations are nonphysical. Indeed we do not need to prove apodeictically that there are no nonphysical mental events. We can make it plausible that there is no good reason to postulate Xs by examining all the reasons the philosophers have given for supposing that there are Xs, and by showing that these reasons are bad ones. Of course, it may be that there are better reasons that someone may discover later, and perhaps there may be good reasons that no one has thought of or will think of. However, the mere *possibility* of this does not matter: one could not accept even a well-tested scientific theory if one were prevented by the mere possibility that an unknown experimental refutation of it exists.

Following U. T. Place (Place 1956) and in agreement with D. M. Armstrong (Armstrong 1968, 1980) and others, my way of getting rid of the nomological danglers was to argue that sensations are *identical* with brain processes and are not extra-psychical entities merely *correlated* with brain processes. Mental events are individuated by their typical environmental causes and their typical behavioral effects. But brain processes have these environmental causes and behavioral effects. And so far, then, it would seem to be a simple and uncontroversial use of Ockham's Razor to chop off the nonphysical and simply *identify* the mental with the physical. But if we let it go at that, the real work has not been done and the dualist will not be convinced.

There is indeed an obstacle to using Ockham's Razor to deny the existence of *X*s if it seems that we are immediately aware of *X*s. We need to give reasons for thinking that when people report an apparent awareness of the nonphysical, they are in some way deceived. In the case of perception of the external world, we can often give scientific reasons for thinking that a supposed perception of putative entities is no such thing: these reasons will contain an explanation of how the mistake is brought about by normal physical and physiological causes. Consider, for example, the optical explanation of mirages. Sometimes the explanation will be psychological (in a sense compatible with physicalism) rather than, say, optical. This would be the case, presumably, with an explanation of the headless woman illusion, which has been discussed by D.M. Armstrong (Armstrong 1968–69). He argues that the apparent phenomenology of consciousness as nonphysical comes from an illusion analogous to that of the headless woman. The headless woman illusion is achieved by placing black cloth over the woman's head and by illuminating the woman's body against a black background. Spectators, not seeing that the woman has a head, jump to the conclusion that the woman has no head. (Not seeing that *p* gets confused with seeing that not *p*.) Similarly, it can be argued that the properties that are presented in inner sense are neutral ones that could be possessed alike by physical and nonphysical entities, and so our inner sense is not an awareness of things as having *specifically* physical properties. Just as with the headless woman, we jump from this to an unwarranted negative judgment: we are not aware that our inner experiences are neurological processes and we jump to the conclusion that they are *not* neurological processes. Armstrong does concede that the consideration about the headless woman illusion will not completely satisfy the objector who relies on the phenomenology of inner experience, so that more needs to be said.

However, I find it very hard to put much weight on such phenomenological objections. The neutral properties do seem to be the ones of which I am aware in inner sense. It is up to the philosopher who appeals to phenomenology to tell us more and I do not think that he succeeds.

Of course, if sense data and mental images were part of the world, they would be things with phenomenological properties, such as blueness, for example. A sense datum can not be identified with a neurophysiological process, since such a process presumably can not be blue. However, I hold that there are no sense data or images as such, but only the havings of them, and the having of a blue sense datum is not itself blue. Of course, I do have to give a physicalist account of the blueness of physical objects, for example, cornflowers. (Smart 1975, which replaces the also physicalist account in Smart 1963.)

The pattern of my argument is therefore as follows. I use plausibility considerations of simplicity, in an attempt to soften up the dualist, by getting him to wonder whether the arguments against the materialist theory of mind are as good as he thought they were. If he can be convinced that they are not good arguments, then it is only a mere uncontroversial application of Ockham's Razor to chop away the immaterially mental, since it is then agreed that there is no necessity to suppose that it exists. But my plausibility arguments came *before* the argument that the immaterially mental was *praeter necessitatem*. Are my plausibility arguments heuristic only? What I have said so far suggests that the answer to this question is in the affirmative. In conclusion I should like to suggest (contrarily to the position I have taken up earlier in this paper) that a case could be made out that plausibility arguments can have a more than heuristic role. Perhaps we should have more faith metaphysically in considerations of plausibility in the light of total science than we have in attempts at apodeictic argument. Philosophical arguments are notoriously slippery. If they lead us to conclusions that do not fit in well with our scientific picture of the world, then we should distrust them. Since a philosopher can question anything whatever, complete apodeictic refutation of a philosophical position is hardly possible. Philosophical arguments can be gotten around, though at the cost of perhaps implausible extra premises. So it could be that plausibility in the light of total science is the best touchstone of metaphysical truth, and that formal philosophical arguments and clarifications play a somewhat ancillary (though necessary) part. But all this is another story (Smart 1966).[5]

Notes

1. In this paper I shall use the more appropriate Anglo-Saxon spelling, rather than the Latinized "Occam" that I used to use.

2. The infelicity was noted in Routley 1980, p. 412.

3. Lewis S. Feuer has argued that the principle of Ockham's Razor is part and parcel of scientific method since it counsels the rejection of unverifiable and hence arbitrary elements. (Feuer 1957, and 1959. However, see also the discussion of this in Schlesinger 1959, and Schlesinger 1963, pp. 20–23.) In Schlesinger 1974, ch. 2, there is an argument that without appeal to a principle of simplicity, the inductive method would not enable us to pick out a unique hypothesis and so we would be completely paralyzed in choosing between them.

4. For a striking illustration of a similarity in complexity between Copernicus's system and the geocentric one, see the illustrations on pp. xii–xiii in de Santillana 1955. I am indebted to the reference in Lakatos 1978b, p. 174, n. 8.

5. I should like to thank my friends D.M. Armstrong, K.K. Campbell, F.J. Clendinnen, F.C. Jackson, P.N. Pettit, and H. Price, who read an earlier draft of this paper and made useful comments.

PART TWO

Philosophy and Science

7 Scientific and Philosophical Argument

Henry E. Kyburg, Jr.

Is there a difference between scientific and philosophical argument? I shall argue that in an important sense there is no difference, not on the gound that philosophical conclusions are to be construed as empirical generalizations (though perhaps of a particularly rarified sort), but on the ground that much of our "scientific" knowledge is no more to be construed as comprising empirical generalization than our philosophical knowledge.

To put the thesis more precisely, I shall suggest that there are three basic forms of argument. Two of them concern transformations within a given language—represented by deductive inference and by statistical inference—and one of them concerns transformations between languages—the replacement of one language by another. The application of each of these three forms of argument requires that we take seriously the notion of a body of knowledge expressed in a certain language. (In fact, I shall argue that they require that we take into account two distinct bodies of knowledge.) Simultaneously, we must take into account the ambiguities surrounding the terms "certain," "infallible," and "incorrigible." There need be nothing particularly problematic about deductive inference—at least, we shall not focus on those problems. There is a lot that is problematic about statistical inference, but for our present purposes, we shall not focus on those problems either. Statistical inference does not play a role in philosophical argument, and deductive inference (we shall suppose) is not controversial, either in science or in philosophy. But if we construe a language as embodying certain relations of meaning, certain *a priori* connections, then the choice between alternative languages is simultaneously a choice between systems of *a priori* truths, and is clearly relevant to the question of philosophical argument.

Philosophical inquiry has long been characterized by the search for certainty. Aristotle sought to found knowledge on the basis of deduction from necessary first principles. Descartes abjured us to seek indubitable knowledge. Philosophers have in recent generations developed a healthy skepticism regarding necessary first principles from which substantive knowledge can be derived by deduction. New variations on this theme may still be found, however, particularly among those who insist that induction or scientific inference must rest on presuppositions. Arthur Burks (1977) and Bertrand Russell (1948), for example, have argued that scientific inference rests on certain material assumptions. From those assumptions, together with observational premises, we can obtain probabilistic knowledge of the empirical world. These presuppositions play a role in a probabilistic framework similar to the role played by first principles in a deductive framework.

Many writers now suppose that scientific inference rests on presuppositions of a far less general character than those proposed by Burks. According to Kuhn (1970), for example, scientific inference can only be carried out in a disciplinary matrix—where a disciplinary matrix embodies the assumptions and presuppositions of a course of scientific inquiry in a particular field and at a particular historical period. According to an older version of Kuhn's view (1962), it was a paradigm that embodied these assumptions and presuppositions. For Lakatos (1970), it was a research program that embodied them. Such suggestions fall on fertile ground in some of the social sciences. To call something a presupposition or a paradigm may seem to eliminate to some extent the need for critical scrutiny or rational support.

It may be questioned whether it is appropriate to approach empirical scientific inquiry in this way. My own view is that it is not appropriate. For our present purposes, that is beside the point. The question is whether it is appropriate to approach philosophical inquiry that way. Few philosophers seem to agree that it is. Most philosophers seem to argue from clear and precise intuitions, by means of classical deductive logic, to their conclusions.

This claim should be clarified and substantiated. The intuitions that serve to ground philosophical argument come in two main forms that may be conveniently differentiated, though they are not independent of one another. One form consists of the intuition of the meanings of words in ordinary or technical language. In its extreme form it resulted in the "ordinary language philosophy" that was prevalent a few decades ago. It is still popular in certain varieties of formal philosophy. Thus in the theory of measurement it is suggested, even when it is not argued explicitly, that the relation of "being the same length as" is transitive simply in virtue of its meaning. Discussions of causality, and of action, and of rationality also often seem to embody, explicitly or implicitly, arguments based on intuitions of the ordinary meanings of certain special terms.

The other form of intuition concerns the intuitive import of particular examples or instances. This is more prevalent now than the dependence on intuitions of the meanings of ordinary words. It underlies the development of philosophical theses by means of argument and counterexample: present a thesis, defend it or modify it in the face of intuitively understood counterexamples, and stand back while others present their counterexamples. The force of a counterexample, I am suggesting, lies in its intuitive impact.

Of course, there is a point of view, or a set of points of view, from which this is the correct way to do both science and philosophy: a kind of naive Popperian view (Popper 1959) according to which we can do no more than propose daring hypotheses and then valiantly attempt to refute them. But there are few naive Popperians in philosophy—certainly Popper is not among them—and most people suppose there is more to the search for truth than unbridled creativity, even when combined with the cold-blooded search for refutation. In philosophy, even more than in science, definitive refutation is hard to come by, even though there are intuitions so nearly universal and so powerful that only a fool would fail to give them their due. And in philosophy, as in science, creativity must be bridled by a judicious respect for what we already have good grounds for believing.

I have said that the basis of many philosophical arguments is intuition, combined with classical deductive argument. I say this despite the plethora of intensional logics and their models that currently fill the more formally oriented of the philosophical journals. It is therefore necessary to say a little more about what I mean.

For several decades, we had a number of modal logics in the literature of philosophy that had no other basis than their intuitive appeal. Since there were several distinct logics, the intuitive appeal of any one of them was obviously not overwhelming. Although it was possible, through interpretation, to establish the consistency of these logics, it was not at all clear that one could go much further. In 1959 Saul Kripke devised a semantics of possible worlds and relations among them that would distinguish among these modal logics, and which could provide a basis for discussing "completeness." Kripke thereby established a new industry (Kripke 1959).

Begin by considering a philosophical domain. Consult your favorite intuitions regarding that domain. Present axioms that embody those intuitions. Then provide a semantic interpretation of the system; if the axioms and the interpretation are suitably related, you will be able to prove that your system of axioms is consistent and (relative to that interpretation) complete. This can be relatively complicated, and doing it will earn you points in the ingenuity competition. Note, however, that your arguments will be in ordinary first order logic. The system you present may be as intensional as you please; nevertheless, the arguments you present to establish its consistency and completeness will involve sentential logic, ordinary first order quantification over possible worlds and their relations and whatever other entities your semantic interpretation requires. No more than classical deductive logic is involved in the philosophical part of the argument.

There is more to defending the philosophical thesis involved, of course. Objections may be brought to the axiomatic embodiment of your original intuitions. The objections have the form of counterexamples. The force of the counterexamples is intuitive. You defend your system by attacking the intuitive soundness of the counterexamples, by presenting contrary intuitions, or (most likely) by showing that the system presented does, after all, and contrary to first appearances, embody those very intuitions.

The greater part of contemporary philosophical argument thus hews to a classical line: it is the attempt to derive necessary philosophical conclusions from clear and distinct intuitions by means of classical deductive argument. Disputation consists in the conflict of contrary intuitions and intuitive argument about their centrality and importance. That this does not often lead to progress in philosophy is no more surprising than that a similar approach to theorizing in science would tend to produce sterility rather than progress. It will be argued below that there is a better way. It is not that counterexample and formalization are useless tools—on the contrary, I shall argue that they are essential—but that they are no more than tools and, however clever the carpenter, the tools alone will produce no useful artifacts without some substance to work on.

In scientific inference, a way out has commonly been proposed: that we should look not to certainty or necessity, but to probability. No theory, law, or hypothesis, it is argued, can be rendered certain by empirical evidence; but empirical evidence can render them probable. Transposed to the philosophical domain, the thesis would be that philosophical conclusions cannot be definitively "established" but that, by philosophical argument, they can be rendered so highly probable as to be worthy of acceptance.

As an article of faith, and stated thus broadly and vaguely, the idea has a certain appeal. But it is an idea we don't know how to apply in science, and one that participants in the scientific enterprise rarely employ explicitly. How to flesh out the idea of providing an inductive logic and an interpretation of probability so that we can tell when a general conclusion has been "rendered probable by the evidence" is highly problematic. That it has not been done, one might say, provides inductive evidence against its feasibility.

Attempts have been made, of course, but in general they have rested on intuitions less clear and more suspect than those they are designed to formalize and rationalize. There is another problem, more general in character, that has led some writers—Kuhn (1962) and Feyerabend (1965), to name two prominent examples, and more recently Hempel (1970)—to doubt that any such approach can be self-sufficient. One aspect of this problem is the difficulty of providing a clear demarcation between "observation" predicates and "theoretical" predicates. If there were a set of observation predicates that could be definitively and incorrigibly applied, that would give us a foothold. But it is hard to imagine any predicates that have empirical content and that satisfy this condition. Intuitively, one would like to be able to talk about cats and trees, ammeters and stars, and even the results of measurement, in the basic observation language. But such predications are always corrigible. It does no good to say that quantitative statements should always concern intervals—that we should say that the length of a rod is 7.6 plus or minus .015 cm, rather than saying that it is 7.6 cm long—because on any ordinary theory of errors of measurement, no matter how large the allowance for error, there is a finite probability that the measurement is in error by more than that amount.

Alternatively, one might retreat to an ever more phenomenological level: I am being appeared to 7.6 centimeterly and rodly. But this retreat multiplies the difficulties of getting to the sort of abstract and general knowledge that we all suppose we have, and if it is carried far enough, it is possible that one can't get there at all.

Another aspect of the same difficulty arises whatever the character of observational knowledge is taken to be, and wherever one draws the line between observational and nonobservational. We constantly use general and theoretical knowledge as premises in arguments. If those arguments are to be sound, their premises must be true. If we are to believe that those arguments are sound, we must believe that their premises are true. To have warrant for accepting the conclusions, we must have warrant for accepting the premises. But this is not at all the same as having grounds for taking the premises to be probable. Take it as probable that all ravens are black, and that Tom is a raven. Under certain circumstances this may deductively render it probable that Tom is black; but under no circumstances will it yield "Tom is black" as a deductive conclusion. The same is true even of probabilistic inferences. Almost everybody claims to accept some form of direct inference: If you know that half of coin tosses yield heads, there are circumstances under which this entitles or obligates you to assign a probability of a half to the next toss yielding heads. But this inference, like the inference concerning Tom's color, depends on the acceptance of a statement that clearly and obviously goes beyond the observational.

The idea that we can simply suppose that the items in our bodies of knowledge can be construed as having the form "the probability of h is high," although it has a certain superficial appeal, simply will not do what we need done, either in science or in philosophy. If deduction is to serve the function in our rational economy we think it serves, we must have grounds for accepting nontrivial premises—not only premises representing the routine results of observation, but premises that quite clearly go beyond any historical sum of observations. This is so whether those premises are regarded as universal or statistical in character. The notion of rational acceptance, however, has its own problems. If a statement is accepted in a body of knowledge, its probability relative to that body of knowledge can only be one. There is therefore no purely Bayesian way in which it can come to be rejected. Suppose it is a general sentence, and we observe a counterinstance? Still there is no way to eliminate the accepted generalization. The probability of the counterinstance must be zero, and there is no way to raise that probability to a level of acceptance. Suppose we have an observational routine that simply provides for the acceptance of certain statements on the basis of certain procedures of observation. Then we are led to an inconsistent body of knowledge. As Levi (to whom the idea of routine acceptance is due) points out (Levi 1980), this is not necessarily a disaster. When our body of knowledge becomes inconsistent, we are (strongly!) motivated to contract it so as to eliminate that inconsistency. But Levi's suggestion is that we should so contract our corpus of knowledge as to preserve the greatest informational content in the process of achieving consistency. To apply this to our example is easy: there is no question but that the generalization has more content than the observation. We must reject the observation.

Perhaps we should institute an ordering procedure that will indicate which statements have priority in the process of purifying a body of knowledge of inconsistency? It seems unlikely that this would lead to acceptable results. On some occasions the observation of a counterexample should lead to the rejection of the generalization; on other occasions the counterexample itself should it be rejected.

As in science, so in philosophy. It is not at all clear that an alleged counterexample should constitute a definitive refutation of even a philosophical theory. It may be that the theory has enough to recommend it so that the counterexample can be left to one side for future consideration, be dealt with in some roundabout way, or in general just disregarded. As an example, the semantics of the ordinary conditional connective of logic are at variance with some of the uses of "if . . . then ———" in English. Most logicians have sensibly decided that these variant uses are just not those captured by the truth functional conditional. It would be perverse to reject the use of theories embodying the truth functional conditional on the grounds that sometimes the English conditional is regarded as false when the "corresponding" truth-functional conditional is regarded as true. But what *are* the standards of rational acceptance?

In the sections that follow, I shall first defend and clarify the assumption that knowledge, both philosophical and scientific, consists of accepted propositions or statements. Second, I shall argue that this requires at least a two tiered system. Third, I shall attempt to characterize the required two tiers. And fourth and finally, I shall try to show that both trans-statistical scientific argument and philosophical argument employ the same general principles.

Suppose we are considering rolls of a die. A person under ordinary circumstances who does not regard the occurrence of a one on the next roll as having a probability of about a sixth is properly regarded as "irrational" in our culture. Why? Because everybody in our culture (as opposed to some aboriginal culture to which dice have not yet been introduced) knows that about a sixth of rolls of dice land with one up. Note that this does not depend on every individual in our culture having extensive firsthand experience in rolling dice. There is the testimony of those who have that experience; there is the theoretical physical knowledge that leads to that result; and most important, there is the known and accepted fact that dice are designed and manufactured to exhibit this property. In this context it is an accepted fact that dice behave this way; it is not a proposition that we should call "probable" or "well supported" by the evidence. It is *itself* evidence, relative to which the rational and educated man should judge the likelihood of a one on the next roll of this die.

Consider a simple measurement—say the measurement of the mass of a sample of uranium. We observe the result R: our scale reads 1.37462 grams. This is the result of our observation. This is what we write down in our laboratory notebook. But we do not attribute a weight of 1.37462 grams to the sample of uranium. Rather, we take account of the distribution of error characteristic of our scale, under ordinary circumstances, and use our *knowledge* of that distribution of error to characterize the probability that the mass of our sample falls in any given interval. Our knowledge of the distribution of error may be based on firsthand experience with that particular scale; more likely it is based on the testimony of others; and ultimately it is based on the claims of the manufacturer, which in turn are based on trials with similar scales and on the theory underlying those scales. The error distribution is, in any event, something that we typically just accept, in this context.

In much the same way, we ordinarily accept the evidence of our senses, the testimony of our teachers, and (I hope with somewhat more discrimination and circumspection) the written reports we read. We accept, rationally, the pronouncements of experts on quantum mechanics, genetics, astrophysics, chemistry, and (at least in certain respects) of experts on economics, psychology, and sociology. In ordinary circumstances, we accept these pronouncements and the testimony of our senses and our teachers in a very strong sense: we accept them as *evidence* or *premises* on which we base our probabilities and predictions.

Of course, items like this may be in error. We may be suffering from hallucination, our teachers may be misguided. The experts can be wrong. The distribution of error in our weighing device may not be what we think it is. The die may not be one that is accurately made, or to introduce a "philosophical" possibility, it may remember its past tosses and behave so as to confirm the gambler's fallacy and to confute rational wisdom. Furthermore, these are things we could learn about; by inquiry we can discover them.

How can we account for both of these facts: that we simply accept as evidence a large body of knowledge; and at the same time we can regard any given item as questionable, and subject to rejection in the light of new or more complete evidence? A distinction that may be helpful here is one introduced by Isaac Levi between incorrigibility and infallibility. Each of the items in our body of knowledge—including our knowledge of the stochastic behavior of dice, our knowledge of the distribution of errors in the weighing device, such knowledge of physics and chemistry as we may have—is regarded as infallible. This is the ground on which we can use it as a premise in a deductive argument or in direct inference. But at the same time, each of the items in our body of knowledge is regarded as corrigible: given new evidence, it may be rejected as false, or replaced by a new and corrected item.[1] To claim to know something is to claim to know that it is true: not probable, but *true*. Such claims may be undermined by subsequent events. They do not need to be supported by evidence, since, while they are accepted, they *are* evidence.

Nevertheless, such claims can be questioned. To question such a claim is to call for evidence justifying its inclusion in a body of knowledge. Here is where Levi and I begin to part company. For Levi, to question an item in a body of knowledge requires deleting it from that body of knowledge (contracting) in order to give alternatives to that item a serious hearing. It is difficult, in circumstances in which the body of knowledge contains no inconsistency, to motivate contraction: we are deliberately throwing away knowledge that, on Levi's view as well as mine, is infallibly true. On my view, what is infallibly true in one context may be "merely" probable in another, and it is that probability we are being called upon to defend when an item of knowledge is questioned.

Levi's view is dynamic. He sees the corpus of knowledge as expanding and contracting. It is expanded deliberately through inductive inference, and routinely through observation, through the reports of others, and so on. Should it become inconsistent, it is contracted through the removal of enough items to become consistent. Should we wish to question some item in the corpus, the corpus must be contracted so as to exclude that item; then we may see whether expansion to include that item is justified.

Obviously we cannot pull the Cartesian trick of trying to question everything at once. But more than this, we cannot even consider expansion unless we already have a lot of material in our body of knowledge. We require not only the sort of contents we can obtain by observational routine, but quite general knowledge about the world, including knowledge of chance. In this respect Levi's approach bears a certain resemblance to the presupposition theories previously mentioned. It is importantly different, however, in that no item of knowledge is immune from critical assessment.[2]

On the other hand, it is not clear that Levi's system can handle what is popularly called "conceptual change," and what I would prefer to construe as a change in basic vocabulary—i.e., as a linguistic change. It may be questioned how important this is in science. According to some who hail revolution in science, the revolutionary changes that involve new conceptual frameworks occur only rarely; if this is so, the inability to handle such changes may be a relatively minor defect compared to the ability to handle the everyday business of scientific inference. But our main concern here is *philosophical* knowledge, and on the face of it philosophical knowledge has a lot to do with concepts, conceptual change, and conceptual frameworks.

Where Levi considers a single body of knowledge and its dynamics, I consider a two-tiered system. This introduces a number of complexities, but enables us to clarify a number of epistemological puzzles, including some peculiar to philosophical knowledge.

Consider the first example, in which the rational man (a) assigns a probability of a sixth to the occurrence of a one on a specific roll of a die, on the grounds that he *knows* that a sixth of the rolls of dice yield a one; and simultaneously (b) can defend that item of knowledge on the grounds that he has evidence that renders that item of knowledge overwhelmingly probable.

To fix our ideas and to simplify the analysis, let us abandon reality and suppose that the evidence that supports his knowledge concerning the stochastic behavior of dice is directly statistical in character. Let the two tiers of knowledge be called evidential and practical certainty. Evidential certainty is to be construed as more demanding: every evidential certainty is a practical certainty, but not conversely. Our rational agent assigns a probability of one sixth to the outcome one on the basis of his practical certainty that a sixth of rolls of dice yield a one. He applies *direct inference* to his stochastic knowledge to obtain a probability applicable to the specific case with which he is concerned. We leave to one side the formulation of the principle of direct inference; it suffices for our purposes here that most writers agree that, in some circumstances, direct inference is an appropriate way to arrive at probabilities.

This accounts for (a). But we wish also to account for (b); we wish to be able to explain, in turn, the grounds on which our rational agent can accept the statistical statement that a sixth of the rolls of dice yield a one. The explanation will be that relative to his evidential corpus, that statistical statement is so probable as to be practically certain. I have argued elsewhere (1974) that *all* probabilities are based on direct inference. In this case the argument might go something like this: it is a set-theoretical truth (and therefore to be incorporated in the agent's corpus of evidential certainties) that practically all large samples from a set closely reflect the relative frequency of a distinguished subset of that set. In particular, practically all large samples of rolls of dice closely reflect the relative frequency of the outcome one.

We also suppose that in his evidential corpus he has the data from a large sample of rolls of dice, in which a sixth (approximately) are ones. *By direct inference* the probability is high ("practically all") that this sample closely reflects the relative frequency of ones in general. But the sample closely reflects the relative frequency of ones in general if and only if the relative frequency of ones in general is (about) a sixth. The probability is therefore very high that the relative frequency of ones in general is about a sixth. This is the very item of statistical information that was in question.

Thus we can both use direct inference to justify the agent's assignment of a probability of a sixth to the occurrence of a one on a specific roll of a specific die, and also use it to justify the occurrence of the required generalization in his corpus of practical certainties.

This procedure suggests that the corpus of practical certainties can appropriately be indexed by a number representing the minimum probability a statement must have in order to be regarded as practically certain. The index r characterizes the corpus of practical certainties consisting of exactly those statements whose probability, relative to the evidential corpus, is at least r.

It is natural to allow the index to vary with context: under some circumstances practical certainty might require only a probability of .90; under others (perhaps with more at stake) it might require a probability of .999.

How about the corpus of evidential certainties? It is not clear that there is as natural a rationale for assigning an index to this corpus as there is for assigning a rationale to the corpus of practical certainties. But it does seem clear that just as items in the corpus of practical certainties can be questioned and justified, so it should be possible to question and justify items in the corpus of evidential certainties. To do so, I suggest, is to regard those items as items in a corpus of practical certainties of higher index. That is, we are asking for justification relative to a corpus that is evidential, relative to the corpus in which the questioned items appear. This amounts to a shift of context. What is questioned, in any context, is something that is claimed to be practically certain. What practical certainty amounts to, in probability, also varies according to the context.

The evidential corpus (since the same set of statements may also be in another context construed as a set of practical certainties) must also be indexed. We might regard the context as setting this level as well, but in (1974) I offered an alternative suggestion: For acceptance into the corpus of practical certainties of level r, we require that the probability of the statement in question be at least r relative to some corpus of evidential certainties of level higher than r, and also relative to every corpus of evidential certainties of level lower than that but higher than r.

There is nothing difficult or impossible about this. In order to justify the inclusion of the statement S in the corpus of practical certainties of level r, all we need is to exhibit a set of statements constituting a corpus of higher index r^*, relative to which the statement S has a probability of at least r, and claim that no intermediate level of evidential statements undermines that assertion of probability. Remember that we are only being asked to *justify* the inclusion of S among the practical certainties of level r.

To be asked to justify the membership or nonmembership in the evidential corpus of the statements that *lead* to the justification of the inclusion of S in the corpus of level r is another matter altogether. It is a request we should be able to satisfy, if our original justification is sound. But it is a different request. In particular, it changes the context so that practical certainty becomes a matter of the level r^* rather than r. For example, part of the problem of justifying the inclusion of S in the corpus of practical certainties of level r is to exhibit an appropriate statistical statement as a member of level r^*. To be called upon to justify the inclusion of this statistical statement in the corpus of practical certainties of level r^* is to be called upon to show that relative to an evidential corpus of level r^{**} greater than r^*, the statistical statement in question is practically certain.

This regress—for regress it admittedly is—is only a problem if it cannot terminate. That it can terminate can be demonstrated as follows. There are statistical statements that can be accepted in the evidential corpus of level 1.0. These are simply set theoretical truths, such as: almost all subsets of the set D contain a proportion of members of the set T that is close to the overall proportion of members of R that belong to T.

We also need empirical statements—for example, that the object a (itself a set, in this case) is a member of the set of subsets of the set *R*, and that the proportion of members of *a* that belong to *T* is *p*. We now consider two cases:

First, we suppose that there are empirical statements that can be accepted in the corpus of level 1.0. These must be incorrigible statements. Many philosophers suppose there are such statements. If there are, we're home free. I tend to think there are no such statements, or at least no such statements that are useful in science, ordinary life, or philosophy. So the other case is that there are no empirical statements that can be accepted in the corpus of level 1.0. But even if there are no *empirical* statements that can be accepted in the corpus of level 1.0, we may yet suppose that there are empirical statements that can be accepted in corpora of lower levels.

Consider a garden variety observation statement—e.g., that there is a squirrel on the roof. Can it be included in the corpus of level 1.0? I doubt it. But there is a *reason* for my doubt. It is that in a certain small percentage of cases in which I am moved by my experience to accept such a statement, it turns out that the acceptance is subsequently undermined.

This itself is something I have learned. The process by which I have learned it, however, is quite different from the process by which I learn statistical generalizations on the basis of samples. There is no way in which I can acquire a sample of squirrel-on-the-roof perceptions, note which ones are veridical, and use that relative frequency to determine the proportion of veridical perceptions of that sort. ("Of that sort . . . ," "similar," and the like, are dispensible in a formal account. What we need is not a direct positive account of similarity, but a set of conditions under which "relevant difference" can be spelled out. The syntactical notion of randomness yields a specification of those conditions.)

The procedure works as follows. We suppose that bookkeeping is error-free. (This condition could be eliminated at the cost of yet further complications.) We thus suppose that we can keep track of our empirical judgments. Why shouldn't we regard them as all veridical? Why should we suppose that any of them are in error? Only because some of them conflict deductively with generalizations and theories we accept. Thus, for example, I may judge that *a* and *b* are rigid bodies, that *a* is longer than *b*, and that *b* is longer than *a*. Given the generalization that for any *x* and *y*, if they are rigid bodies then it is not the case that both *x* is longer than *y* and *y* is longer than *x*, one of my judgments *must* be wrong. I may judge that there is a squirrel on the roof, and I may watch it tumble down at my feet, and I may judge that the object at my feet is a leaf. This conflicts with the generalization (is it conceptual or empirical?) that squirrels don't turn into leaves.

Where do these generalizations come from? The answer to this question provides the last link in the chain of argument from ordinary experience to philosophical knowledge as well as scientific knowledge.

Let us begin by considering the predictive observational content of a corpus of practical certainties. Suppose an individual undergoes (or participates in) a certain course of experience. This course of experience can be codified in statements of a certain language. It is well known that what a person experiences depends on his past experiences, on his beliefs, and also on his language. If we focus on what is communicable in a given linguistic community, however, we can ignore the effects of some of these dependencies. Given a language, then, we can represent that body of experience by a set of statements in the language representing judgments based directly on experience. Following Levi, we might say that these are statements that are accepted on the basis of observational routine.

Let us consider two cases. Case I: These statements are taken to be incorrigible; they are entered into the evidential corpus of level 1.0. Given the variability of human experience, we may conjecture that there are no universal generalizations of interest that hold of these statements. But there will be statistical generalizations that can be accepted as practically certain on the evidence they provide. These statistical statements, in turn, if they are construed evidentially, can support observational predictions as practically certain.

Illustrative examples are hard to generate since our language already embodies so much in the way of generalization. But we might suppose (to pursue an example already alluded to) that we have only rarely seen squirrels turn into leaves. This could warrant the acceptance in our corpus of practical certainties of level, say, .95, that squirrels almost never turn into leaves. Suppose that we see a squirrel. If we regard the statistical generalization as an evidential certainty (of level .95) we may take it to be practically certain (at, say, the .90 level) that this squirrel will not turn into a leaf. This is a prediction about the course of our experience.

Case II: Alternatively, we may suppose that we have accepted (perhaps as a principle of "meaning") that squirrels just don't turn into leaves. Then we have no choice but to suppose that our "observation" of a squirrel that turned into a leaf was erroneous. If error is possible in our identifications of squirrels and leaves, again we cannot be more than "practically certain" about the course of our future experience. We can only be practically certain that what we are looking at is a squirrel. But since we have accepted it as a principle that squirrels don't ("can't," for that matter) turn into leaves, we can be just as sure that we will not be led by experience to make a leaf judgment as we are that our original judgment was veridical.

Note that in either case our practical certainty is derived from experience: In the first case it is the observation that only rarely do squirrels turn into leaves that warrants our belief that it won't happen this time. In the second case it is the observation that we are only rarely mistaken when we judge something to be a squirrel that warrants our belief that we are not mistaken this time, and that therefore what we see will not turn out to be a leaf.

Are these equivalent ways of viewing the matter? Should it be taken as mere convention whether we use language in such a way that we take our attributions of squirrelhood to be incorrigible, or whether we use it in such a way that the principle that squirrels can't turn into leaves is *a priori* and incorrigible?

I suggest that it *is* a matter of convention—linguistic convention, if you will—but not a matter of "mere" convention. These are not equivalent ways of viewing the matter. If you look at the body of predictive statements that are certified as practically certain in the case of an "appearance" language and in the case of a "reality" language you will find (as I have tried to show in the mistitled "All Generalizations are Analytic" [1977a]) that the body of practical certainties is larger in the second case.

This suggests a second principle of scientific inference. Given a choice between two languages, choose that language that yields the corpus of practical certainties containing the greatest number of predictive observational statements. To allow comparisons, we must ensure that there are only a finite number of such statements in any corpus of practical certainties. There are a number of ways in which one might accomplish this. We might take a "predictive observational statement" to be a statement that occupies the place of S in "If X were to do A, then X would judge that S," and suppose that there are only a finite number of acts A that are potentially open to X. What concerns us here is primarily the relation between scientific inference and reasoning, and philosophical inference and reasoning. We will therefore not concern ourselves with the details of specifying in a finite way the contents of a corpus of practical certainties. We will suppose that some plausible measure of the predictive observational contents of a corpus of practical certainties can be devised. We will also suppose, though this, too, requires argument, that we will be led to the same results with regard to a choice between languages whatever level of practical certainties we focus on. Let us simply suppose, hypothetically and for the sake of the argument, that some such scheme tied to the predictive observational content of the corpus of practical certainties is appropriate in science.

There are thus two forms of scientific reasoning or argument that can alter our bodies of knowledge. One we may call statistical inference: within the framework of a given language, finite empirical data can render an approximate statistical generalization highly probable; the *inferential* move is to accept that generalization in the corpus of appropriate level. The second form of scientific reasoning or argument consists in the reasoned replacement of one language by another, on the grounds of the enrichment of the predictive component of the corpus of practical certainties.

How do these forms of reasoning or inference bear on philosophical argument? The first form, statistical inference, has relatively little to do with philosophical knowledge. Philosophical theses are not presented as approximate statistical generalizations. In fact, one might characterize philosophical theses as necessary but arguable. To the extent that scientific reasoning is statistical, philosophical reasoning is quite different.

It has been thought that another form of scientific reasoning concerns the confirmation and acceptance of universal empirical generalizations. I have argued elsewhere ("A Defense of Conventionalism," [1977b] and "All Acceptable Generalizations are Analytic" [1977a]) that such generalizations are hard to find, and that the "empirical" generalizations usually cited are in fact better construed as *a priori* features of the scientific language we speak.

If I am right about this, much of the motivation for drawing a sharp distinction between philosophical and scientific reasoning is undermined. This would suggest that both science and philosophy are pursuing the same goal. Some evidence for this should be apparent even from the examples I have used. The distinction between appearance and reality is a classical philosophical one. When we argue for a realistic language, in which our observational judgments are subject to error, as opposed to a phenomenalistic language in which our judgments are incorrigible and infallible, but in which no universal generalizations obtain concerning relations among such terms, we are reasoning in a manner appropriate to philosophy as well as to science.

Note that in this instance as well as in others, empirical evidence is "involved." It is in virtue of the experience we have, the judgments we have made, that we can distinguish between the corpus of useful predictive observation statements we obtain in the two cases. The generalizations are *a priori* features of our language, so evidence is irrelevant to them. But the choice between two languages rests on the consequences for our corpus of practical certainties of the combination of experience and language.

It is not hard to see how such forms of reasoning can be regarded as appropriate to certain disputes in the philosophy of science— realism versus instrumentalism, for example. It is not quite so easy to see the outcome: it takes a certain amount of ingenuity to figure out what realism and instrumentalism amount to, and a certain amount of argument to show that, as thus construed, one of them yields more useful content to our corpus of practical certainties. I have claimed, but I have not presented any detailed argument, that reasoning of the sort I am endorsing leads to support of the metaphysical thesis of realism as opposed to the metaphysical thesis of phenomenalism: we observe squirrels, not squirrel appearances.

But it is less clear that this is also the form of reasoning appropriate to philosophical disputes in ethics or meta-ethics, to questions about freedom and determinism, to theological questions, to questions of ontology, to problems concerning the foundations of language itself, or of logic and mathematics.

As an example, consider ethics. An ethical or moral theory, let us suppose, consists of certain principles from which, it is alleged, follows a standard for judging human conduct. These principles may be defended in a number of ways. They may be defended on the basis of intuition, on the basis of conformity to ordinary judgment, on the basis of conformity to the ordinary usage of moral terms, etc. The usual form of counterargument consists in exhibiting hypothetical instances of human behavior, to which the principles lead to the "wrong" result.

On the view of philosophical reasoning and inference I am suggesting, this is the wrong way of looking at the matter. To propose moral principles is to propose that certain statements be taken as *a priori* in our moral language. They are not "derived" from anything—they are free creations of the human mind. But, as scientific generalizations are weighed against immediate but corrigible observational judgments, so moral principles may be weighed against immediate but corrigible moral judgments. The force of a counterexample against proposed moral principles lies not in the particular case, but in the fact that the particular case represents a broad class of cases. The claim is not merely that there exists a particular case in which our moral judgment would have to be construed as erroneous, but that there is a whole class of judgments that would have to be construed as mistaken.

Just as in the case of empirical judgments we can, by hewing to a tight phenomenological line, eliminate mistakes in observation, so in the case of moral judgments, we can hew to a phenomenological line and argue that there are no general moral principles, and therefore no errors of moral judgment. I would suggest, as in the case of a scientific language, that the adoption of such a language would impoverish our corpus of moral judgments.

It is of greater interest to inquire as to whether the principles of rationality briefly suggested here can themselves be defended in its own terms. Consider first classical deductive logic. Most of what each of us knows—most of the contents of our corpus of practical certainties, at any level—comes from the testimony of others. Classical deductive logic can be construed as providing constraints on argument and assertion that are necessary for the communication of knowledge. At least one justification for imposing these constraints on our public language is that it allows me to adopt (some) of your practical certainties as my own.

Consider statistical inference. If we allow no form of rational acceptance, our corpus of practical certainties will be empty. If we are too liberal, we undermine the possibility of useful communication and thus the possibility of enriching each other's corpora of practical certainties. The principles I have proposed—put otherwise, the *a priori* constraints I have suggested putting on the terms "probability" and "random"—are intended to reflect a judicious compromise between these extremes.

Finally, there is the principle proposed for choosing between languages. It is automatic that this principle leads to the maximization of predictive observational practical certainties for an individual. But as the previous considerations suggest, we must also take into account the social dimensions of knowledge. It is possible that two individuals, in virtue of their different funds of experience, should be led to different choices between two languages. I do not deny that this can happen, particularly when the difference between the two languages lies in the esoteric reaches of scientific inquiry. But I think it is rare. It is rare because of our shared biological inheritance, and even more rare among those with a shared culture. The standards of rationality suggested are intended to enhance both the acquisition and the communication of knowledge among featherless bipeds.

Notes

1. This is not quite correct, for Levi does allow for incorrigible items in the corpus of knowledge. These include truths of mathematics and logic, and perhaps some other items. But incorrigibilia are not my present concern.

2. See note 1.

8 The Method of Counterexample

George Schlesinger

(I)

It is probably safe to state that no technique is more frequently employed in philosophy than is the technique of counterexamples. At the same time, it is also obviously true that there are hardly any discussions of this method in the literature. This is not very surprising. It has simply not occurred to many people that the straightforward method of counterexample presents problems that require close study. Most of the other methodological rules employed by philosophers are not easy to state precisely, nor is there agreement as to the scope of their application and as to their ultimate justification. However, the method under discussion amounts to little more than producing an example e of which '$\sim Fe$' is evidently true, thus providing conclusive proof that the generalization '$(x) Fx$' some wished to defend must be false. This is a fully effective, unproblematic, and therefore safe method, which hardly allows for much discussion.

After studying a certain number of examples of its application, however, it becomes apparent that, while this method constitutes a considerably potent tool, it is in fact a two-edged weapon that in many cases does more harm than good. Its potential for harm may be said to lie in its great vitality. That is, because its formal credentials are beyond question, it is applied freely and indiscriminately and, because it is such an efficient thought-saving device, it is often employed as a complete substitute for thought.

To be more specific: the technique is most frequently used to refute a generalization without analyzing what lies at the root of the trouble, i.e., without investigating precisely what is wrong with the generalization that permits the construction of counterexamples. Consequently, the move that usually follows is devised in similar spirit to introduce a proviso specifically constructed to render the counterexample harmless rather than to remedy whatever really ails the generalization of which these counterexamples are merely symptomatic. The following is a familiar scenario of the way philosophical discussions involving the technique of counterexamples often develop:

The story begins with a philosopher advancing a given thesis *T*, which someone wishes to oppose. The most readily available weapon is usually to construct an example whose inclusion or exclusion seems implied by *T* and hence whose existence may be seen as evidence for the inadequacy of *T*.

Since neither the opponent nor the defender of *T* might have any idea what is wrong with *T* except that it clashes with such an example—which is clearly a symptom and not the root of *T*'s malady—it is most natural for those who want to save *T* to introduce qualifications designed to protect it from these particular examples. Unfortunately, there is no guarantee that this sort of revision will bring us closer to an adequate formulation of *T*. The situation may be compared to one in which I notice blue smoke issuing through an opening in the back of my television set and seal the hole so no smoke can escape. Not only have I failed to repair the set, but I have probably made the situation worse.

Yet the typical philosophical situation is more complicated than this. Producing a counterexample, followed by the revision of *T*, is usually only the first step in an extended process with which the reader is surely familiar: a second counterexample is then produced, which is followed by further revisions, and so on. In the course of this process, it quite often happens—and understandably so—that each revision produces a reformulated thesis *one step further away from* a correct thesis than what we had before the revision. It may also quite naturally occur that at each successive stage it becomes increasingly more difficult to recognize an adequate formulation of the thesis originally pursued, since we are increasingly further away from it. In addition, it is also quite natural for a philosopher to seek an ultimate answer to the question of how to formulate his thesis in more or less the same direction we have so far been proceeding. No one likes to admit that a complicated chain of arguments, which has been generated by the process of counterexample followed by reformulation, by which we have reached our present position, may be devoid of all validity, where not a single one of the many steps we have taken so far are of any use because the actual solution lies in quite a different direction.

The end result of this process is that we settle for a formulation that we have reached after we seem to have run out of further counterexamples, whose defects we have managed to paper over for a while. The version of *T* we end up with is considerably more encumbered than the one we started out with as well as containing more inadequacies than did our original version.

(II)

A singularly apt illustration of this kind of a process is provided by the decades-long debate over the notion of scientific explanation. Probably the most famous account of explanation is associated with the name of Carl G. Hempel. To put it informally, what he has suggested amounts roughly to saying that an explanandum *E* (a statement describing the event to be explained) is explained when it is shown that a description of the relevant laws of nature and initial conditions *C* logically imply *E*. In other words, *E* is explained when it is shown that *E* has to be true, for the universe is such that it is inevitable that the event referred to by *E* should occur.

It would be too much to cite all the counterexamples that have been produced to this account, but I shall recall some of them. The result of these examples has been the enlargement of Hempel's simple criterion through the addition of several extra conditions. Ackermann and Stenner (1966, p. 78) for example, suggest the adoption of a criterion with seven conditions, some quite elaborate. Each of their conditions seems to have been formulated in response to a particular kind of counterexample. It is no longer easy to evaluate the extent to which their criterion embodies the notion of explanation, as it is so complex that it is not at all easy to see what it amounts to.

The important point, however, is that, if we cease to worry about counterexamples *per se* and instead ask ourselves what exactly an explanation is for and what it is supposed to achieve, it is not hard to see what aspect of explanation Hempel has failed to capture by his account. For once Hempel's account is supplemented in the appropriate way by taking this aspect into account, all the different objections disappear. Let us begin by looking at several of the most important counterexamples:

Counterexample 1: This objection is raised by Hempel himself. He asks us to suppose:

  E: Mt. Everest is snowcapped;
  T: All metals are good conductors of heat;
  T_s: If the Eiffel Tower is metal, then it is a good conductor of heat;

where T (and therefore T_s, which is an instance of T) is true.

Let C: $T_s \supset E$

then, since E is true, so is C. But T and C logically imply E, while C alone does not; thus, all the conditions for a Hempelian explanation are satisfied. Yet we feel it is absurd that T, which has no apparent bearing whatever on E, should form an essential part of an adequate explanation for E.

Counterexample 2: Hempel has focused his account upon the explanation of singular explananda. He acknowledges, however, that it would be of the utmost importance to provide a clear account of the way in which general regularities reflected by laws of nature are explained. It seems to him that laws of nature are explained when they are shown to follow from more comprehensive laws of nature. But he finds himself confronted with a difficulty that he is unable to resolve. He observes:

> The core of the difficulty can be indicated briefly by reference to an example: Kepler's laws, K, may be conjoined with Boyle's law, B to form a stronger law $K \& B$; but derivation of K from the latter would not be considered as an explanation of the regularities stated in Kepler's laws; rather it would be viewed as representing, in effect, a pointless "explanation" of Kepler's laws by themselves. The derivation of Kepler's laws from Newton's laws of motion and gravitation, on the other hand, would be recognized as a genuine explanation in terms of more comprehensive regularities in so-called higher-level laws. (1965, p. 273)

Hempel is at a loss as to how to set up a general criterion whereby these two cases may be properly distinguished. As a result, he believes that he cannot account for the ways law are to be explained. This, of course, amounts to a crucial defect in his explication. After all, the explanation of events by subsuming them by means of generalizations is only the beginning of science. To explain why this raven is black by citing the generalization that all ravens are black is not to engage in sophisticated scientific work. The interesting stage begins when we go deeper and manage to show that there is something in the constitution of ravens which requires that they all be black. The really important matter is the explanation of instantiable generalizations, which likewise results in more illuminating explanations for the observed instances of that generalization.

Counterexample 3: An ingenious example has been constructed by Kim (1963, p. 288) and has also been discussed by Morgan, (1970, p. 435) which shows that the received account of explanation is inadequate: Given that there are no mermaids, "All mermaids are good conductors of heat," e.g.,

$$T: \quad (x)(Mx \supset Cx)$$

must be true, simply because its antecedent is false. Similarly,

$$C: \quad \sim Me \supset Ce$$

i.e., 'If the Eiffel Tower is not a mermaid, then it is a good conductor of heat,' must also be true, since 'Ce' is true. Now suppose we attempt to explain E: 'Ce.' Then T and C could legitimately be suggested as explanans, since T and C entail E, while C alone does not. But surely the fact that the Eiffel Tower is not a mermaid cannot be relevant to the fact that the Eiffel Tower is a good conductor of heat.

The point I want to make is that the correct thing to do is not to try and tackle each counterexample separately (with the narrow aim of seeing what would render it harmless) but to examine more closely the nature of explanation in order to discover what deficiency in Hempel's account may underlie the symptoms that have been brought to our attention.

We should begin by asking ourselves: what is the basic function of an explanation; what is it supposed to accomplish? Surely, when we are confronted with an explanandum E and want it to be explained, what we are seeking is information concerning facts that render it inevitable that E is true rather than false. The relevant facts—the description of which is called "the explanans"—are such that anyone who was not informed that E is the case could thereby anticipate that E, rather than its denial, is true. It is therefore obvious that when the explanans advanced, T & C, is such that though it logically implies E, if everything remained the same except that instead of E, E', a contrary of E, were true, then at once T' & C' became available, where T' & C' were true and their relationship to E' was parallel to that of T & C to E, then those explanans are inadmissible.

A part of the assertion that we can explain E is the claim that anyone knowing the circumstances prevailing is not at all surprised that E, and not E', is true. An act of explanation essentially consists in pointing out the unique conditions that exist which unequivocally require that E be true. These conditions are such that, if we learned that instead of E, E' were true, we would regard it as inexplicable. This inexplicability would consist of being driven to disbelieve the report that E' were true, since the accepted description of the prevailing circumstances T & C logically implies E, that is, the falsity of E'.

It immediately follows that if we should find that a putative explanation lacks this vital feature (since the conditions described by the explanans do not demand not only that E should be true but also that E' should be false), then we have no genuine explanation. Thus a very simple and compelling principle suggests itself, which I shall formulate with the aid of these definitions:

(1) p implies q in a fashion paralle to which p' implies q' = $_{df}$ p yields q by application of the same sequence of logical rules R_1, R_2, . . . R_n that p' yields q'.

(2)   The explanans T & C are the counterparts of T' and C' = $_{df}$ T & C imply E in a fashion parallel to which T' & C' imply E'.

(3) T and C tend to explain E = $_{df}$ T and C satisfy the set of conditions T and C may reasonably be expected to fulfill in order to qualify as a legitimate explanans of E (e.g., Hempel's original set *without* adding any of the complicated extra conditions divised to neutralize the numerous counterexamples concocted by various philosophers.)

This then appears to be an essential principle restricting the validity of explanations:

(P)   If T and C tend to explain E, then we have to ask what would the situation be like if instead of E, a contrary of E, E', were true but otherwise nothing else changed. If in that case counterparts of T and C would inevitably become available, namely T' and C, which imply E' in a fashion parallel to the way T and C imply E, then T and C do not actually explain E.

Thus, to fix the precise meaning of "counterparts inevitably becoming available," suppose that

$$T = (x)(Ax \equiv Bx)$$
$$C = Ai$$
$$E = Bi$$

Clearly T and C qualify as adequate explanans for E. Imagine now that the world changes in a single respect, namely, that instead of E, $E' = `\sim Bi$' is true. It would seem that in this case an appropriate C' namely, '$\sim Ai$,' becomes automatically available since T and E' logically imply C'. Hence, it might seem that here too we have a typical violation of (P).

We must realize, however, that, since it is given now as a fact that 'Ai' is true, then if no physical aspect of i changed except that instead of having B, it loses it and '$\sim Bi$' is true, instead, then clearly, since we are confronted with Ai & $\sim Bi$, we have a counterexample to T, which must be regarded as falsified. In all those cases in which we really have a violation of (P) when E is replaced by E', there are no independent facts to prevent the immediate availability of an appropriate C'.

Now we shall look at the objections we have cited against Hempel's account and demonstrate how the application of (P) quickly dissolves them.

(1) Given: $E = $ Mt. Everest is snowcapped; we saw that (after picking an arbitrary T) E may be used in conjunction with $T_s \supset E$ (where T_s results from the Universal Instantiation of T) a premise from which E may logically be derived. Thus, an entirely irrelevant T seems to qualify as an essential part of a legitimate explanation of E. In fact, however, what we must ask is, what would be the situation if instead of E,

E':   Mt. Everest is *not* snowcapped

were true, while everything in the universe otherwise remains the same. While physically impossible, this is a coherently describable situation. It is clear that in this case,

C': $T_s \supset E'$

which is logically implied by E', must be true. But T & C' implies E' in exactly the same fashion (i.e., by Universal Instantiation T and then Modus Ponens) as T and C implied E. Thus, the mere fact that instead of E, E' is true, ensures that a usable C' becomes available, that is, ensures that C' is true (simple because a material conditional is true when ever its consequent is true). But, of course, T & C' tend to explain E' in the same fashion as T & C tend to explain E. T and C therefore do not express any particular feature of the universe which specifically demands that E be true. Thus, it clearly violates Principle (P).

Before moving on, I would like to draw special attention to the phrases "exactly parallel explanans" and "in the same fashion" that occur in the wording in Principle (P). What is being implied is that an explanation is defective when explanans of E' are symmetrical counterparts of explanans of E, which means that the former are logically related to E' exactly as the latter are to E (or, to be more precise: the derivation of E' from T and C' is a mirror image of the derivation of E from T and C as the former may be directly obtained by substituting C' for C and E' for E in the latter). Figuratively speaking, it may be said that the two opposing tendencies balance out and thus cancel one another. It therefore follows that if there is an additional explanans for E that has no similar counterpart tending to explain E', then this explanans is not cancelled out and may be adequate to explain E. Let me illustrate this point. Let us consider for a moment a situation in which the following obtain:

T: All metals are good conductors of heat
E_r: Rod r is a conductor of heat

and,

C_r: Rod r is a metal

are all true. Then unquestionably T & C_r both logically implies and adequately explains E_r. Thus, any principle that disqualfies this explanation must be invalid. Yet it might occur to some that (P) disqualifies it, nevertheless. For suppose:

E'_r: Red r is a *bad* conductor

were true. Then automatically

K': $T_s \supset E'_r$

would become true. But T & K' logically implies E'_r and therefore tends to explain it. Should not this tendency be regarded as cancelling the tendency of T & C_r to explain the contrary of E'_r, E_r? The answer, as we have said before, is, no. T & K' are the symmetrical counterpart of T & K, where

K: $T_s \supset E_r$.

They are counterparts in the sense defined above, because E_r logically implies K and E'_r (which is the consequent of the conditional K) has exactly the same logical relationship to K'. Consequently, the tendency of T and K followed by combining the result with $K = T_s \supset E_r$ (yielding E_r by Modus Ponens) is exactly counterbalanced according to (P) by the parallel tendency of T' and K' to explain E_r (since these explanans imply E'_r via the same logical steps that has led us from T & K to E_r). Therefore by (P) the two tendencies cancel one another. However, there are additional explanans that tend to explain E_r, namely, T & C_r. These explanans have no counterparts that tend to explain E'_r. Consequently, T & C_r adequately explain E_r.

(2) It is not hard to see the solution to Objection 2. It was not necessary for Hempel to despair of giving an account of how laws of nature are explained. If we add the proviso that Principle (P) must be obeyed, we may very well say that a law of nature is explained when it is shown to follow from a set of other laws not implied by it. It seems to me that no undesirable explanations will then remain admissible. Newton's laws—which, let us assume, imply Kepler's laws but are not implied by them—are a legitimate explanans of the latter. But we are not permitted to explain Keplers's laws K by its conjunction with Boyle's law, i.e., by K & B. The simple reason is that such an explanation would violate (P). In our universe, we took K & B as tending to explain K because K & B entails K by the Rule of Simplification. But in the K' universe, K' & B (which is the exact counterpart of K & B) entails K' by

the Rule of Simplification and hence tends to explain K', precisely as K & B tend to explain K. By (P), therefore, K & B are disqualified from adequately explaining K.

(3) I believe once again that there is no need for the relatively elaborate extra conditions that have been suggested by various authors in order to rule out this example. Our simple principle will do the job. For let us consider what the situation would be if instead of 'Ce,' '$\sim Ce$' were true? Obviously T: $(x)\,(Mx \supset \sim Cx)$ would be available to us, since T' must be true for the same reason that T is true, i.e., because 'Mx' is false for every x. '$\sim Ce$' of course entails C': $\sim Me \supset \sim Ce$. But T' and C' logically imply '$\sim Ce$' by the following steps.

(i)	$Me \supset \sim Ce$	from T' by Univ. Inst.
(ii)	$Ce \supset Me$	from C' by Counterposition
(iii)	$Ce \supset \sim Ce$	(ii) & (i) by Hypothetical Syllogism
(iv)	$\sim Ce$	from (iii) by Implication and Tautology.

Thus T' and C' yield E' through exactly the same four steps by which T and C yield E. That is, T' and C' tend to explain E'—the negation of E—in a fashion which is precisely parallel to the way T and C tend to explain E. Consequently, (P) disqualifies T and C from actually explaining E.

Thus, the three objections we have considered—as well as many others raised in the last three decades—vanish as soon as we free ourselves from the patterns of thought acquired through an over-reliance upon the method of counterexample.

(III)

Not all cases develop along the lines we have just depicted. Sometimes the supply of counterexamples does not seem to dry up. When they continue to arise, philosophers may conclude that, in view of the repeated failure of attempts to formulate an acceptable version of T, the whole enterprise was misconceived. Thus, instead of looking further for the solution, they may conclude that no solution exists.

A most dramatic illustration of this kind of misuse of the method of counterexamples is provided by the history of Verificationism discussed in Chapter 4 of this book. The unfortunate results in this case were most far-reaching and, as there explained, they were also easily preventable. Logical positivists have advanced the basically sound and important insight underlying Verificationism; however, they did not succeed in providing a precise, flawless formulation of their idea as has become evident through the production of counterexamples. Unfortunately, but quite typically, instead of examining more thoroughly the aim and scope of Verificationism so as to put themselves in a position in which they would be able to articulate a more authentic expression of this principle, they at once rushed into formulating an amended version, while focusing primarily on the need to neutralize the counterexamples that were raised. In the subsequent stages of this process, their reaction when faced with new counterexamples was a virtually automatic and precise repetition of the first reaction, thus ensuring that the verifiability principle was getting further and further away from its proper formulation.

In the face of a never-ending succession of failures to come up with adequate wording for the verifiability criterion, eventually most critics came to the conclusion that the whole enterprise was doomed and the principle should be abandoned. We have seen, however, that on an unblinkered approach it is easily seen that the very first attempt to offer a brief formulation of the verifiability principle was not too far off the mark and that by conjoining it with a relatively elementary and rather obvious proviso, such a principle is rendered unquestionable. It would be regrettable if philosophers were to reject such a basic and sound idea concerning the empirical significance of sentences as a result of decades' long frustrating wild-goose chase, which there was no need at all to embark upon in the first place.

(IV)

A different kind of by-product of the untempered practice of the method of counterexample has been the squandering of large amounts of fruitless ingenuity to tackle what are practically make-believe topics and pseudoproblems. It so happens that the uncritical use of this methodological tool is particularly conducive to the creation of an illusion of importance to what may be essentially trivial. It is not hard to see why. It is when confronted with the fancied task of explicating a concept, criterion, or principle that does not exist, that fertile ground is provided for a whole philosophical industry to spring into being. Clearly, no matter how numerous and brilliant a suggested explication may be, we would then never run out of counterexamples, since their unending supply is guaranteed by the simple fact that there is no truthful formulation of what is false. Hence, there is scope for suggestions, counter-examples, amendments, and reformulations, and, in turn, the demonstration of their inadequacy, and so on and so forth, *ad infinitum*.

A look at the incredible size of the literature of what has become known as the Gettier problem, for instance, may convince the skeptical reader that I am not exaggerating. This problem concerns efforts to provide an adequate definition for '*S* knows that *p*.' Traditionally, three conditions have been thought to be sufficient and necessary for such statements to be true: (1) *p* is true; (2) *S* believes that *p*; and (3) *S* is justified in believing that *p*. In its essentials, the problem was raised by Russell back in 1912 in his *Problems in Philosophy*, where he explained that situations are possible where all three conditions are satisfied, yet it seems inappropriate to ascribe knowledge to *S*. Wisely enough, Russell devoted no more than half a page to the matter and then went on to deal with issues of substance. But subsequent to Gettier's restatement of the problem in 1963, there has been an avalanche of articles attempting either to set up extra conditions or to produce new counterexamples showing the inadequacy of these attempts. It is fair to state that no other aspect of epistemology has received as much attention in the last twenty years as has the problem of formulating conditions for knowledge that are immune to Gettier's counterexamples.

To gain an impression of what is going on, let us consider an example devised by Harman to show the inadequacy of the pre-vailing definition of "knowledge":

> While I am watching him Tom takes a library book from the shelf and conceals it beneath his coat. Since I am the library detective, I follow him as he walks brazenly past the guard at the front door. Outside I see him take out the book and smile. As I approach he notices me and suddenly runs away. But I am sure it was Tom, for I know him well. I saw Tom steal a book from the library and that is the testimony I give before the University Judicial Council. After testifying I leave the hearing room and return to my post in the library. Later that day, Tom's mother testifies that Tom has an identical twin, Buck. Tom, she says, was thousands of miles away

at the time of the theft. She hopes that Buck did not do it; but she admits that he has a bad character.

Do I know that Tom stole the book? Let us suppose that I am right. It was Tom that took the book. His mother was lying when she said that Tom was thousands of miles away. I do not know that she was lying, of course, since I do not know anything about her, even that she exists. Nor does anyone at the hearing know that she is lying, although some may suspect that she is. In these circumstances I do not know that Tom stole the book. My knowledge is undermined by evidence I do not possess.

Harman considers the suggestion that the reason why I cannot be said to know that Tom stole the book, in spite of the fact that the three traditional conditions for knowledge have been satisfied, is that there is a fourth relevant condition:

(4) One knows only if there is no evidence such that if one knew about the evidence one would not be justified in believing in one's conclusion. (1973, p. 215)

He argues however that (4) cannot be correct since:

Suppose that Tom's mother was known to the Judicial Council as a pathological liar. Everyone at the hearing realized that Buck, Tom's supposed twin, is a figment of her imagination. When she testifies no one believes her. Back at my post in the library, I still know nothing of Tom's mother or her testimony. In such a case, my knowledge would not be undermined by her testimony; but if I were told only that she had just testified that Tom has a twin brother and was himself thousands of miles away from the scene of the crime at the time the book was stolen, I would no longer be justified in believing as I now do that Tom stole the book. Here I know even though there is evidence which, if I know about it, would cause me not to be justified in believing my conclusion. (1973, p. 215)

So the problem, as Harman sees it, is how to devise a fourth condition that will disqualify me from knowing that Tom stole the book in the first case in which the Council believed the testimony of Tom's mother, yet will allow that, in the second case in which they did not believe her, I do have knowledge.

I am quite certain that not everyone will agree with Harman's judgments. There will be some who will deem it proper to attribute knowledge to me even in the first case, since, after all, it is true that Tom stole the book and I am fully justified in believing it. So what does it then matter that evidence contradicting my belief was presented to the Council when that evidence was false, even though the Council happened to believe it? Then there might be others who would say that in both cases I fail to know that Tom stole the book. And others, quite reasonably may maintain that it is just not clear whether I do or do not know and that there is no way to sort things out. But Harman does not address these possibilities, since his mind is made up and he is confident that in the first case I do, and in the second case I do not, know that Tom stole the book. Thus, he is solely concerned with the problem of finding a single general condition that will fit all cases. But as to the more basic question—Does he think that he can decide in any case that may present itself whether it is a case of knowledge or not?—the answer seems to be, yes.

Harman's position strikes me as untenable. He happens to consider two cases, but between those two there lies a whole spectrum consisting of indefinitely many cases. What if, for instance, Tom's mother was not known to the Judicial Council as a pathological liar; however, (unbeknown to me, of course) Dick testifies (out of spite and without really knowing) that Tom's mother was lying and the Council accepts this testimony? Suppose Harman still retains his confidence and claims to be sure that in this case, too, my knowledge would not be undermined by the testimony of Tom's mother. We may then ask: If the Council accepts Dick's testimony but later reverses itself when they find out that Dick's testimony has violated some technicality by virtue of which it is inadmissible, do I now possess knowledge? Are we to say that, in this case, the testimony of Tom's mother does undermine my knowledge or, perhaps, that prior to the Council's reversal the mother's testimony was counteracted and therefore did not undermine my knowledge? Thus, I was to be regarded as knowing that Tom stole the book, but I ceased to know this after the Council decided not to accept Dick's testimony?

It should be amply clear by now that we could go on indefinitely and construct as many cases as we wish, in each of which my knowledge is undermined to a slightly different degree. It is inconceivable that Harman could feel confident that he knows in every case whether it represents an instance of knowledge or not. Thus, it is not true that all he is confronted with is the task of devising an adequate fourth condition that will exclude those cases, and only those cases, which we want to exclude from qualifying as instances of knowledge. There is a more basic problem: We simply do not always know what we want to include and what we want to exclude. Nor shall we ever know. There are many situations with respect to which it is entirely futile to look for a definition that will help us to decide whether or not they qualify as cases of knowledge, since these are intrinsically indeterminate cases.

The crucial point to be realized is that '*S* knows that *p*' is of interest chiefly because it presupposes '*p* is true,' '*S* believes that *p*,' and '*S* is justified in believing that *p*.' Now, it goes without saying that the question of whether or not *p* is true is of importance. So is the question of whether or not *S* believes that *p*, because belief is a mental or a brain state, the absence or presence of which makes a substantial difference. Also the question of whether *S* is justified in believing that *p* is of great interest, since it is intimately related to profound issues of evidence, inference, confirmation, and the like. But the additional question of whether or not *S* qualifies for the *title* of 'knowing that *p*' is of no great importance and no concrete feature of the universe may be relevant to it.

This, of course, does nothing to diminish the significance of any of the really substantial issues in epistemology. For example, scepticism is a major topic of interest. This is not because the sceptic refuses to honor anyone with the label of distinction of ascribing knowledge to an agent, however, but because of his genuinely devastating claim that no means for discovering the truth are available to us, and thus none of our beliefs are sufficiently well grounded. Then again, fallibilism is a substantial issue, but not because the fallibilist claims that the title of 'possessing knowlege' is subject to revokement, but because of his concrete assertion of the limited power of all justification, i.e., that no justification establishes anything beyond all doubt.

(V)

The previous example illustrated the remarkable effect that addiction to the method of counterexample may have; how it can lead to a gigantic wild-goose chase and to the squandering of philosophical ingenuity on a topic with little substance. Still, the participants in the enterprise were at the least clear-headed to the extent that they made an effort to ensure that their suggested amendments to the definition they pursued should answer some requirement due to the nature of the concept to be defined and not merely that it should effectively block a particular counterexample. However, there are also more severe cases of our malady, where a philosopher may become so carried away with trying to meet a counterexample that he neglects to ask himself altogether whether his amendment has any genuine bearing on the issue at hand. An example that so strikingly illustrates this as to appear almost bizarre is provided by Plantinga's efforts to provide an accurate definition of elementary induction. Plantinga has claimed that what is commonly regarded as valid inductive reasoning, namely, to argue that the unobserved will be like the observed, is an untenable form of reasoning, as is evident from the following counterexample:

(R) = Every physical object of which it has been determined whether or not it has ever been conceived (i.e., perceived or thought of) has been conceived. Therefore: probably every physical object has been conceived. (Plantinga 1966, ch. 10)

The conclusion of (R) is quite absurd; reason tells us that there must be a great many objects in this vast universe of ours that have not been, and will never be, conceived. But the premise of (R) is indubitably true and implies the conclusion by (what is taken to be) the rule of induction. How then are we to avoid an unacceptable conclusion? Plantinga suggests that we achieve this by amending that rule by adding to it the following proviso:

(A) = A simple inductive argument is acceptable only if it is logically possible that its sample class contains a counterinstance to its conclusion.

Plantinga is certainly right in thinking that (A) is effective in disqualifying (R). The sample class of argument (R) is the class of objects each "of which it has been determined whether or not it has ever been conceived"; thus it is logically impossible to claim that any of these constituted a counterinstance to the conclusion, that is, that it has *not* been conceived. Subsequently, Plantinga advances an argument—which we need not describe here—that the standard inductive argument supporting belief in the existence of other minds, which goes back to John Stuart Mill, violates (A) and is therefore invalid.

Plantinga's position seems to have a number of extraordinary features. First of all, simple inductive reasoning is something that has been in use ever since human beings existed and is employed by each of us innumerably many times every day; yet before Plantinga, no one noticed that it is not at all valid the way it is normally formulated, but only in conjunction with the additional basic proviso (A). However, what is really startling is that, apart from (A)'s capacity to block (R), it does not appear to have anything else to recommend it. Unfortunately, Plantinga did not feel at all obliged to show why (A) follows from a correct understanding of the nature of induction to lend plausibility to (A) as performing some function relevant to what induction is all about. We are familiar with certain other so-called 'canons of induction,' which have all been introduced on the basis of arguments claiming to show that they are indispensible to the proper function of inductive logic. Lastly, of course, it is hard to swallow that, in spite of the fact that it lacks all visible support, Plantinga is willing to lend it so much weight as to reach the momentous conclusion that because of it the inductive argument supporting belief in other minds is invalid and that, as a result, there are no rational grounds upon which to hold this belief.

Anyone willing to pause before rushing into formulating novel rules of induction specifically designed to disqualify (R) may ask himself: Is (R) an acceptable conclusion on the basis of familiar rules of induction? Brief reflection should suffice for one to see that (R) violates a widely acknowledged basic rule against the use of biased sample classes. For example, we would not feel entitled to conclude that all Americans hold that the best solution to the energy problem is greater use of coal, even though each one of several thousands of respondents might have asserted this view, if all of them were coal-miners. The members of this sample class are obviously biased, since they have a special interest in coal being in high demand; hence it is wrong to extrapolate and to maintain that all Americans, including those whose livelihood does not depend on coal, hold the same opinion. Indeed, in the case of (R), the sample class is biased in the strongest sense: logic demands that each member of the sample class for which it *has* been determined whether or not it has been perceived that it *has* been conceived. It is illegitimate to extrapolate from this generalization to maintain that it extends to other when there is no known reason why it should.

It is quite obvious, therefore, that proviso (A) is entirely unwarranted; in fact, the rules of induction need not be amended at all. Confrontation with (R) leads to no conclusion whatever that should affect the state of our belief in other minds: the whole house of cards seems to collapse and, with it, the central thesis of the well-known book, *God and Other Minds*.

(VI)

Our last example illustrates another highly dangerous trap that, fortunately, ensnares philosophers less frequently. Pollock, a leading expert on the topic of counterfactuals, claims:

> There are some natural (i.e., intuitive) laws that do not hold for simple subjunctives. Transitivity fails. Consider our study of dynamite again. If it were dropped, it would explode; and if it were soaked in water and dropped it would be dropped; but it is not the case that if it were soaked in water and dropped it would explode. (Pollock 1975, p. 56)

Here the elementary error is that the alleged "counterexample" is nothing of the sort. When an expert on explosives assures me that if I drop this stick of dynamite, it is sure to explode, his assertion is to be understood to carry any number of qualifications. In particular, he means to postulate that, provided the stick is not rendered harmless first by something like being soaked in water. Thus, Pollock thought that what he had was:

$$(S \ \& \ D > D) \ \& \ (D > E);$$

and yet $(S \ \& \ D) > E$ was false, which would indeed amount to a violation of transitivity. But, of course, the second conjunct when spelled out says something like $(D \ \& \sim S) > E$. On the other hand, the first conjunct cannot be rewritten as $[(S \ \& \ D) > (S \ \& \sim D)]$ since that would amount to a contradiction. Thus, what we really have is,

$$(S \ \& \ D > D) \ \& \ (D \ \& \sim S > E);$$

from which, of course, $(S \ \& \ D) > E$ does not follow, even if transitivity definitely holds.[1]

Some might wish to object that, given the precarious nature of philosophical reasoning, everyone, including prominent logicians like Pollock, is accident prone, and that the error under discussion is not related to any feature of the method of counterexample. It was simply the result of an oversight that the statement asserting the occurrence of an explosion really meant to convey only that this could come about if the stick of dynamite were dropped *without* first being rendered harmless by something like being soaked in water. A person who has never employed the method of counterexample should be no less prone to commit such a mistake than is a habitual practitioner of that method.

I submit, however, that the fallacy under review is a typical side effect of one's addiction to the method of counterexamples. One of the basic symptoms of the malady that requires treatment is that its victims tend to substitute this method for reasoning things through. This means that, when attempting to find out whether a certain thesis *T* is adequate or not, then instead of subjecting *T* to close scrutiny through thorough internal examination, as reason would dictate, one mechanically puts it through the counterexample test. In the case before us, a sane approach should have been, when facing the question, 'Does transitivity apply to counterfactuals?,' to examine the intrinsic nature of counterfactuals and hope to find the answer as soon as it is properly grasped.

One of the most conspicious features of counterfactuals that is bound to be noticed on a closer look is their strong resemblance to predictive conditionals and, to a somewhat lesser extent, to material conditionals. Now transitivity, of course, is known to hold in the case of the last two families of sentences; thus, one who bore this in mind would tend to assume that it holds in the case of counterfactuals as well. Hence, should he come across an alleged counterexample to this thesis, he would tend to treat it with suspicion.

Had Pollock started out in this manner, then upon being confronted with his 'counterexample' he might very well have asked himself: What is the situation in the case of material conditionals with respect to this kind of counterexample? He would have found, of course, that it is similar to the situation that obtains in the case of counterfactuals. For we may have,

$$(S \mathbin{\&} D \supset D) \mathbin{\&} (D \supset E)$$

where $(S \& D \supset E)$ is false. But of course no one is going to question the applicability of transitivity to material conditionals. Consequently, Pollock would likely have become alerted to the fact that there simply is no scope for transitivity here, since the antecendent of the second conjunct, when fully stated, turns out not to be identical with the consequent of the first. But this he failed to see. It is therefore reasonable to place the blame for that failure upon unfortunate habits of thoughts engendered by over-reliance on the method of counterexample.

(VII)

The remedy that suggests itself is fairly accessible and is by no means overly painful. The first step is to reiterate the truism that there is no substitute for thought. No method is good enough to be left on its own to do philosophy for us. To examine the adequacy of a theory, we must make every effort to subject it to close analysis and, in doing so, the method of counterexamples may play at most an auxiliary role.

It is especially important to realize that, when presented with counterexamples to a theory, thesis, or criterion we wish to defend, we should resist the temptation to focus on these counterexamples and to tailor revisions to the need of neutralizing them. Counterexamples should be recognized for what they are, namely, symptoms of some more deeply rooted malady, which it should be our main concern to uncover.

Those wishing to discredit a theory should ideally use counterexamples only for the sake of illustration. That is, after having clearly diagnosed what really ails a given theory T, they should construct a counterexample that highlights the defect they have discovered. This means, of course, refraining from presenting counterexamples without giving indications of what basic flaw made the construction of counterexamples possible.

I submit that those who produce counterexamples are virtually always in a good position to offer a diagnosis of the malady underlying the symptom. It is said that a famous preacher was once asked by his admirers how he always succeeded in producing such illuminating ideas with the aid of such entertaining parables. In reply, he told them a parable involving a group of hunters who were target practicing. A bystander was struck by the fact that the target-board of one of the participants had dozens of bullet holes and each of these holes was exactly at the center of one of the circles drawn on the board. He approached the hunter and begged him to reveal how a person can succeed in getting such a perfect score. The hunter explained that, unlike the others, he started by shooting holes in the board and only then drew circles around them. This, he assured him, was not too hard at all. The preacher concluded by claiming that he adopted a similar methodology, which made his task not too difficult. He began by working out the thought he wished to put across and only when that was accomplished did he make up a story specially tailored to appropriately illustrate his idea.

I believe this shrewd technique is also the one that is almost always practiced by those who produce counterexamples to some suggested principle. As a rule, one does not simply stumble upon an effective counterexample by chance. One has to be aware, to some extent at least, of some defect in the proposed definition under review and proceed to construct such examples according to a preconceived plan. This being so, it is possible to ask philosophers to make an extra effort to diagnose more fully the defect in question of which he is already half aware in order to articulate it explicitly. Then, of course, one stands a good chance of dealing with the real issue, which may lead to a genuine solution that will indirectly eliminate the possibility of counterexamples as well.

Notes

1. More succinctly: Pollock's second conjunct is patently false since
$$D \leftrightarrow (S \,\&\, D) \vee (\sim S \,\&\, D)$$
and once we represent that conjunct as
$$[(S \,\&\, D) \vee (\sim S \,\&\, D)] > E$$
nobody should mistakenly take it to be a true statement.

9 Explanation in Philosophy and in Science

Paul Humphreys

Explanations used to play a central role in metaphysics. Descartes certainly assumed so when he offered his famous tree metaphor, with its metaphysical roots, its trunk of physics, and its branches of the various special sciences. So, too, did Leibniz when he asserted that "all phenomena are indeed to be explained by mechanical efficient causes, but that these mechanical laws are themselves to be derived in general from higher reasons."[1] Yet these views seem to trade upon an ambiguity that is now widely recognized within the literature on explanation, and which originates with the fact that 'explanations' can be of two forms. They can be construed as answers to epistemic why-questions ("Why should we believe that X?") or they can be construed as answers to explanatory why-questions ("Why is X true?"). The early philosophical explanations have a strongly foundational flavor, for the explanatory sentences were more secure epistemologically than were the things to be explained.

Empiricists have naturally been reluctant to accept such justificatory metaphysical explanations, and metaphysics as an explanatory activity almost disappeared in the first half of this century. Typical of the views then current was that of Hans Reichenbach, who insisted that the only genuine explanations were scientific explanations, and that earlier attempts at 'explanation' were merely reflections of philosophy's origins in the human tendency to prefer pseudo-explanations to no explanation at all. And so, for a while at least, the 'scientific' in 'scientific explanation' became pleonastic.

Philosophical explanations have begun to resurface, and not surprisingly, they tend to be modeled on what are perceived to be well-entrenched accounts of scientific explanation. Many of these 'philosophical' explanations are actually naturalistic or scientistic explanations of what have traditionally been taken to be philosophical matters, but not all are.[2] The feature that they share is that they are based upon versions of what has loosely been called "inference to the best explanation," which is, in its essential details, nothing more than a variant of the conjectural account of hypothesis confirmation. Because the justificatory direction in many such inferences is from the empirical phenomena to the philosophical explanatory material, such explanations would seem to avoid the empiricists' principal objection to the older style of justificatory explanations, where the explanatory and justificatory directions were in the same direction, from the metaphysical to the physical.

The use of explanations in philosophy is to be welcomed, for it provides a useful integrating device to counteract the tendency of analytic work to degenerate into puzzle-solving.[3] There is, however, a world of difference between allowing explanations in specific circumstances, and advocating philosophical explanations as a general philosophical method. It is no coincidence that the reappearance of philosophical explanations has been contemporaneous with the widespread acceptance of various kinds of realism, and we must be sure that requests for explanations do not presuppose an unwarranted tolerance for dubious forms of realism. One further caveat must be added here. The tendency to model philosophical explanations on scientific explanations is a natural one because of the quantity and quality of systematic work that has been done in the latter area, and the widespread perception that hypothetico-inferential accounts of scientific explanation are essentially correct. I must emphasize that the logically oriented model of scientific explanation that has been closely associated with the work of Carl Hempel is, in my view, seriously inadequate as a correct account of scientific explanations, primarily because of its inability to deal successfully with causal explanations, and the reader is urged to review the arguments against that particular approach before using it as a starting point for approaching philosophical explanations.[4]

In particular, the criteria of adequacy that were provided with that model are not only insufficient as a characterization of an adequate scientific explanation, but are also flawed as necessary conditions as well. This latter deficiency stems from the use of a regularity theory of causation and the consequential commitment to explanations as particular kinds of arguments.

Having recognized this we need not ignore that approach altogether, for causal considerations will be absent in many philosophical explanations, and indeed, by dropping the requirement that explanations contain laws, we can avoid one of the most obvious barriers to the existence of philosophical explanations. Causal considerations are important, of course, for many arguments for realism take the form of causal arguments, as do explanatory theories of reference.[5] For this reason, I shall devote much of this article to a discussion of arguments for realism, and scientific realism in particular.

1. What is a Philosophical Explanation?

Philosophical explanations seem most frequently to occur at the interface between science and philosophy. The line of demarcation is not easy to specify precisely, of course, if at all, but that in itself has made the possibility of philosophical explanations at the highest level of theoretical science more plausible. Indeed, even Karl Popper, champion of the separation of science and philosophy, is willing to allow the existence of nonscientific explanations to account for the growth of knowledge: "In seeking pure knowledge, our aim is, quite simply, to understand, to answer how questions and why questions. These are questions which are answered by giving an explanation. Thus all problems of pure knowledge are problems of explanation."[6]

Because of this difficulty in sharply separating scientific and philosophical explanations, I shall not attempt to impose a line of demarcation here. But we can isolate where the difference between the two will lie if we have a criterion for separating sentences with philosophical content from sentences with scientific content. It is not the form or the content of the explanandum sentence, nor the form of the request for an explanation that distinguishes the two, but the nature of the explanatory sentences that determines the character of the explanation. Both science and philosophy can provide answers to why-questions, to how-possibly questions, to why-necessarily questions, and, as we shall see, to certain kinds of why-cannot questions as well. Furthermore, what are clearly scientific explanations of what used to be traditional philosophical issues can be given (see the citations in note 2 for examples), and various cosmological explanations of why there is something rather than nothing appeal to *a posteriori* premises to establish their conclusions. I shall thus count as a philosophical explanation any explanation in which at least one of the explanatory sentences or facts has philosophical content. There is little doubt that such things are and have been proposed as philosophical explanations, for attempts to explain why freedom of the will is impossible, or why our attitude toward space and time must be one of transcendental idealism are examples of philosophical explanations, if any are.

2. An Aside on Negative Results

I listed above a number of questions to which the appropriate response seems to be an explanation. One of these is a form of question commonly asked in a philosophical exchange, and which, although logically reducible to a why-necessarily question, sometimes elicits a reply that has origins different from responses to traditional why-necessarily questions.

Typically, *A* is arguing against *B* who is advocating the truth of some sentence that may or may not follow necessarily from other sentences already accepted. *A* and *B* are sufficiently open-minded and share enough common ground that their disagreement is over specifics and not fundamentals. *A* then asks (perhaps rhetorically) "Why can't it be the case that *X*?" where *X* is some situation that undermines *B*'s position. Often, even though *A* may have only a weak justification for asserting the possibility of *X*, perhaps only that he believes he can conceive it, the burden of proof is generally supposed to have shifted to *B*, and an inability to answer the why-cannot question in itself makes *B*'s position deficient in some way. For example, in challenging the supposed universality of the principle of causal determinism, we might legitimately ask "Why couldn't something occur spontaneously?" without providing a specific physical counterexample. Now this may not be a desirable way of arguing, but it is sufficiently prevalent for it to be useful to know what kind of response is appropriate.

Here, A is asking a particular form of an epistemic why-question, i.e., "Justify to me (A) why not-X," because A does not yet believe not-X, whereas B, who already holds not-X to be true, and often to be necessarily true, will be providing an explanation for himself, but a justification for A. By far the most effective way to do this is to provide A with an impossibility result. Such results have been prominent in the history of philosophy, with skeptical arguments against the possibility of knowledge, Kant's arguments against the possibility of knowing things-in-themselves, McTaggart's argument demonstrating the impossibility of an A-series analysis of time given the existence of a B-series, various arguments purporting to establish the impossibility of a noncircular justification of a global inductive rule, Zeno's arguments for the impossibility of change, and so on. This negative thread runs strongly through the mainstream of philosophy, and although unappealing to those of a positive frame of mind, nevertheless has produced results that seem quintessentially philosophical in nature.

One of the appealing features of science used to be that it was heavily oriented toward positive results, but this is no longer so, and the kind of impossibility result just mentioned has spread to science and logic. Important examples are Pauli's Exclusion Principle, Heisenberg's Uncertainty Principle, the relativistic upper limit on the velocity of causal signals, the undecidability of first order logic, Godel's incompleteness results and their effect on Hilbert's program, Tarski's result on the undefinability of truth, the various results showing the impossibility of consistently adding hidden variables to current quantum theory, and so on. Whether it is their negative aspect that has made them so appealing to the philosophical community, I would not care to speculate. But they are different from the kinds of impossibility derivable from classical physics, for example.

Classical deterministic laws of nature can be seen as showing that given certain initial conditions, the state of a system must necessarily evolve in only one way, or, to put it differently, that given the particular initial conditions, other later states are impossible. One interesting and general version of this is the positive result that for a system with two absorbing end-states, if the state of the system at t is a continuous function of the state at t_0, then whatever the influences on the system, for any final state, there is an initial state that will lead to that final state. So, the answer to

"Why can't the system be in state s' at t'?" was traditionally "Because the system was in state s at t, and s' cannot be reached from s given the laws of development of the system (although it could if the initial state had been different)." There were impossibility results of another kind—that no two particles could have the same initial position state (although they could be in the same momentum state), but these were, revealingly, taken to be analytic. Impossibility results of the form that Pauli's Exclusion Principle has are empirical, and demonstrate the impossibility of certain kinds of initial state of the system. Whereas the traditional empirical impossibility results were relative impossibility results (relative to some intitial state), the modern empirical results are absolute impossibility results. Not even God could nonmiraculously put two fermions in the same state in this universe, or in any other with the same physical laws.

Impossibility results of any kind are important for placing constraints on the possibilities that need to be considered. It is worth noting that if the alternatives are $X_1, \ldots, X_n$ and an impossibility result showed that X_1 was impossible, we should have an explanation of why we can't have X_1, although we may not have any explanation of why X_i, for $i \neq 1$, as for example when there is a uniform distribution of chances over the remaining possibilities. (We might call these negative results underdetermination or antidetermination results to illustrate their connection with more obviously philosophical concerns.)

3. Explanation and Truth

A fundamental feature that we ought to require of any general philosophical method is that it be free, as far as is possible, from presuppositions that automatically exclude particular philosophical positions. Logical analysis has this invariance property to a greater extent than most, whereas the Cartesian method does not. More specifically, a virtue supposedly possessed by Tarski's method of defining truth is (although this is disputed) its philosophical neutrality, which in part accounts for its wide use. It appears, however, that by insisting upon explanations in philosophy, and especially if we adhere to criteria adopted from scientific explanations, that we shall commit ourselves to some form of realism. Furthermore, if the widely held view that realism and empiricism are incompatible is true, then the method of philosophical explanations will exclude idealism, other forms of antirealism, and empiricism.

The reason seems simple. Adequate explanations require truth. Models of scientific explanation may be scientifically invariant—the legacy of the Unified Science movement makes most of them applicable to the subject matter of any science—but an appeal to falsehoods, or even worse, to things lacking truth values at all, ruins any attempt at explanation. Or so it is claimed. Falsehoods are bad because they make explanations epistemically defeasible (when it is discovered that they *are* false) and, more importantly, because they block further explanation. We simply cannot explain things that are not true, and hence no further explanation via the transitivity of explanation will be possible.

Let us suppose that adherence to bivalence and a correspondence theory of truth for a set of sentences commits us to a realist position regarding those objects referred to in those sentences. How much realism is then necessary to have explanations? Little enough, it seems, that some versions of instrumentalism, for example, are not excluded from giving explanations. This is illuminating, because historically instrumentalists have disclaimed science as an explanatory activity, arguing that the function of science is accurate prediction and description rather than explanation, one of the principal reasons for this being the inability to provide satisfactory models for certain kinds of theoretical laws. Instrumentalists must be willing to allow the truth of sentences reporting observations, however, and what is denied a truth value is any lawlike generalization referring to unobservables, such things being regarded as inference devices instead. Although this seems to be incompatible with a covering law model of explanation, it is not. For example, Mill, who is often seen as the originator of the covering law account, and was cited to that effect by Hempel, would have taken an inference device approach within the modern logical form of the deductive-nomological model (although he would, of course, have refrained from classifying it as deductive). This is because:

> All inference is from particulars to particulars: General propositions are merely registers of such inferences already made, and short formulae for making more: The major premise of a syllogism, consequently, is a formula of this description, and the conclusion is not an inference drawn *from* the formula, but an inference drawn *according* to the formula. . . .[7]

More important than this historical fact is the possibility of modifying the deductive-nomological model's four conditions of adequacy so as to allow lawlike regularities as inference rules rather than premises in the explanatory argument. Three of these conditions are logical in form (the essential use of lawlike generalizations in the explanans, the correctness of the explanatory argument form, and the need for testable content in the explanans) and these three alone lead to the (modified) symmetry thesis of the structural identity of explanations and predictions, which allows that at least some predictions are potential explanations, as well as that all adequate scientific explanations are potential predictions.[8] The difference between the two is merely pragmatic, according to Hempel, and the derivation of the thesis does not depend upon the fourth condition of empirical adequacy, which requires the truth of the explanatory material. Even the modified symmetry thesis would, it appears, commit the rule-using instrumentalist to the position that at least some of his predictions were potential explanations. But traditionally, instrumentalists have been unwilling to allow even some of their predictions to be explanations. This position appear to be logically unjustifiable, not only for the reason just given, but because general rules, leading from specific facts to specific facts, seem able to pass analogs of traditional tests of lawlikeness. They can support counterfactual and subjunctive inferences, and some rules can be shown to be derived rules (i.e., that any conclusion reached by them can be reached without them by using other rules) hence satisfying a property that explanatory laws have, of intermediate level laws being dispensable within a hierarchy of laws by the transitivity of explanation rendering them redundant. Indeed, instrumental explanations will look very much like elliptically formulated covering law explanations, where the laws have been left implicitly stated. And so, leaving other motivations aside here, there seems to be no structural reason why instrumental explanations cannot be given. This not only removes one possible entailment relation between explanation and realism, but it also removes one of the most powerful arguments against the possibility of philosophical explanations: the fact that there seem to be no philosophical analogs of natural laws. What has just been shown is that, at least logically, there can be explanations via inferential principles, even if they are methodological in character.

I have provided this argument simply to indicate the possibility of such explanations within certain philosophical positions, and not because I believe that either the instrumentalist construal of laws or the modified symmetry thesis is correct. I shall now turn to another argument purporting to show the connection between explanation and realism. Whereas the one just discussed connected them via truth, this one emphasizes the principle of explanatory completeness. It is at the interface between philosophical and scientific explanations that a commitment to explanatory completeness is supposed to take us over the admittedly ill-defined boundary between science and philosophy, and from the realm of the empirically acceptable to the realm of the dubiously real.

4. Explanatory Completeness and Realism

Perhaps the most common use of philosophical explanations has been as a justification of claims concerning the existence of certain kinds of entities, on the grounds that postulating their existence provides the best, and perhaps the only, explanation for a specified set of phenomena. I shall here examine in detail one particular version of this kind of explanatory realism, which in many ways is not only the clearest, but is exemplary of features possessed by other versions. This is the argument from the principle of the common cause.

First, let us be clear that we are discussing *scientific* realism in this context. And so, in evaluating arguments claiming to show that scientific realism is incompatible with empiricism, we must insist that we are discussing *scientific* empiricism. This certainly means that we need not discuss extreme empiricist views involving various kinds of phenomenalism, for whatever the referents of theoretical terms in scientific theories are, the areas in dispute between scientific realists and scientific empiricists are so far removed from everyday experience that it would seriously misplace the real division between the two were we to worry about the truth of physicalism. Even if one believes the view that everyday perceptions are filtered through the lens of a theory, the correct and interesting locus of the scientific realism debate is certainly not to be placed at the level of tables and chairs, however legitimate that may be for the traditional realism debates.

Of course, once we have allowed this move, it is not at all easy to see how much realism is too much realism for a scientific empiricist, but the objective existence of chance (referred to *perhaps* by a probabilistic function within an indeterministic theory), unactualized possibilities appearing as elements of the state space of the kind of theory just mentioned, and nonreductive dispositions of various kinds would do as examples. The argument I am about to discuss does not depend crucially on where the scientific empiricist draws the edge of his world. For heuristic purposes, it is best to think in terms of things that are presently observable with the aid of whatever devices one is willing to allow, versus "things" that are presently (and perhaps essentially) unobservable, rather than in terms of the kind of ideal theories discussed in the context of convergent realism, because this particular argument does not require ideal theories for its force. We then need to accept the truth of the principle of the common cause, which asserts that if a collection of phenomena occurs with a frequency higher than would occur by sheer chance, (less contentiously, than they would have were they stochastically independent), and there is no direct causal connection between them, then their joint occurrence *must* be explained by appeal to a common cause. There are a number of things to be said regarding this principle.

First, we can note that this principle is weaker than the principle of sufficient reason, for it admits of explanations that are not deterministic in form, and hence could be probabilistic or aleatory in character.

Second, it is weaker than a principle of universal explanation, for it asserts only that certain kinds of regularity, rather than everything, must have an explanation. In particular, it allows for a fundamental set of phenomena, all of which occur in a fashion that makes them statistically independent of one another. This is important, for the argument from the common cause principle supposedly will take us over the epistemological line at which the empiricist has decided to halt, but if a lawless set of fundamental entities was reached before that line was crossed, the realist would not differ from the empiricist in that situation. Is such a situation possible? Mill and Peirce claimed (for different reasons) that it was not, but their arguments are too weak. Recall that our scientific empiricist is willing to allow regularities in the form of the existence of at least some semi-permanent entities. But then, by a minimal adaptation of a construction I gave in an earlier paper,[9] such objects could be causally independent and give rise to data sequences that were covered by neither deterministic nor probabilistic laws. The original model provided deterministic sequences (deterministic in the sense of Montague) that violated a consequence of standard axioms for probability, and this latter property can be preserved while making the sequences indeterministic by the simple expedient of making the state function no longer single valued at some point. Of course, one could conclude from this that deterministic and probabilistic regularities are not exhaustive of what should count as a lawlike regularity, but as the common cause principle is stated, it would not apply to such cases because of the way that dependence is stated in terms of probability functions. Furthermore, given the current absence of any alternative characterization of regularities, I shall not pursue that issue here, although it is important to bear in mind. What this example does show, I think, is that in a certain kind of situation the universal application of the common cause principle does not lead to an infinite regress that would take us across the empiricist/realist boundary.

Third, because of its causal form, the principle does not cover certain kinds of cases where regularities among observable phenomena are (said to be) philosophically explained by reference to common abstract entities. Examples of this might be the explanation of correlations between the use of sentence tokens in different languages by means of appeal to propositions, the explanation of our grouping of individuals by appeal to natural kinds, and perhaps even the explanation of Church's Thesis applied to Turing machines and formalist accounts of recursive functions, by appeal to a suitable class of abstract functions.

Fourth, two quite different uses of the principle have been made by realists. The first use is to explain specific coincidences located in a particular spatio-temporal region. This is the traditional use made of it to explain, for example, why each individual standing around a table receives closely correlated sensory experiences, and to infer that it is far simpler to assume that the sensory experiences are all caused by a single common object than it is to assume that multiple independent causes are present, or that there is no explanation at all. The second use has been to explain general regularities that are not spatio-temporally specific. An example of this is the explanation of the fact that the value of Avogadro's number obtained from the analysis of Brownian motion agrees closely with the value obtained by electrolytic measurements.[10]

Here the common cause is a common underlying type of molecular structure present in both kinds of situation. Although this second kind of situation does require an explanation, it is quite different in kind from the first. Indeed, although in the second kind of regularity the common kind of structural cause interacts with other causes to produce different kinds of effects, which here are Brownian motion and electrolysis, the common element in these effects, which is the constancy of Avogadro's number, is in fact the result of the more traditional 'same (kind of) effect, same (kind of) cause' principle that formed part of Newton's Rules of Reasoning. In the first kind of regularity, with specific, spatio-temporally localized effects, the principle used will often be 'same kinds of effects, same cause.' I have discussed here cases in which the effects are of the same kind to bring out this point, but of course correlations between any two kinds of variables or events can serve to invoke the common cause principle.

Fifth, is the principle necessarily applicable to every regularity? A recent writer has claimed that it has to be: "the realist will need his special extra premise that every universal regularity in nature needs an explanation. . . . And it is just this extra premise that distinguishes the realist from his opponents."[11] On the basis of this claim, two things are argued: (1) That such an insistence on the universal applicability of the principle is inconsistent with well-established results of quantum theory, and (2) that such a principle leads to the postulation of unobservable entities and processes that are necessary in order to have the required explanations. From (1) it is concluded that the principle must be abandoned, and from this and (2) that a commitment to unobservables and realism is avoidable. If this argument is correct, it shows that there is a connection between a particular type of explanation and scientific realism, but that such explanations have to be abandoned as a regulative principle of science, and if they must be given up there, then either explanations that are not based upon common causes must be given or it is likely that philosophical explanations will have to be curtailed as well.

Now, I think it is evident that (1) is correct, but that (2) has a peculiar status that sheds serious doubt on the claim that a commitment to explanatory completeness is what differentiates a realist from an empiricist. I have already shown above how the world could have been such that the principle of the common cause had no application, simply because there were no regularities of a form that would distinguish a scientific realist from a scientific empiricist on the basis of the principle. Furthermore, it is clearly a contingent matter that the use of the principle leads to the postulation of unobservables. The world might have been structured in such a way that "smaller" phenomena were explained in terms of "larger" phenomena. The regularities which would then be incapable of being explained would be those involving the largest entities, and those incapable of doing any explaining would be the smallest. That is, the "most fundamental" laws would be those involving huge objects such as galaxies, and such objects would be covered by "accidental generalizations." This is, after all, the kind of picture that holds within a modified Aristotelian celestial mechanics, with a mechanical Prime Mover as the common cause of planetary and stellar orbital motions. Observability is not just a matter of size, of course, but this kind of example is useful in avoiding the trap of taking explanatory or logical reduction to mean *literally* ontological reduction. There is, however, obvious evidence that, as a matter of fact, empiricists are constantly pushed toward having to postulate unobservables in order to explain observable regularities. Why is this? The answer is surely that by the very nature of why-questions, empiricists will rarely, if ever, be confronted with the kind of why-question that would give an explanation proceeding in the opposite direction. It is a standard feature of why-questions that they are only asked where the questioner has reason to believe that the explanandum sentences to which they give rise are true. And if there are unobservables of the kind that an empiricist would rule out as unacceptable, then he certainly would not be asking for the reasons why sentences about them are true.

This does lead to a slight advantage for the empiricist in terms of explanations, however, because within the realm of empirically legitimate sentences, we often have alternative routes to the truth of an explanandum sentence that are relatively independent of one another. We can justify them by means of direct observation or we can justify them by means of deductive arguments from other sentences whose truth value has been established by independent observations. This will not hold true of all scientific claims, of course, and all direct observation claims use theories in some elementary sense, but not one that always plays a central role in their acceptance. These alternative routes are usually not open for the kind of sentences featuring as explanandum sentences in philosophical explanations, and this poses a minor difficulty for such explanations. Suppose that we have a request for an explanation of a particular sentence, which has, under some agreed upon standard, some nonempirical, philosophical content. (As I noted in section 1 above, this will not by itself require that the explanation itself be philosophical, but that is irrelevant here.) The request for the explanation must be made by someone who has reason to suppose that the explanandum sentence is true, and in this case, because direct empirical confirmation is impossible, this justification will have to be through an argument from already accepted premises. This argument would thus be an answer to a possible epistemic why-question. (I am ruling out direct access to philosophical truth by intuition or some other dubious method here.) We could not then, of course, answer the explanatory why-question by providing that same argument, for the questioner is already familiar with it via the justification of the explanandum sentence. Hence for explanations where the explanandum sentence has philosophical content, there must always be at least two routes leading to the explanandum sentence, or there can be no explanation. Furthermore, given that there are two such routes, which will be the explanatory route and which the justificatory? It seems quite arbitrary to select one rather than the other as the explanation because it will usually be quite accidental which was provided first. In particular, where explanatory and justificatory claims must take place by argument, and this includes almost all classical philosophical explanations and justifications, it appears that all justificatory arguments ought to be explanatory and vice versa, providing a symmetry claim for the philosophical case.

Returning to the issue of whether explanatory completeness is entailed by realism, I think that we can see that it is not by appeal to a necessarily fanciful example. Suppose that we are all inhabiting an apparently platonic realm where we have direct acquaintance with mathematical objects and abstract entities of various kinds. We know that there are regularities governing many of the relationships between these objects, and we are certainly realists about them. Indeed, up to this point, we have never appealed to empirical phenomena, although we have the faculties for experiencing them. The consensus that they are a hopelessly unreliable source of knowledge has prevented anyone from bothering. We then realize that there are *fundamental* regularities between some of these objects, which seem to have no explanation, for they cannot be derived from any logically more general regularities. We also have up to that point used the method of inference to the best explanation (although not in a causal form), and it has been highly successful, but now seems to have failed us. A desperate philosopher amongst us suggests that rather than living in a platonic realm, we are actually inhabiting Popper's World 3, and that the explanation for the source of these objects and their regularities is the scientific activity of individuals in the empirical World 1.[12] One can imagine that such a suggestion would be received with less than enthusiasm, and that the platonists would settle for the view that there simply were fundamental, irreducible regularities amongst the objects of which they had knowledge. They would thus have abandoned their principle of explanatory completeness, but they would certainly still be realists. Hence realism cannot entail that every regularity has to have an explanation.

This example does show that explanations of the fundamental regularities in the platonic world would have to be in terms of phenomena that were 'unobservable' for its inhabitants (but observable for us as humans). It also brings out the most unsatisfactory feature of opposing realism and empiricism—that the epistemologist can stake out his territory first and hence can fix the limits on what he will consider real. This has a tendency to make even moderately liberal scientific empiricists indistinguishable from scientific realists (as opposed to metaphysical realists). Once we have abandoned the attempt reductively to define unobservables in terms of observables, and switched to a form of causal explanatory realism, the main focus of the dispute about scientific realism has to be about the causal underdetermination of realistically construed theories, for all the common cause principle asserts (at least in Reichenbach's form) is that there exists a common cause that will make the effects probabilistically independent. Claim (1) above is primarily interesting because it affects even this weak version of the principle, but in general, the issue of realism will come down to whether or not the explanans sentences are true, rather than to bare existence claims.

One further point is relevant here. Consider the traditional distinction between lawlike regularities and accidental generalizations. It is often supposed that one ground for distinguishing between the two is that laws can serve as the basis of explanations, whereas accidental generalizations cannot. This is, at least in part, one of the reasons for insisting upon the use of laws in the criteria of adequacy for covering law models of explanation. This dichotomy is not only based upon poor terminology, which when revealed, shows the need for a trichotomy, but it has the connection between laws and explanations reversed. Take the simplest form of a generalization "All *F*s are *G*s." A generalization of this form will be 'accidental' not if it cannot explain, but when it itself has no explanation. The commitment to the universal applicability of the principle of the common cause entails that a scientific realist cannot allow such accidental generalizations, and that even when the properties *F* and *G* are logically but not statistically independent of one another, there will need to be an explanation.

Suppose that we do find an explanation for the regularity, so that it is no longer 'accidental.' This will not by itself turn the regularity into an explanatory law, for in the case where there is an explanation in terms of a common cause of things being both *F*s and *G*s, we should still not be able to use the generalization "All *F*s are *G*s" to explain why some *F* is a *G*. Hence the correct division ought to be into accidental generalizations or correlations, and nonaccidental generalizations or correlations, with explanatory laws being a special subclass of the latter group. Of course, the inability of a generalization to provide an explanation is weakly connected with the inability to explain that generalization, for providing an explanation in terms of something for which there is no further explanation will often make the offered explanation unsatisfactory to a certain extent, but it is clear that an inability to explain is not a correct characterization of a generalization as accidental.[13] One important conclusion that we can draw from this is that if we combine the condition that to be a law a regularity must have an explanation with the criterion that in order to be explanatory a regularity must be a law, then if every hierarchy of regularities rests upon fundamental but inexplicable regularities (with the hierarchical ordering having only finitely many levels), there will be no laws at all. This Humean result indicates another reason for breaking the connection between causes and laws, for even though there may be no laws in such a world, there can still be causal connections in terms of which explanations can be given.

This is the approach I would advocate, although it is worth noting that if there is an infinite regress of explanations in the traditional law-based sense, then the combination of the two conditions above will allow at least some regularities to be lawlike, contrary to the widely held view that ungrounded explanatory regresses are essentially flawed.

5. Conclusion

I have dwelt at length upon one particular kind of philosophical explanation concerning realism and empiricism because I believe that an argument via causal explanations cannot satisfactorily deal with the important difference between these two positions within the scientific realm. It is with the dispute over whether supra-evidential truth conditions exist for theories, not over a condition of explanatory completeness or an explanatory regress where the break between empiricists and realists must occur. Explanations still play a central role in that dispute because the realist connections between theory and the world ought to have some explanatory power. As I have tried to show, imposing an explanatory requirement does not exclude certain kinds of nonrealism about the explanatory principles, but it does leave us still requiring the truth of some of the explanatory material, and that is exactly what recent antirealists have suggested makes no philosophical sense. Indeed, philosophical underdetermination results seem to provide one of the most convincing responses possible to the question "Why can't I be a (metaphysical) realist?"

Notes

1. *Specimen Dynamicum*, Loemker, p. 722.
2. There are many modern examples of specific claims along this direction. Quine's insistence that epistemology can be naturalized and provided with a philosophical explanation (Quine 1969); Putnam's former view that scientific realism, as a philosophical position, has a scientific explanation; Dummett's claim that deduction can be justified by an explanatory argument (Dummett 1978, p. 296); Nozick's question "Does the philosopher who explains how p is possible by putting forward potential explanations of p differ from the scientist who puts forth and tests potential explanations of p in order to explain why p is true?" (Nozick 1981, p. 12); and J.L. Mackie's claim in his Introduction (Mackie 1982) that most of the important arguments for and against the existence of God have been instances of inferences to the best explanation. Many more examples could be given.

3. Compare here, for example, A.J. Ayer's view that philosophy is a puzzle-solving activity in his *Introduction* (Ayer 1946, p. 26, n. 2), with some more recent "discoveries" about the nature of science. *Plus ca change, plus c'est la meme chose.*
4 See, for example, Fetzer 1981, Part II; Humphreys 1983; and Salmon 1984.
5. For a general argument against such views, see Putnam 1981, ch. 2.
6. In Popper 1972, p. 263.
7. In Mill 1872, b. II, ch. iii, section 4.
8. See Hempel 1965a for an extended discussion of this, and Humphreys 1981b, p. 231.
9. In the Appendix to Humphreys 1981a.
10. Given in Salmon 1979, pp. 418–19.
11. In van Fraassen 1980, p. 21.
12. For an account of these worlds, see Popper 1972, ch. 3.
13. A noncausal logical version of this view was advocated by R.B. Braithwaite (1953).

10   Transcendental and Dialectical Thinking

Douglas C. Berggren

There are two kinds of thinking, I would like to suggest, that tend to be uniquely philosophical: transcendental thinking, which attempts to establish the diverse presuppositions that would legitimate our various nonphilosophical modes of thinking; and dialectical thinking, which attempts to reconcile these diverse presuppositions with one another. In other words, philosophy tries, as it were, to be both the father and the mother of its academic offspring. It strives to provide at least some of the intellectual enterprises it has spawned with independent birthrights of rational respectability. But, at the same time, it tries equally hard to get these purportedly independent enterprises to cooperate harmoniously with one another. What I would also like to propose, however, is that both transcendental and dialectical thinking are irreducibly tensional in character. Transcendental thinking culminates in certain basic ontological oppositions, which dialectical thinking can never entirely resolve. The most that can be hoped for is that these two related modes of philosophical thought might find a way to qualify each other in an intellectually fruitful manner, thereby making some sort of human intellectual integrity a legitimate possibility.

I. Transcendental Thinking

In contrast to dialectical thinking—which is always a thinking in opposites, a thinking that transforms the premises with which it begins—transcendental thinking is essentially linear. It does not transform the premises with which it begins, but looks for premises whose necessary truth will guarantee the equally necessary truth of the conclusions it seeks to defend. Thus, transcendental arguments are clearly very different from ordinary deductive arguments and explanations, as these have recently been defined by Nozick.[1] Nozick thinks that deductive arguments, useful primarily in the context of debate, merely try to show that a given claim being attacked by someone follows from something else he may happen to believe even more strongly. So he is logically forced to withdraw his attack, whether he wants to or not. But, needless to say, what may eventually be agreed upon can still be false. Similarly, what Nozick calls "deductive explanations" may result in a set of beliefs that are equally false. Used primarily in the context of a debate with oneself, rather than with others, deductive explanations try to eliminate apparent inconsistencies in one's own beliefs. Nevertheless, whether this end is accomplished by giving up certain beliefs or by discovering how the apparent inconsistencies can be removed, it does not follow that the upshot need in any sense be true. What transcendental arguments seek to establish, by contrast, is that their conclusions follow from certain premises whose denial would be self-refuting, no matter what anyone may happen to believe.

This feature also distinguishes transcendental arguments from scientific explanations. Admittedly, scientific explanations likewise try to derive various necessary truths from certain premises that are themselves taken to be true. Given the truth of the lawlike statements of thermodynamics, the claim that copper expands when heated must be true, necessarily. But, on the one hand, it would not be logically impossible to deny the truth of the lawlike statements of thermodynamics. And, on the other hand, neither would it be logically impossible to find some other scientific theory that might explain the same data. In contrast to both of these features characteristic of scientific explanations, however, it must be logically impossible to deny the premises of transcendental arguments, whose premises are also conditionally entailed by the conclusions that are categorically derived from them. Apart from these formal differences, moreover, the subject matter of transcendental arguments is significantly different from the subject matter of scientific explanations. The conclusions that transcendental arguments seek to defend are the very assumptions that must be made before any scientific explanation can be given. In particular, scientific explanations presuppose that there are factual necessities of some sort that can be discovered. And it is precisely the logical necessity of there being such factual necessities—whatever they might turn out to be—that transcendental arguments seek to establish.

The historical source of this conception of transcendental thinking is, of course, Kant's transcendental deduction of the categories. But the conception of transcendental thinking I wish to explore tends to differ from Kant's in at least one important respect.[2] The same sequence of arguments, I contend, can be used to defend three quite different kinds of factual necessity, or three very different conceptions of the world, depending on how the form of these arguments is filled in. And the choice of interpretation, I suggest, in turn depends on which of three types of explanation one might wish to employ. The three types I have in mind, together with that way of understanding the world from which all three seem to have emerged historically, can be loosely compared with Aristotle's four causes. Or such a comparison can be made at least if Aristotle's four causes are not simply taken to be distinct features of one common world, but are instead construed to be four distinct ways of interpreting the world. Thus, Aristotle's material cause, *hylê*, rather than being the physical matter of things, would become that original mythic way of thinking about things that potentially held within itself all three of the other modes of understanding I wish to consider. Myths performed—and may continue to perform—three distinct functions that were not initially separated from one another.[3] In line with Aristotle's efficient cause, *archê*, they were introduced to explain what antecedently made things be the way they were found to be. But, in line with Aristotle's final cause, *telos*, they also served in some sense to justify what they explained. And, in line with Aristotle's formal cause, *eidos*, it must in addition be kept in mind that myths, after all, are stories that were understood and enjoyed as such. In other words, mythic thinking contains the seeds of what I call "archaeological," "teleological," and "semiological" thinking, respectively. Nor are any of these modes of thinking uniquely philosophical, despite the fact that philosophy has historically aligned itself, at different times, with all three of them. Instead of being either transcendental or dialectical, they are empirical, *a posteriori* modes of thinking.

What they are, in effect, are simply three different ways of looking at temporal occurrences. Archaeological thinking, which is essentially the mode of thinking that currently prevails in the natural sciences, attempts to understand both the present and the future in terms of their relative past. Not only are its predictions mere extrapolations from previously observed regularities, it is also the case that archaeological explanations construe any of the occurrences they explain as inert events that happen *as the result of* certain antecedent conditions that are sufficient to account for their occurrence. In other words, the kind of factual necessity that archaeological explanations presuppose is an objective *causal* necessity. Whatever is causally explained must happen, given the existence of the antecedent conditions that actually made it occur. Or, conversely, it is counterfactually claimed that whatever happened would only have failed to happen if the antecedent conditions that made it happen had in fact been different. Thus archaeological explanations are also completely value-neutral. They need not even mention value terms, let alone use them.

On the other hand, teleological thinking, which is currently most pervasive in the social sciences, attempts to understand both the present and the past in terms of their relative future. Even historians tend to construe any of the occurrences they teleologically explain as self-initiating actions that were performed *in order to* realize certain ideal objectives in the future. Nor is this to suggest, as Aristotle might have thought, that actions that are teleologically explained must somehow be caused by what does not yet even exist. Indeed, teleological explanations do not entail that the actions they explain are themselves caused by anything. Rather, they properly perform two quite different functions. First, in trying to discover what the basic reason or the main objective for an action was, that action is placed within a means-end framework of values, not a cause-effect framework of facts. And second, insofar as teleological explanations also place actions within some context of causality, what is being claimed is simply that the sort of action performed might be a necessary—even though not sufficient— condition for the realization of the end in question. In other words, the kind of factual necessity that teleological explanations presuppose is an objective *instrumental* necessity. If they are correct, certain types of actions must be performed—or ought to be performed—not as the result of antecedent causes, but only if certain ideal objectives are to be historically realizable. Or, conversely, what is now being counterfactually claimed is merely that various objectives would not be achievable if certain types of actions were not initiated. And, this being the case, there is an obvious sense in which teleological explanations are essentially value-laden, rather than value-neutral. To be sure, teleological explanations need only point out what was considered necessary for the achievement of what was considered valuable. They need not go on and try to justify an action by establishing that these opinions were correct. Nevertheless, teleological explanations cannot be given without at least mentioning what people do value, as well as what they think necessary for bringing what they value into being.

Semiological thinking, however, most characteristic of the humanities, attempts to understand both the past and the future in terms of what can be said about either in terms of their relative present. Thus semiological explanations construe any of the occurrences they explain as being mere signifieds, whose occurrence is made possible only *because of* the operation of certain conventional signifiers.[4] Yet it by no means follows that semiological explanations must therefore be merely exegetical. They may well begin with explications of texts. But what a semiological explanation then tries to do is to explain how it was possible for such a text to have occurred when it did, with the sorts of signifiers and signifieds that define it. And the explanation offered will in fact be semiological, rather than archaeological or teleological, only if it confines itself to accounting for the historical possibility of the text's occurrence—not its actual occurrence—by pointing to the indispensable artistic and social conventions that prevailed at that time. In other words, the kind of factual necessity semiological explanations presuppose is nothing more nor less than objective *conventional* necessity. All they purport to establish is what types of things must be said—or can be said—given the techniques, rules, and practices that situate the text or any other cultural product, in the cultural world contemporaneous with it. Or, conversely, what is in this case being counterfactually claimed is simply that a very different sort of text would have been possible only if significantly different conventions had prevailed at the time.

Thus, while semiological explanations may also be value-laden, rather than value-neutral, they are not so in the same sense in which teleological explanations are. Certainly they need not mention what the artist might have intended but failed to accomplish anymore than they must look for what might conceivably have caused him to *try* to do what he either did or did not succeed in doing. Rather, they need only show how the values that are actually inherent in the work—in contrast to the value of the work—are grounded in the broader cultural world they either champion or attack.

Thus, causal necessities, instrumental necessities, and conventional necessities are all taken to be factual necessities, which presuppose the truth of certain counterfactual conditions. But the sort of counterfactual conditionals presupposed in each case is obviously not the same, which is why each type of explanation, though falsifiable, would have to be falsified in a different way. What would falsify an archeological explanation is if supposedly sufficient antecedent conditions occurred, but the predicted effect did not. Conversely, what would falsify a teleological explanation is if supposedly necessary types of action did not occur, yet their ideal objective was nevertheless realized. And, in contrast to both of these test conditions, what would falsify a semilogical explanation is if some quite different sort of text could be situated in very similar techniques, rules, and social practices. Even if specific explanations of any of these types were not falsified, however, this still would not prove that they were in fact true—and for two very different reasons. First, it is always possible that they might yet be falsified sometime in the future, given an ever increasing quantity of evidence. And second, even assuming that this were never to happen, it of course could be argued that the assumed necessities do not in fact exist. It is at least logically possible, it would seem, to insist that what are taken to be necessary connections are actually only accidental correlations, no matter how constant they may happen to be. Nor, quite clearly, can these two very different objections be handled in the same way. The only response to the first objection is to keep trying to gather more evidence that might falsify the type of explanation being given. This is what being responsibly involved in any *a posteriori* mode of thinking continually demands. Nor can the results—no matter how supportive—

ever warrant complete certainty. If there is an answer to the second objection, however, it cannot really come from empirical investigation at all, but must be sought in that kind of *a priori,* transcendental thinking that is uniquely philosophical.

To return, then, to Kant's transcendental deduction, my contention is that each of the above types of factual necessity can be transcendentally defended by the same sequence of arguments, provided those arguments are intially divorced from Kant's special, archaeological interpretation. Purified in this way, Kant's transcendental argument can be formulated in terms of three quite simple steps.[5] What seems to be, so the argument runs, cannot even seem to be, unless what is in fact generally the case must necessarily be the case. (1) More specifically, the first step in the deduction is the *argument for self-ascription.* The claim that this argument is advanced to defend is that no conception of immediate experience—whether that experience is veridical or illusory—can be made intelligible without admitting that the experience in question must belong to someone. Or, conversely, what this first argument claims to establish is that anything like Hume's conception of unowned experience is self-refuting. Any experience must at least be an experience of some sort. What is experienced must have some identifiable properties. But if no distinction could be drawn between the act of experiencing (a representing) and the datum experienced (a represented), it would be impossible for there to be any recognition of the datum as being the sort of datum it is. The recognitional component could not be contrasted with what is recognized. Nor could any datum be identified as being the sort of datum it is, if it were not possible in principle to identify some other instance as being an instance of the same sort of datum. Yet this would not even in principle be possible if distinct recognitional acts could never in any sense truly be said to belong to the same consciousness, or to be part of a temporal sequence of recognitions that conceivably could be both remembered and compared. Consequently, the supposition that there can be experiential data of any identifiable sort, even though they are not in principle identifiable by any sequentially unified consciousness, is self-contradictory.

(2) The second step in the deduction is the *argument for independent reality.* What this argument points out is that the very

possibility of referring to some subjective experience in turn entails that at least some of the data experienced must exist independently of their being experienced. If all data had the purely dependent status of dream contents—if no instance of any identifiable datum could be simultaneously identified by two distinct acts of identification, belonging to two different routes of experience—it would be impossible to distinguish the temporal sequence of the data (the idea of succession) from the temporal sequence of their recognition (the succession of ideas). Given my dreaming that I was first old and then young, I could not contrast the order of my dreaming with the order of my life that I was dreaming about. Furthermore, even intersubjective agreement is not enough to establish the difference between subjective appearance and objective reality. If no datum had any more literal reality than the visual depth of a Cézanne painting, it would still be impossible to distinguish between what we all might recognize and what is independently there, whether we recognize it or not. But if such a distinction could not be drawn—if nothing could be truly said to be independent of experience—then neither could anything be meaningfully said to be dependent upon it. Both sides of the distinction between *seems* and *is* must either stand or fall together. Thus, any solipsistic attempt to reduce all that is, or can be, to what only seems to be is no less self-refuting than is any attempt to reduce whatever seems to be to unowned experiences.

(3) The concluding step in the deduction is the *argument for objective coherency,* which not only conditionally entails the previous two steps but is also categorically entailed thereby. The thrust of this argument is to establish that nothing which is independently so could be inferentially or theoretically known to be so, unless what usually is so in some sense necessarily has the properties it has. Certainly, if all of the data experienced were completely wild or unruly—if everything continually changed in ways that were entirely incomprehensible—there would be no grounds for distinguishing what is independently real from what is merely apparent. But neither are purely accidental regularities sufficient to justify a distinction between appearance and reality. If no true claims could be justified concerning what must be so, given that something else is in fact so, neither could any true claims be justified concerning what is in fact so to begin with. At

the very least, the truth of any statement must exclude the truth of any statement it excludes. But more than that, if there were no significant body of disparate claims that mutually supported one another, there would be no rationally defensible way to decide which of two competing claims was in fact objectively true. The very possibility of there being any story about the world presupposes the legitimacy, as well as the necessity, of adding rules of compossibility, or of interdependence, to the ordinary formation and transformation rules of extensional logic.[6] If there were no factual necessities in the world, in other words, there could be no ascertainably true story of the world at all. Therefore, the claim that any world is a Tractarian world of objectively existing, but atomic, facts cannot possibly be defended. Nor could it even be intelligibly believed, since if there could not be said to be any objective world, neither could there be said to be any subjective opinions about it.

Needless to say, all three steps of this transcendental defense of factual necessity warrant a much fuller treatment. My special concern, however, is to show that each of these three steps can be interpreted in three radically different ways. And depending on which interpretation is adopted, any one of the three kinds of factual necessity previously discussed can be justified transcendentally. The crux of the matter is how immediate experience is to be understood. (1.1) In relation to the argument for self-ascription, the identifiable properties of immediate experience might be exclusively taken to be whatever can be explicitly recognized, or consciously attended to, whether by perception or introspection, independently of language. (1.2) But the identifiable properties of our most immediate experience might instead be taken to be whatever can be tacitly recognized, or consciously oriented from, whether perceptually or self-consciously, independently of language. (1.3) And in contrast to both of these interpretations, it might be argued that most, if not all, of the identifiable properties of immediate experience, whether explicitly or tacitly recognized, would in fact be unrecognizable apart from the use of some set of conventional signifiers.

Given the first of these interpretations, language would not only tend to become a mere device for communicating perceptual experiences that could be quite determinate prior to acquiring the ability to articulate them: what is equally far-reaching is how desires and beliefs would have to be construed. Insofar as they could be explicitly recognized at all, in any immediate sense, they would have to be attended to by a process of introspection. In other words, they would become represented mental events for some introspective act of representing that would itself have to remain unrecognizable. Consequently, desires and beliefs would necessarily acquire the status of being inert states of consciousness that are simply there to be discovered, already receding into the past. Subsequently, perhaps, they could be introduced to provide causal explanations for actions. But they could not themselves be actions or be in any sense self-initiating. As detached spectators of our own lives, we would simply find ourselves having whatever desires and beliefs we in fact find ourselves having. Nor could we suppose that it would be in our power, at the moment in question, to desire or believe anything else. Some different antecedent event would first have to occur to bring such a change about. Thus, what is produced by this first interpretation is a rather passive sense of self, a consciousness of just *having a position,* the having of which can potentially be explained archaeologically.

Given the second interpretation, however, a quite different story of immediate experience can be told. If the identifiable properties of our most immediate experience are taken to be only tacitly recognizable, none of them would have to be construed as mental representeds that are introspectively attended to. As Polanyi points out, the blind man who explicitly follows the curb with his cane is not explicitly attending to the pressures of the cane on his hand.[7] If he did, he would tend to lose the curb. Nevertheless, if he were not at least tacitly aware of those pressures, he could never find the curb in the first place. In Sartrean terminology, his ability to follow the curb seems simultaneously to entail a positional *consciousness* of the curb and a nonpositional *consciousness (of)* the pressures of the cane on his hand.[8] And far from saying that he cannot immediately recognize what he is only conscious (of), or is consciously orienting from, it could easily be argued that it is precisely this kind of tacit awareness that is most immediate, since it does not posit any explicit relation to a represented datum. But then consider what happens when this kind of interpretation is trained on desires and beliefs. When they are oriented from, rather than introspectively attended to, they cease being represented events and instead become representing acts. In other words, what previously had to be explicitly construed as inert mental states can now be tacitly construed as intentional acts of valuing and believing whatever it is that is valued and believed. So rather than just finding ourselves passively having a position, we can begin to rescue the tacit awareness we have had all along of actively *taking a position.* And this in turn would begin to make it much more plausible to suppose that we conceivably could have taken a very different position from the one we in fact took, even though everything remained antecedently the same. We could simply have weighted our alternatives in some other way. Indeed, even perceiving can be tacitly construed as a valuational act, selectively attending to whatever is taken to be more important. Thus, a much more obviously active sense of self emerges whenever we become involved participants in our conscious lives, rather than detached spectators of them. Or, as Heidegger puts much the same point, we are all preontologically aware of ourselves as actively orienting toward the future with care, sometimes even with resolve.[9] We tend to lose this fundamental awareness only when we explicitly turn upon ourselves and start reflectively attending to our initial prereflective experiences.

Yet in opposition to both of the above interpretations of immediate experience, what the third interpretation insists upon is that our immediate recognition of most, if not all, identifiable properties, whether explicitly or tacitly recognized, is inseparable from our manner of articulating what we experience. Clearly we could not see a touchdown if we were not already familiar with the rules of football. But neither, it seems, does the monolingual Zuni Indian normally discriminate between what we call orange and what we call yellow given the fact that his language employs the same word for both.[10] As the later Wittgenstein emphasized, all seeing involves the mastery of certain techniques, many of which are linguistic, just as all *seeing as* involves the learning of new techniques.[11] Hence, the conception of language as a mere device for communication is rejected. We do not just publically name what we already personally recognize, but tend personally to recognize what has already been publically named. Even our silent monologues and imaginings are made possible by a language we did not create,[12] And quite a similar objection is also raised in relation to our tacitly recognized feelings or attitudes. There may be some sense in which the poet is vaguely aware of his emotions before he manages to express them in his poetry. But as Croce and Collingwood have argued, like Vico before them, it is only in the process of deliberately expressing his emotions, in some medium or other, that any artist becomes fully aware of the feelings he is orienting from.[13] As a matter of fact, it could even be argued that artistic expression, no less than ordinary expression, does not merely sharpen a feeling of which we are already tacitly aware, but tends to constitute it as the kind of feeling that it is.[14] As conventional styles of expression change, so do styles of feeling. Yet neither need be construed as either preceding or following the other. Both changes may be simultaneous and inseparable. In other words, what begins to emerge from this third interpretation is what Foucault refers to as a decentered sense of self, a sense of ourselves not as just passively *having* a position, nor of actively *taking* a position, but of tacitly *accepting a position* that has already been defined by others.[15] We may at least be dimly conscious (of) the fact that what we normally orient from are, in effect, interpersonal representings. Not only can we never entirely escape the feeling of being with others; we also tend continually to see ourselves through their eyes, even when we reject them.

Moreover, each one of these interpretations of immediate experience entails an equally different interpretation of independent reality. (2.1) If the identifiable properties of immediate experience are restricted to what can be explicitly recognized, independently of language, the entities that are inferentially taken to be independently real will tend to be either observable or theoretical objects, juxtaposed in value-neutral, spatio-temporal relations. (2.2) But if the identifiable properties of immediate experience are understood to be what can only be tacitly recognized, independently of language, the entities that are inferentially taken to be independently real will tend to be tools and obstacles, as well as other persons, existentially grounded in goal-oriented situations, or in value-laden, spatio-temporal relations. (2.3) And if the identifiable properties of immediate experience, whether explicitly or tacitly recognizable, are understood to be inseparably bound to the use of some set of purely conventional signifiers—mere conventional classifications—then the entities that are inferentially taken to be independently real will tend to be nothing more nor less than symbolic constructs, conventionally rooted in various social roles, rules, and institutional practices, or in culturally defined spatio-temporal relations.[16] Each of these inferential moves to independent reality necessarily involves some kind of distinction between what is and what only seems to be. But what lies on either side of this distinction is obviously very different in each case.

In line with the first interpretation, if the blind man were simply to feel along his cane with his fingers, all he would find would be a more or less smooth, cylindrical object, which appears to possess a certain hardness and flexibility. And if he then, with his other hand, were to touch those fingers that were touching the cane, all he would find would be one set of objects on top of, or enclosing, another. True, he might also go on to theorize about what could conceivably make it possible for any object to be hard, yet flexible. And he might even try to understand how tactile sensations are possible, in contrast to mere spatial juxtaposition. Thus he might arrive at various theoretical conceptions of physics and neuro-physiology that not only account for the sensations in question, but also account for the properties of hardness and flexibility. Yet, no matter how he might finally decide to relate theoretical objects to observable objects and observable objects to sensations, he could never end up with anything like the simple notion of a tool. The most that he could do would be to try to define a tool as some observable object that is spatio-temporally juxtaposed to other observable objects as the result of certain electro-chemical impulses that these other observable objects posses. But when defined this way, so would any target become a tool for the guided missile that explodes it. Clearly, what is crucially missing here is the entire means-end framework of instrumental values, without which nothing could conceivably either be or become a tool. Whether just observable objects are taken to exist independently, or just theoretical objects, or somehow both, they could only be given what Heidegger calls a purely *vorhanden* mode of existence.[17] They would be independently present-at-hand. As such, their properties could exist categorically or dispositionally, essentially or inciden-tally, constantly or transiently. But they could not have any inherent properties of utility, even though all such properties may well be in some sense dependent upon properties that are present-at-hand. Independent reality would have to be what the natural sciences take it to be.

Not until the blind man uses his cane to find the curb, and uses the curb to find his destination, will tools and obstacles emerge, as well as other people. In Heideggerian terms, what is scientifically only present-at-hand now becomes *zuhanden,* or ready-to-hand.[18] And it becomes ready-to-hand only in the process of using it, of tacitly orienting from and through it toward some explicit objective. Indeed, given this practical orientation, the entire world, not just man-made tools, can now be ready-to-hand in one way or another. Not only do trees become potential timber for building houses: the wind becomes good or bad for sailing, the water becomes good or bad for swimming, and one's own body becomes either a tool or an obstacle for accomplishing whatever objectives one might value. Other people, on the other hand, are not mere tools or obstacles, but are essentially the users of tools, and should not be confused with the tools they use. Nor, given this practical orientation, are either tools or other people mere observable objects that are somehow invested with value form outside the world.[19] On the contrary, mere things must now be construed as entities whose inherent values have been ignored for certain scientific purposes, purposes which can themselves be understood only from this same practical orientation. Granted, what may be a tool for one person may well be an obstacle for another. This does not mean, however, that no distinction can be drawn between what merely seems to be useful and what really is useful. Finding something to be useful need not always be analogous to the mere perspectivity relation of finding that a tree looks smaller from farther away, but may also be analogous to the respectivity relation of being taller than someone else who is shorter.[20] And in so far as the latter is the case, something may really be useful or not, no matter how it might seem to the person who is trying to use it. Even here, of course, a given implement may really be useful for accomplishing some end that is not itself really ideal. Thus, something parallel to the contrast between the manifest, observable world and the inferred, theoretical world of the natural sciences must no doubt be introduced into this practical sphere as well, as has in fact been attempted from Plato and Aristotle, down through

Kant and Hegel, to Rawls and Gewirth. No matter what ethical theory might prove to be most adequate, however, the kind of independent reality they all presuppose can only be defined in terms of the practical existentialia of Heidegger, not the categories of Kant, or the purely factual relations of Wittgenstein's *Tractatus.*[21] Only insofar as we dwell in the world with others—in contrast to being just located alongside of them—can we meaningfully cooperate with them, or refuse to do so.

Suppose, however, that one were to focus on the fact that the cane the blind man was carrying was white. If this is not merely seen to be so, but the white cane is itself taken to be a signifier that the man is blind, then the third sense of independent reality begins to take hold.[22] Here, too, it is possible to be mistaken. The man may only be pretending to be blind. Nevertheless, the white cane could be of no assistance in such a plot if it were not for the fact that certain social conventions have been established which have a reality that is quite independent of any use to which they might be put. Indeed, from this perspective of an already established cultural world, even the purposes that people might have can be seen to be largely constituted by the social practices that prevail. Nor can a cultural world be changed if it does not in some way allow for that very possibility within the practices which define it.[23] What is most interesting, though, is the sense in which the symbolic constructs that comprise this third kind of independent reality are neither present-at-hand nor even ready-to-hand, but are, as it were, *abhanden,* or missing.[24] They are not missing, of course, in the sense in which a tool might be missing, or accidentally misplaced. Rather, they are missing in the sense in which Foucault agrees that semiological explanations (which he misleadingly calls "archaeological") dispense with things, or depresentify them.[25] It is impossible to lay one's hands on the Presidency of the United States, marriage, property, crime, insanity, or sexuality. Nor is this simply because these are abstract nouns. Obviously one cannot lay one's hands on cylindricality either. Unlike what are taken to be either observable objects or tools, no occurrence of actually occupying the office of the President, or of being married, or of illegally taking something that rightfully belongs to someone else, would be possible were it not for the social conventions that constitute such possibilities. Nor can anyone be officially called insane without appealing to the combined authorization of legal and medical institutions.[26] Even sexual roles, it can be argued, are in many ways conventionally defined. As a matter of fact, just as everything in the world can be ready-to-hand, in relation to practical, instrumental purposes, so everything we either practically or theoretically take to be in the world can likewise be regarded as mere symbolic constructs of some cultural enterprise. Not only God and the devil, or witches and phlogiston, but also neutrinos and electro-chemical impulses, or even tables and chairs, can all be construed as only conventional ways of characterizing whatever it is that might occur and endure. And if this is all they are, one could not literally lay one's hands on anything that was recognizably real apart from such conventions. We would be forever confined to the depresentified things that are simply said in our various ways of talking about the world. We could never really get beyond our talk to any of the supposedly inherent characteristics of what is purportedly being talked about.[27]

Finally, each of these quite different conceptions of independent reality in turn entails an equally different conception of objective coherency, without which the kind of independent reality in question would not be possible. (3.1) If *vorhanden* objects are taken to be independently real, whether observable or theoretical, the coherency of the present must be sought in the past, in the interrelated causal laws that make the present be what it is. (3.2) If *zuhanden* tools and obstacles, as well as other persons, are taken to be independently real, however, the coherency of the present must be sought in the future, in the interrelated objectives that give the present direction. (3.3) And if only *abhanden* symbolic constructs are taken to be independently real, the coherency of the present must be sought in the present, in the interrelated conventions that currently prevail. Each one of these conceptions of coherency is pitted against a correlative notion of mere chance occurrences. But what chance is taken to mean in each case must obviously be different. What the first conception of coherency maintains is that not all real events can be uncaused. What the second conception of coherency maintains, by comparison, is that not all actions can be only inadvertently or incidentally performed. And what the third conception of coherency maintains is that not all current signifieds can be purely coincidental. What is common to all three of these claims is the argument that what really is so, at least for the most part, must be explainable. But the modes of explanation which are relevant are at least *prima facie* not the same. They are the archaeological, teleological and semiological modes of explanation previously introduced, whose transcendental defense must now be completed.

If the blind man were to ask himself how he knew that the cylindrical object he was holding in his hand was real, rather than illusory, the only way he could proceed to answer this question would be to try to insert it into a causal order of events. He has not only been feeling it all along and making sounds with it as it hits the sidewalk; he also remembers where he found it in the hall at home, and when he first got it. Nor does his cane ever behave like a Dali watch, suddenly going limp in his hands, with no apparent causal explanation. It is a relatively stable part of the causal order. In other words, the basic principle he is using to define the real coherency of things he finds present-at-hand is the *principle of inertia*. The claim he is relying upon is that everything, or at least almost everything, will necessarily go on being the same, unless it is transformed by the operation of antecedent forces— only now it can be seen why this is not merely an assumption. If it were not so, he could not distinguish appearance from reality, and therefore could not even ask himself whether the cane in his hand were merely an illusion. But suppose he were then to ask himself whether he himself was real. Would he not have to try to answer this question in the very same way? Would he not have to be able to insert himself into the same causal order that he inserted his cane? Not only must it be possible to know when he was born and who his parents were, but also what caused him to be blind, and cvcn what caused him to be on the sidewalk where he currently finds himself, tapping his cane. Yet if his real location in the world must be causally explainable, must he not conlcude that he is no less inevitably where he is, and no less inevitably the way he is, than his cane? If he is as real as his cane is, the principle of inertia must presumably apply to him as well. He, too, will go on being the same, unless he is transformed by the operation of antecedent forces.

If he were to ask himself why there are real canes, however, or how it was possible for him to go out and buy one, quite a different sense of coherency would start to come into focus. He bought it at a store, which sold it for a profit. And the store could do this only because people like himself are willing to pay more for canes like this than the store had to pay manufacturer for them. Nor would the manufacturer have tried to secure the raw material for making such canes if he didn't think he should have made a profit as well. Thus, the reality of the cane now seems to be dependent upon the historical possibility of inserting it into a relatively stable, instrumental order of interlocking plans for the future, not into a mere natural order of past events. Admittedly, canes like this would remain as hard and flexible as they are whether or not anyone wanted to purchase them. Yet if no one did want to purchase them, they would simply lie around and eventually cease to be made. The being of what is ready-to-hand, therefore, in this sense depends on the existence of human projects, as well as on some degree of cooperation—at least on a division of labor. And the principle that governs human projects does not seem to be the principle of inertia, but the *principle of progress.*[28] People continually try to change things for the better. In a narrow, tactical sense, we might simply try to maximize our own gains or minimize our own losses. Or, in a broader, more strategic sense, we might also try to devise schemes that will allow us all to maximize our gains or minimize our losses, especially given the realization that in many cases we ourselves cannot be winners if others are losers. Or, in a more absolute, ethical sense, we might even move beyond the strategic notion of a mere harmony of interests to some conception of what kinds of interests we think people really ought to have, as well as to some consideration of how we might persuade them to agree. Whichever of these versions of the principle of progress is adopted, however, the upshot is in one sense the same: it is assumed that we can weight the alternatives before us in one way or another and act accordingly. But if this is so, then it would seem to follow that the blind man need not be inevitably where he is, any more than he must inevitably be the way he is. He is not merely inadvertently walking down the street or just incidentally doing so. Rather, he has promised to meet his friend for dinner. And, having the ability to keep a promise, like having the ability to walk, would seem to entail the simultaneous possibility of either exercising such an ability or not.[29] True, he may well be the sort of man who keeps his promises. Yet, if this is true, it could be argued, this is only because he continues to value what he has valued in the past. Teleologically speaking, our actions are not the effects of our already formed character. Rather, they form and either preserve or change our character by the values they posit.[30] Consequently, the blind man presumably could have stayed at home instead.

What if the blind man were to think again, however, and realize that the buying and selling of canes itself presupposes the existence of certain human conventions, in particular the convention of a more-or-less free enterprise system? If he is to understand the reality of this practice, as it currently exists, what he must presumably now begin to do is to see how it is related to various other practices that are contemporaneous with it. Without a certain kind of political system, this specific kind of economic system might well not be possible. And without various social and educational values, no doubt this specific kind of political system might also be impossible. Nor could any of these practices proceed the way they do without being interpreted and facilitated by various cultural texts or by certain oral practices of ordinary discourse. In other words, what would seem to be involved is something similar to what Foucault calls a vertical system of dependences, a system in which the dependency relation works both ways simultaneously.[31] Cultural practices are dependent on the very economic practices they also make possible. Thus, instead of trying to define the coherency of the present in terms of either the principle of inertia or the principle of progress, both of these would tend to give way to the *principle of permissiblity.* This principle itself, however, entails two complementary principles that conjointly define what is meant by permissibility. As the later Carnap emphasized, the principle of permissibility entails the principle of tolerance.[32] What can be legitimately said will depend upon what specific framework of discourse one is operating within. No cultural world authorizes only one way of talking, but allows for different sorts of enterprises, each with its own rules and supporting practices. Yet as both Foucault and Barthes have emphasized, the principle of permissibility also entails the principle of rarity.[33] Not only is there a restricted range of legitimate types of positions that can be occupied in any given cultural context; there are also certain conventional restrictions concerning what sorts of individuals are entitled to occupy them. Consequently, not everything can be legitimately said, or legitimately done, especially by the same individual. As Kuhn has argued, moreover, this principle of rarity applies to the scientific enterprise as well.[34] What can be legitimately said about the physical world, at any given time in history, is no less dependent upon authorized paradigms than is what can be legitimately said about man's economic and religious existence. So what happens to the blind man's being-in-the-world under these conditions? In addition to pointing out that he could neither break nor keep his promise if various social conventions did not prevail, including the convention of making promises, it would seem to follow that it can legitimately be said not only that he is inevitably on his way down the street, but also that he could have stayed home instead. The former claim seems to be authorized by the current scientific framework of events and causes, while the latter claim seems to be authorized by our practical, instrumental framework of actions and values. Only now, of course, presumably neither of these stories can be taken to be literally true, at least in any realistic, nonconventional sense.[35] Semiologically speaking, they are merely different ways of talking, which are currently found useful for different accepted purposes.

In short, transcendental thinking appears to have reached an impasse that it cannot itself circumvent. On the one hand, the same set of arguments, differently interpreted, can be used to defend archaeological, teleological, and semiological explanations. Nor might this initially seem to be unfortunate. When we are dealing with human behavior anyway, all three types of explanation do seem to be applicable in different senses. The types of military formations that are generally used in battles at certain times in history might be semiologically accounted for, while the tactical or strategic objectives of any given battle might be teleologically explained. And typical aggressive responses to certain sorts of stimuli, rooted in human instincts of territoriality, might be archaeologically traced to our genetic makeup. Yet on the other hand, as should by now be clear, the ontological presuppositions of each of these three types of explanations do seem to be mutually exclusive. How can the same occurrence be not only unavoidable and value-neutral, but also both avoidable and value-laden? As Nietzsche

The Purified Transcendental Deduction	The Archaeological Interpretation	The Teleological Interpretation	The Semiological Interpretation
1. The Argument for Self-ascription:	1.1 Having a Position	1.2 Taking a Position	1.3 Accepting a Position
2. The Argument for Independent Reality:	2.1 *Vorhanden* Observable and/or Theoretical Objects	2.2 *Zuhanden* Tools and Obstacles, as well as Other Persons	2.3 *Abhanden* Symbolic Constructs
3. The Argument for Objective Coherency:	3.1 The Principal of Inertia	3.2 The Principal of Progress	3.3 The Principal of Permissibility

pointed out in the *Twilight Of The Idols,* archaeological and teleological thinking are direct inversions of one another. Furthermore, how could either of these more realistic conceptions of the ontological nature of things be necessarily true, if it is also necessarily true that whatever we might say about occurrences is nothing but the reflection of certain linguistic, social conventions? To claim that all three of these positions are equally defensible would appear to be absurd. But simply to opt for one of them would appear to be transcendentally arbitrary. Therefore, if this dilemma of transcendental thinking is to be resolved, we must look to dialectical thinking for any possible resolution. These relations may be represented in the figure above.[36]

II. Dialectical Thinking

In contrast to the linear character of transcendental thinking, dialectical thinking is essentially a thinking in opposites that in some sense transforms the premises with which it begins. More specifically, it tries to overcome what appear to be necessary oppositions, not merely contingent differences of opinion. And it tries to do so in a way that is itself necessary—or rationally defensible—rather than arbitrary. Thus, contrary to what is sometimes taken to be the Platonic meaning of dialectic, dialectical thinking is not mere dialogue, or debate, moving from conflicting hypotheses toward some agreement that may simply happen to come about. Nor is it a mere collecting and differentiating according to essential presuppositions, another Platonic meaning of dialectic, which is actually the function of transcendental thinking.[37] Rather, the central function of dialectical thinking is to demonstrate, in a somewhat Hegelian sense of the term, how apparently unavoidable conflicts not only can, but must, be mitigated. But then, as Gadamer points out, this may not be so different from the Platonic sense of dialectic after all.[38] Even Plato believed that a dialectical resolution must be one whose truth can withstand any possible counterargument. This is why he put such emphasis on dialogue in the first place.

There are at least three different ways, however, in which dialectical thinking might try to accomplish this objective. First, it might try simply to merge what seems to be disparate. Each of the modes of thinking that have been transcendentally defended might try to include, or subsume, the other two modes of thinking within itself, by explicating their essential presuppositions in terms of its own presuppositions. This is the dialectical *method of reduction,* in whichever direction the reduction is pursued. It tends to be the most dogmatic of the three and is also subject to the counterargument that it seriously distorts the meanings that are purportedly being explicated. Second, dialectical thinking might also try to employ the ancient Eleatic *method of elimination* instead of the method of reduction. Each of the modes of thinking that have been transcendentally defended might try to exclude, rather than to include, its competitors. Beginning in this case with those presuppositions that seem to challenge its own presuppositions, each mode of thinking might try to show that, insofar as the other two modes are not reducible to itself, they are logically self-refuting or reduce themselves to absurdity. This is obviously a much less dogmatic way to proceed. But whichever mode of thinking employs this method of elimination is subject to the possible counterargument that it reduces itself to absurdity as well. Nor, it might be suggested, are there any completely decisive proofs of this *reductio ad absurdum* sort outside a purely formal calculus.[39] Third, however, dialectical thinking might also try to show that the three modes of thinking, which exclude one another and cannot be reduced to one another, nevertheless presuppose one another, and therefore must each be qualified by the others in certain specific ways. This is the *method of tensional transformation,* the method I myself intend to support in opposition to nontensional thinking. Yet before attempting to do so, the basic inadequacies of the other two methods must first be exposed, at least in a very general way.

No doubt the most obvious instance of the first dialectical method of reduction is semiological reduction. It is already implicit in the semiological principle of permissibility. The claim that it makes is that the essential archaeological relation *as the result of* and the essential teleological relation *in order to* can both be explicated in terms of the purely conventional, semiological relation *because of.* In other words, causal necessity can be interpreted as a mere logical deduction from certain lawlike statements within some scientific theory that is currently accepted. And instrumental necessity can likewise be interpreted as merely what is thought to be required by various social roles, rules, and institutional practices. But needless to say, neither of the other two modes of thinking would find these explications to be at all adequate. The archaeological realist does not think of causal laws as mere inference tickets that have simply been validated by his theory.[40] Rather, he thinks that his theory in some sense truly maps various causal connections that exist independently of it. Nor do teleological explanations simply focus on what people feel is expected of them, given the fact that they are occupying certain positions in society. On the contrary, they focus on what various individuals themselves consider to be both necessary and valuable, whether or not their commitments are found socially acceptable. Nor, of course, are the individuals whose behavior is being teleologically explained merely reporting what they happen to believe. Rather, in believing what they believe, they in effect claim that certain actions really are necessary for the achievement of what really is valuable. Thus, neither archaeological nor teleological thinking can be subsumed within, or reduced to, the presuppositions of semiological thinking without seriously distorting their initial import.

Teleological reduction, on the other hand, tries to explicate both of the other relations in terms of its own notion of instrumental necessity. It might initially accept the semiological claim that what can be legitimately said to be so in the natural sciences, the social sciences and the humanities may be relative to some currently accepted framework. And in line with Carnap's distinction between internal and external truth, it might also agree that different frameworks are useful for different purposes.[41] But what teleological thinking must then insist on emphasizing is that no framework can be said to be useful for any purpose without relying on something like Heidegger's fundamental ontology, in terms of which the very notions of utility and purpose could be themselves defined.[42] Moreover, cultural conventions can be teleologically construed as social strategies for harmonizing human interests and maximizing human satisfactions, just as Toulmin has shown that scientific theories can be teleologically construed as instrumental in advancing the aims of the scientific enterprise.[43] Indeed, a teleological reduction might go so far as to insist that causal necessities, as well as conventional necessities, really are instrumental necessities. Conventional necessities, it might be argued, are necessary only to the extent that they actually do promote, or are indispensable to, the ideal objectives they were introduced to achieve. And causal necessities, so at least Aristotle, Hegel, and Whitehead would argue, likewise involve some notion of subjective aim, even in the inanimate world.[44] Yet once again, these explications seriously distort what they claim to be explicating. Social laws may be quite legal, or conventionally legitimate, whether or not they are either expedient or moral. And the causal explanations of physics and chemistry, if not also biological explanations, do not generally appeal to any teleological, projective principles.[45]

Nor is archaeological reduction any more successful. It might begin by accepting the teleological reduction of conventional necessities to instrumental necessities. But it would then go on to insist that instrumental practices can in turn be defined in terms of the antecedent desires and beliefs that causally produce the behavior in question. And admittedly, it can do this in one of three ways. (1) Actions might be defined as the effects of those mental events we call desires and beliefs.[46] (2) They might also be defined as the mere exercise of certain behavioral abilities, which may in turn involve an actualization of certain behavioral propensities, which are causally triggered by some external stimulus.[47] (3) Or mental desires and beliefs might in some sense be identified with electro-chemical impulses in the central nervous system, thus providing a physiological account of both dispositions and their causal instantiation.[48]

But at least two things demonstrate the inadequacy of these explications. First, as Davidson, Goldman, and so many others have come to admit, intentional performances cannot be successfully defined as the simple effects even of relevant desires and beliefs. Of the many counterexamples that have been given, one of Davidson's own should suffice.[49] A mountain climber who is holding someone else up by a rope may so fear for his own life that his conscious desire to stay alive, together with his conscious belief that he himself probably will fall if he does not let go of the other person, may cause his hold on the rope to be loosened even though he still may have not intentionally loosened it. As Goldman points out, an action is intentional only if it is performed in the way conceived by the action-plan.[50] Or in other words, it cannot simply be the effect even of relevant desires and beliefs, but must be performed *in order to* accomplish what is desired, given certain beliefs. Thus, this crucial teleological relation, which was purportedly being defined archaeologically, has to be surreptitiously reintroduced. Nor, it would be teleologically objected, should desires and beliefs be in any case construed as preceding the actions they define.[51] If they were antecedent events, the action they supposedly explain would not be an action at all, but a mere body movement. And two events do not make an action, it could be argued, any more than two facts make a value.

Second, the ordinary teleological notion of exercising an ability not only entails that nothing prevents that ability from being exercised at the time in question, but also entails that nothing antecedently made its exercise at that time inevitable.[52] As Austin has so convincingly shown, when we say that someone could have done otherwise, we certainly do not mean that he *could* have *if,* or only if, he had wanted to.[53] Obviously, wanting to do something is not a sufficient condition for being able to do it. If it were, someone who is paralyzed could walk whenever he wanted to. Nor is wanting to do something a necessary condition for being able to do it. If it were, not wanting to walk would produce instant paralysis. But as Austin has also shown, neither does saying that someone could have done otherwise mean that he *would* have *if, or only if,* he had wanted to.[54] Even assuming that someone had both the ability and the opportunity to have done something else, it still does not follow that his wanting to do it would be sufficient to constitute his actually doing it, as Davidson's example of the mountain climber indicates. And conversely, since it is not logically impossible to do something else for no reason at all—at least given the second archaeological way of defining actions mentioned above—it is also not the case that wanting to do something else is a necessary condition for actually doing it. When we say that someone could have done otherwise, we are categorically asserting *on* the basis of certain conditions that actually did obtain that he could have done what he in fact did not do. We are not hypothetically asserting that *if* certain conditions that did not obtain had obtained, he either could or would have done it. Consequently, the archaeological explication of our ordinary conception of human abilities is just as distorting as is the archaeological explication of our ordinary conception of intentional performances. Archaeological reduction is no more adequate than either teleological or semiological reduction.

The dialectical method of elimination, however, is a much more effective weapon. As a matter of fact, the basic ontological presuppositions of semiological thinking can be quite easily seen to reduce themselves to absurdity. If all recognizable occurrences are the mere signifieds of some purely conventional set of signifiers—if nothing can be said to have any inherent ontological nature independently of some stipulated framework—how could there *be* any act of stipulation, or any pragmatic signification, to begin with? Even granting that what may be signified may be nothing more than a symbolic construct, how could the construction of symbolic constructs be itself a mere symbolic construct? How could the real author of any novel be only a character in some other novel? True, semiological thinking at this point might appeal to some metaphorical notion of transcendent acts of constitution, as Cassirer tended to do, in line with Kant's transcendental idealism.[55]

But if such metaphors were to be taken literally—if it were supposed that transcendent acts of symbolic constitution do really in some sense occur—the claim being made would inevitably be absurd. If they were literally to occur, they would have to be construed as spatio-temporal signifieds, which would undo their transcendent status, as well as their constituting power. And yet, if transcendent acts of constitution could not be said to occur in any sense at all, it would certainly appear to follow that transcendental idealism is nonsensical. Thus, the presuppositions of semiological thinking inevitably seem to be either nonsensical or absurd.

Furthermore, the presuppositions of teleological thinking can likewise be seen to reduce themselves to absurdity. As Broad has pointed out, the teleological conception of an action not only entails some degree of indeterminism, or mere probabilistic causation, it also entails some notion of self-determinism, or self-initiation.[56] To claim that I could have moved my arm is not simply to presuppose that it might or might not have moved at the time in question. (Nor is this physically impossible. Kant was wrong to suppose that even archaeological coherence requires that all events must be explainable in terms of strictly universalistic causal laws.[57]) Still, in addition to presupposing that my arm might or might not have moved at the time in question, it must also be presupposed that I in some sense could have moved it. It would obviously not be an action if it suddenly just started to move all by itself. True, moving one's arm need not be construed as a semantically transitive relation, unless of course one moved it with one's other hand. Nor, therefore, must some ghostly self be posited as the hidden cause of its motion, any more than occult volitions must be introduced— or represented desires and beliefs. Here is where Broad himself went awry. Nevertheless, there must be some difference between a self-initiating performance and a mere uncaused event. What is it? It is extremely difficult, if not impossible, for teleological thinking to answer this question. It might be said that a self-initiating performance is not just a chance event, in the archaeological sense, but is one that knowingly brings itself into being. Yet what could this metaphor possibly mean? It would clearly be absurd to suppose that any action can literally precede itself. And even if it could, this would only generate an infinite regress. If this metaphor cannot be explicated in any way at all, however, then the teleological notion of self-initiating performances would seem to be no less nonsensical than the semiological notion of symbolic constitution. Teleological, like semiological, thinking appears to be inescapably caught in either nonsense or absurdity.

Does this leave, then, only the presuppositions of archaeological thinking standing? If so, a dialectical resolution of the problem posed by transcendental thinking would be achieved. Nor would supporting the presuppositions of archaeological thinking be any longer arbitrary, or dogmatic, given the collapse of the other two modes of thinking. The initial interpretation of Kant's transcendental argument would turn out to be the only viable interpretation after all. Unfortunately, however, the archaeological interpretation of Kant's transcendental argument can also be seen to reduce itself to absurdity, no less decisively. Not only must it insist upon the illusory character of self-initiating performances and symbolic constitution, it must in the end admit that it cannot even save the reality of its own inert events. What archaeological thinking champions is what Derrida calls the metaphysics of presence.[58] According to archaeological thinking, both mental and physical events simply are what they are. They do not intrinsically either mean or refer to anything beyond themselves. Rather than being *of* or *about* anything, they are merely the effects of whatever might have antecedently produced them. But how, then, could one set of events ever be literally aware of, let alone come to know or understand, another? Indeed, how could they even be literally aware of themselves? True, it could in a sense be argued that the physical events of the natural order need not be experienced in order to be. And this certainly seems to be so, since there was a natural order long before there were any experiences of it. Still, as both Heidegger and Peirce have argued, albeit in different ways, while such events might be ontically real without being perceived, it is only in relation to some possible perception that they could be justifiably assigned any independent, ontological reality.[59] Given the metaphysics of presence, however, it would seem to follow that the very notion of a possible representation is logically absurd. Literally speaking, there could be no representings in the world. Consequently, there could be no real representeds either. To be sure, some attempt might be made to give perceptual representings their own transcendent status, along with self-initiating performances and symbolic constitution.[60] But then we would be back once more with metaphors that cannot be taken literally without absurdity, yet that otherwise appear to remain nonsensical. Thus, in contrast to the method of reduction, the method of elimination appears to be overly successful. The entire upshot of transcendental thought seems to have dialectically abolished itself. There is no position left to support.

The trouble with the first two methods, however, is that they are not dialectical enough. They both presuppose the initial, Platonic formulation of the principle of identity, which dominated Western thought at least until Hegel, and then reasserted itself after his influence began to wane. According to this initial formulation, *everything is what it is and not something else.* Thus two different things cannot be said to be the same without specifying quite univocally in what ways they are the same, as well as in what ways they are different.[61] Yet this is precisely what produced the difficulties inherent not only in the dialectical method of reduction, but also in the dialectical method of elimination. On the one hand, every attempt to define univocally the basic relation of any one of the three modes of *a posteriori* thinking in terms of either of the other two results in a serious distortion of its meaning. And on the other hand, what generates the *reductio ad absurdum* of all three of these modes of thinking is a certain binary opposition that the Platonic formulation of the principle of identity entails. Anything must be either an immanent presence or a transcendent absence. As has been shown, however, both of these alternatives undermine themselves. Sheer presence can never know itself. And sheer absence can never be.

Nor can these problems be resolved by appealing to the second formulation of the principle of identity, the one that Hegel himself advanced. According to this second formulation, *everything is what it is only by virtue of being other than what it is not.* This does make the mediation implicit in the first formulation explicit, as Heidegger points out.[62] But it also transforms external relations into internal relations. Now nothing can be without being bound in a systematic way to everything else that is. In other words, the basic differences that distinguish archaeological, teleological, and semiological thinking from one another must be construed as abstractions from their concrete unity. Where, however, is this concrete unity to be found? It would seem that the only way in a sense to preserve these differences, while simultaneously sublating them, would be to return to that original mode of mythic thought from which they all emerged. Consequently, despite Hegel's attempt to distinguish the rational concepts of philosophy (*Begriffen*) from the figurative concepts of myth (*Vorstellungen*), he is inevitably driven back to what he wants to surmount.[63] There simply is no way in which archaeological, teleological, and semiological thinking can be discursively integrated in one conceptual framework. The most that can be done, as the later Heidegger tried to do, is to abandon all three of these modes of calculative thinking and open oneself, through meditative thinking, to whatever it is that might be ontologically prior to their separation.[64]

But there is a third formulation of the principle of identity, one that is irreducibly tensional in character. According to this final formulation, *everything is what it is only by virtue of being other than itself.* This is the formulation that Derrida calls the principle of *différance,* in contrast to ordinary difference, whether in the Platonic or the Hegelian sense.[65] In a way, however, it is as old as Heraclitus. And it is the principle that essentially defines the dialectical method of tensional transformation, or what Derrida calls the method of deconstruction.[66] As applied to the three modes of archaeological, teleological, and semiological thinking, it not only involves a series of dialectical reversals concerning which mode is to be regarded as ontologically more fundamental; it also, because of these reversals, entails what Derrida calls an erasure of the simple ontological priority of any one of them. Thus, the claim being made is that whichever of these three modes of thinking might be taken to be most fundamental, it cannot defend itself without appealing to the other two, despite the fact that it cannot help but negate their priority. Nor does this simply mean that the failure of any one of these modes of explanation might lead, in succession, to an employment of the other two. Admittedly, this may in fact be so. If someone is not doing what is expected of him, or is disobeying some social rule, semiological explanations may be abandoned in favor of teleological explanations. And similarly, if the expected realization of some goal does not materialize, even given the appropriate means, teleological explanations may give way to archaeological explanations, or to some account of what the interferring factors might have been. What the phases of reversal and erasure entail, however, is something more than this.

In Anglo-American thought, perhaps the person who comes closest to what Derrida seems to have in mind, even though he does not go far enough, is Popper. In line with Hegel's own account of the material substrate of the world, human action, and its cultural products—not to mention Habermas's account of *the* world, *my* world, and *our* world—Popper introduces the notions of World 1, World 2, and World 3.[67] In effect, these are correlates of what I have been calling archaeological, teleological, and semiological thinking, except for the fact that neither Popper nor Habermas seems sufficiently to realize that teleological thinking is by no means restricted to purely subjective experiences. As I have tried to show, it provides its own instrumental conception of the objective world. Nevertheless, what Popper then goes on to emphasize is both the upward and the downward influences that these worlds exert upon one another. And it is at this point that affinities between Popper and Derrida begin to surface.

True, if only the notion of upward causation were considered, the archaeological realism of World 1 would tend to become ontologically fundamental, without any subsequent erasure. Then all one would be saying is that life and conscioius purposes in some sense emerge from inanimate matter and, in turn, give birth to various cultural constructs. The semiological would presuppose the teleological, which would itself presuppose the archaeological. Yet, as Popper also stresses, this entire process can in a certain sense be reversed. Various conventional signifieds, or symbolic constructs, not only influence how we act upon and transform the natural order, but also influence how we theorize about it. Admittedly, Popper himself only tends to give these downward influences an ontical, rather than ontological, interpretation. He sees that the development of semiological constructs transforms genetic evolution into cultural evolution.[68] But what Popper does not adequately seem to appreciate is the sense in which these downward, semiological influences may serve to challenge any naively realistic conception either of the natural order or of human agency. If one were to take the conventionalist conclusions of Cassirer and the later Wittgenstein or of Carnap, Quine, and Kuhn more seriously, however, one would begin to see the way in which the upward and downward reversals would tend to erase one another. Given a series of upward transformations, linguistic games would somehow simply be played in a natural world that could be quite determinate without them; whereas, given a series of downward transformations, even "the natural world" would tend to become merely another set of games within language. Yet, given both simultaneously, with each erasing the other, what would emerge is the irreducibly tensional notion of what Derrida calls the *game of the world*—in contrast not only to the realist notion of games in the world, but also in contrast to the conventionalist notion of the world of games.[69] Instead of supposing that language either maps or constitutes reality, the linguistic games we play would be construed as disclosing certain aspects of reality, leaving other conflicting aspects hidden, which would then have to be played against one another in an endlessly self-correcting fashion. Truth would no longer be understood as either created or discovered but would come to be understood as a *creative-discovery,* with each side of the hyphen tensionally qualifying the other.

In other words, what this tensional deconstruction of archaeological, teleological, and semiological thinking entails is a further, even more fundamental, deconstruction of the essential relation between the literal and the metaphorical. Metaphorical meaning and truth, especially in philosophy, can no longer be regarded as subservient to literal meaning and truth. Archaeological, teleological, and semiological thinking may all produce their own peculiar conceptions of what is literally the case. But not only would it amount to an absurd category-mistake to suppose that the type of explanans employed by any one of them can explain the explananda of the others; it must also be kept in mind, as the dialectical method of elimination shows, that each of these modes of thinking is rooted in a crucial metaphor that cannot be explicated nontensionally. And the reason for this is that each mode of thinking presupposes the other two, even though they cannot all three possibly be true without qualification. Hence, instead of using a dialectical method to arrive at a nondialectical conception of Being, as Plato tended to do, and instead of using a purely phenomenological method to describe the dialectical transformations of Being, as Hegel tended to do, each of these modes of thinking must be seen as tensionally transforming the others, without any ultimate closure.[70] Or as I said some years ago, if philosophical thought is not to be mythic, nonsensical or literally absurd, it must be invariably and irreducibly metaphorical.[71] It must never lose a healthy sense of irony about its own systematic aspirations.

Fortunately, moreover, none of this is quite as mysterious as it might sound. To claim that archaeological, teleological, and semiological thinking must tensionally transform one another is at least to claim that they must be accommodating enough to be truth-functionally compatible with one another. This much can be understood even in terms of the Platonic formulation of the priniple of identity. It could not be true without qualification to say (in the teleological framework of actions and values) that someone categorically could have done otherwise, if it were also true without qualification to say (in the archaeological framework of events and causes) that his body movements were inevitable.[72] Each of these types of explanation must give a little. Teleological thinking must give up Sartre's notion of absolute spontaneity for something like Merleau-Ponty's notion of habitual sedimentation, while archaeological thinking must grant that it can at best provide only probabilistic causal explanations of electro-chemical impulses.[73] And similarly, semiological thinking must confess that the conventions it appeals to only tend to be in play, given a sufficient degree of pragmatic acceptance, just as teleological thinking must confess that the acceptance of conventions is usually not deliberate.

What these truth-functional correlations do not account for, however, is how any of the truths that are being correlated are themselves possible. This is where, and why, the tensional formulation of the principle of identity is needed. Nor need this formulation be regarded as excessively paradoxical. To claim that a given text can be itself only by virtue of being other than itself is obviously not to claim that it must be different from itself in the sense in which one text may be different from, or dependent upon, another. Rather, what is being claimed is that every text, or work of art, is what it is, a thing to which nouns and adjectives can be applied, only by virtue of being an activity, or artistic process, to which verbs and adverbs can be applied. In other words, just as Marx construed capital as frozen labor, so works of art can be construed as frozen creativity. Far from abolishing the distinction between the work of art as a semiological noun and the work of art as a teleological verb, however, each can only be as the absence of the other. What is represented, expressed, or compositionally exemplified *in* any work of art must never be confused with the absent origins of the work. And yet if the work did not bear the *trace* of those absent origins, it would not be what it is, any more than those origins would be what they are if they did not culminate in something like that work.[74] Thus, given the tensional noun-verb status of all cultural phenomena, neither side of the hyphen can be regarded as ontologically more fundamental. Nor can the hyphen itself, which separates what it unifies, be removed.

Furthermore, physical reality can also be what it is only by virtue of being other than itself. As has already been argued, inert events can be known to be what they are in themselves only insofar as they are in some sense for us, or are representeds for some possible act of representing. They are in-themselves-for-us in an irreducibly tensional manner. And, in opposition to the simple metaphysics of presence, they could not even be for us unless, or until, some physical mode of being emerged whose presence is permeated by absence. Nor is this to suggest that consciousness must be either detachable from the body or in causal interaction with it. Rather, in line with the conception of the lived body developed by Sartre and Merleau-Ponty, what it does entail is that the body lived through—in contrast to the body looked at—must function projectively as both a spatial point of view and a temporal point of departure.[75] In Whiteheadian terms, the lived body must have a single location, but it cannot have a simple location.[76] It must orient from itself not only toward what presently surrounds it, but also toward both the past and the future.

Finally, this helps to clarify in turn what it means to claim that human actions can be what they are only by virtue of being other than themselves in a doubly tensional sense. While it is true that the real author of any text cannot be simply a character in some other text, it is also true that no one creates or thinks *ex nihilo.* And while it is likewise true that mere body movements are not actions, any more than purely physical propensities are intentional, it is equally true that no one acts without a body. Mediating as they do between World 3 and World 1, our teleological performances are influenced by both without being strictly determined by either. On the one hand, we are all to some degree constrained by the conventional codifications that define the cultural world in which we participate. And, on the other hand, we are also to some degree constrained by the genetic code we have physically inherited. Nevertheless, it is precisely because we are to some extent over-determined in both of these ways that some degree of personal freedom can never be ontologically denied, even though it may be politically taken away. Given a possible conflict between enculturation and heredity, as well as possible conflicts among the various social roles we are called upon to play, we all not only can, but must, in the end decide how to resolve such conflicts, in one way or another, within at least some limited range of real alternatives. Consequently, just as we can never get beyond the creative-discovery of truth, so we can never get beyond the *con-strained-freedom* of our own behavior.

In short, what the dialectical method of tensional transformation provides is a proper understanding of what the game of the world is like. To play the game, however, one must turn from transcendental and dialectical thinking to the *a posteriori* modes of archaeological, teleological, and semiological thinking whose possible cooperation—in continually challenging one another—has been philosophically established and theoretically reconciled.

Notes

1. Robert Nozick 1981, pp. 1–24.
2. Immanuel Kant, *The Critique of Pure Reason,* translated by Norman K. Smith London: Macmillan and Co., 1929, pp. 129–79. Even the difference I go on to point out could be questioned, however. Kant's three critiques could be roughly construed as analogous to what I call archaeological, teleological, and semiological thinking.
3. I return in my later discussion of dialectical thinking to the nature of mythic thought. Some of the differences between Hegel and Heidegger can be clarified in this connection.
4. The terms "signifier" and "signified" are borrowed from Ferdinand de Saussure 1960. But I use these terms to encompass various developments in Anglo-American philosophy of language as well.
5. My formulation especially of the first two steps owes a considerable debt to Strawson (1966, pp. 83–93).
6. Sellars makes this point (Sellars 1948).
7. Polanyi 1966, pp. 3–25.
8. Sartre 1966, p. lxiii.

9. Heidegger 1962, p. 32–35.

10. Brown and Zenneberg 1954.

11. Wittgenstein 1953, pp. 193–229.

12. Merleau-Ponty 1962, p. 183.

13. Vico 1948, p. 446.

14. Croce 1955, pp. 1–11.

15. Foucault 1972, pp. 12, 92–95.

16. Cassirer argues for something like this, as well as Foucault (Cassier 1953, pp. 73–144).

17. Heidegger 1962, pp. 121–31.

18. Heidegger 1962, pp. 95–102.

19. Heidegger 1962, p. 96. While the early Wittgenstein was correct in arguing that values cannot be located in a world that is merely present-at-hand, he was wrong in suggesting an emotivist account of value. It makes no sense at all to be either for or against what is initially perceived to be a mere fact. Ludwig Wittgenstein 1961, 6.41.

20. I am borrowing this distinction between perspectivity and respectivity from Lovejoy 1960, pp. 157–58.

21. Heidegger 1962, p. 70.

22. Barthes develops this sense in which a signified may itself become a signifier (Barthes 1968, p. 90).

23. Foucault 1972, pp. 141–48. Foucault's insistence that originality can be no less decentered than conformity would seem to constitute one of the basic differences between him and the early Heidegger.

24. Heidegger does not use this term. But it does seem to be appropriate, especially since it might also suggest the German word *Abhandeln,* or the social process of bargaining and discussion. Moreover, Popper also refers to entities of this sort as unembodied (Popper and Eccles 1977, p. 41).

25. Foucault 1972, p. 47.

26. Foucault 1973.

27. I am alluding here to Heidegger's distinction between *Geredete* (said in the talk) and *Beredete* (talked about) (Heidegger 1962, p. 205).

28. This should by no means be confused, however, with the notion of inevitable progress. That notion involved a mythic confusion of teleological thinking with archaeological thinking.

29. I will return to this point in my subsequent discussion of dialectical thinking.

30. Sartre 1957.

31. Foucault 1972, p. 73.

32. Rudolf Carnap, "Empiricism, Semantics and Ontology," reprinted in Carnap 1956a.

33. Foucault 1972, p. 118; Barthes 1972. In stressing the sense in which our thoughts are confined by social conventions, Barthes suggests that it might be more accurate, if less grammatical, to say not that I have written (J'ai ecrit), but that I am written (Je suis ecrit), or even that one writes me (On m'acrit).

34. Kuhn 1970a, pp. 43–51.

35. Norton 1977, pp. 17–27. Norton contrasts the conventionalism of both Carnap and Quine with more traditional, essentialist ontologies.

36. The downward solid arrows indicate categorical entailment, while the upward broken arrows indicate conditional entailment.

37. Gadamer 1980, pp. 1, 122.

38. Gadamer 1980, p. 96.
39. MacIntyre makes this point (MacIntyre 1981, p. 96).
40. Ryle seems to take this conventionalist approach (Ryle 1949, pp. 122–124).
41. Carnap, "Empiricism," in Carnap 1956.
42. Heidegger 1962, p. 34.
43. Toulmin 1972.
44. Whitehead 1929, pp. 523–27.
45. Monod 1972, pp. 2–44.
46. Davidson 1980, pp. 3–19.
47. Ryle 1949, pp. 86–92.
48. Goldman 1970, pp. 137–69.
49. Davidson 1980, p. 79.
50. Goldman 1970, pp. 59–61.
51. Sartre 1966, p. 478.
52. Ryle, for example, asserts the first condition, but fails to assert the second (Ryle 1949, p. 127).
53. Austin 1961b, pp. 153–80.
54. Austin 1961b.
55. This is what motivates Strawson to reject Kant's transcendental idealism, thereby eliminating any supposedly "subjective origin" for the *a priori* conditions of objective reality (Strawson 1966, pp. 235–73).
56. C. D. Broad, "Determinism, Indeterminism and Libertarianism," in Broad 1952a, pp. 195–217.
57. Strawson argues this quite effectively (Strawson 1966, p. 146).
58. Derrida 1976, p. 12.
59. Heidegger 1962, pp. 244–73; Peirce 1965, vol. I, pp. 173–80.
60. Wittgenstein attempted something like this in the *Tractatus* (1961, paragraphs 5.6–5.64).
61. Gadamer points out not only what the ramifications of this formulation of the principle of identity are in Platonic thought, but also how Hegel completely misunderstood what Plato was saying (Gadamer 1980, p. 22).
62. Heidegger 1969, pp. 23–25.
63. Hegel 1967, pp. 789–808.
64. Heidegger 1966, pp. 43–57.
65. Derrida 1976, p. 23.
66. Derrida 1976, p. 24.
67. Kojève 1969, p. 207; Habermas 1979, p. 68; Popper and Eccles 1977, p. 47.
68. Popper and Eccles 1977, p. 48.
69. Derrida 1976, p. 50.
70. Kojève contrasts Plato and Hegel in this way (Kojève 1969, pp. 179–81).
71. Berggren 1962–63, Parts I & II.
72. Bogen argues this point effectively in opposition to Melden (Bogen, "Physical Determinism," in Care and Landesman 1968); Melden, *Free Action* 1961.
73. Merleau-Ponty 1962, pp. 434–41.
74. Derrida develops this notion of a trace (Derrida 1976, p. 61).
75. Sartre 1966, pp. 303–51; Merleau-Ponty 1962, pp. 148–73.
76. Whitehead 1929, p. 208.

11 Philosophical Refutations

Hector-Neri Castaneda

Philosophical Method has the anti-Augustinian property. When somebody asks me about philosophical method I know what it is. But when nobody asks me and I am philosophizing, I often do not know what it is.

Oscar Thend, *On Philosophical Method*

Ce n'est pas Gäste qui exprime le pluriel, mais l'opposition *Gast:Gäste*.

Ferdinand de Saussure, *Cours de linguistique generale*

Thus, it became evident to me that it was necessary to resort to words (and concepts), sentences (and propositions), and reasonings to study in them the truth of realities.

Plato, *Phaedo* 99E

1. Introduction

The central problems of philosophy are perennial. Why? Problems and views recede from the center of dispute, only to dominate the scene later on. Why don't theories stay refuted, and problems dissolved?

Refutation is more than 80 percent of what goes on in so-called analytic philosophy, yet the theory of refutation of philosophical theories or views has received scanty attention. Attacks on method have, of course, a trailing view on the nature of refutation. And views on philosophical method have an implicit companion view on philosophical refutation. Thus, many valuable remarks on philosophical refutation are dispersed throughout the major philosophical contributions. Here I propose to engage in an exegesis and assessment of some of the most commonly practiced techniques of refutation. I offer a collection of data for the general theory of philosophical refutation.

In particular, I want to examine the scope and function of the following techniques: Appeals to Ockham's Razor; Spurious Demands of Deductive Proof; the Coffee-Pot Approach; Counterexampling; the Divide-and-Conquer Technique; the Bypassing Attacks; Guilty-by-Association Attacks. My diagnosis is that often these refutational techniques create much more obscurity than illumination. The fruitful role of counterexampling is not exactly what some of its practitioners take it to be. Indeed, philosophical refutation is a chimera.

Refutation is the obverse side of method. It is the topic of Negative Meta-philosophy. But it needs to be treated as a genuine topic, not merely by default. Nevertheless, the proper method of a field of study is the entry to the refutation proprietary to that field. However, as my friend Oscar Thend hasn't tired of insisting, philosophical method has the anti-Augustinian property. We must consider a particular problem when we are discussing method. Therefore, we must enter any discussion of philosophical refutation via the exegesis of some philosophical problem. Here we enter the discussion through the well known "Paradox of Reference," which by being well known should provide an easy start.

2. A Perennial Problem: The Structure of the World

A method is good—or bad—depending on the purpose it serves. Philosophical method is no exception. In philosophy there are many fields, and within them many different programs have been pursued. There is, however, *one* philosophical objective that has stood at the center of philosophical activity throughout history, namely: to understand as fully as it is feasible the structure of the world and of our experience of it. This objective has demarcated a network of problems in the field that has been called ontology, more precisely, phenomenological ontology, the ontology of experience. That field is different from metaphysical ontology, the study of the underlying reality of both world and experience as it might be in itself, independently of its being experienced. By experience here is meant the totality of our dealings with the world. Thus, in phenomenological ontology we seek to unravel the most pervasive patterns of the different types of experience: perceptual, scientific, aesthetic, moral, political, religious, erotic, poetic, ludic, etc. We aim, as ontologists, to propose views or hypotheses about the contours of those patterns, which, regardless of the particular contents of a particular experience, are constitutive of such experiences. Our ultimate goal is, of course, to formulate *the* master theory of the world and experience that integrates all those hypotheses into a coherent, comprehensive, and unified picture of the grand design of the world and our experience of it.

But what right do we have to speak of "*the* master theory"? May we assume that our local and unrelated hypotheses about different segments of that grand design will fit together harmoniously? No, indeed. We have *no* right to assume that there *is* one master theory at the end of our research, awaiting the completion of our efforts. Likewise, we have *no* right to assume there is *not* just one master theory at the end as an asymptotic limit of our collective endeavours.

Evidently, the philosophical, structural theories we hypothesize must perforce be *tentative,* subject to the modifications required by their embedding in more comprehensive theories. *Embedment in a more comprehensive theory is, at bottom, the fundamental test of fruitfulness, hence, of genuine adequacy, of a theory.*

The hypothetical character of ontological theorizing, together with the enormous magnitude of the world, demand both humility and respect for *each* of the well-knit comprehensive alternative theories built upon a rich, variegated, and complex data base. Consequently, one of the most important timely theses about the methodology of ontology (and of metaphysics) is this: the most urgent philosophical NEED is the development of *all* the comprehensive theories that the *cumulation* of *all* of the data at present available allow for. This methodological pluralism surges from the idea that *before* we have produced a total theory of the world and of experience, we cannot be sure which of the many partial theories on one problem, even a theory on many problems, can be extended, coherently and adequately, to a total theory. There is at least the thinkable, but unprovable, possibility that there may be not just one, but *many* total theories of the world and of experience. *If* this is so, then our methodological pluralism is undergirded by a deep-seated ontological pluralism. *If* this is how things stand between the world and ourselves, then all the different theories of the world and of experience *must* be developed in full detail. Then, our partial theories should be extended more and more so as to make them more and more comprehensive. These elementary points have several crucial consequences.

For one thing, the most satisfying philosophical experience is to be able to see the world in different ways. In Wittgenstein's analogy with the duck-rabbit design, the one and external reality is better understood if we can see it now as having the full "duck" depicted in a comprehensive theory, and now as being the full "rabbit" depicted in another theory—and, indeed, the whole of the other designs that other master theories depict, or, better, allow to come forth.

Second, the philosophical task of our times should be the enrichment of our arsenal of *comprehensive* theories. The petty disputes between two very local and small theories should be overcome in the process of building larger and larger theories. All the totally comprehensive theories are precisely in the same boat as master designs of the world, through which reality allows itself to appear. The same holds for comprehensive partial theories catering to the same rich data.

For obvious professional reasons philosophers tend to work on fashionable problems within the fashionable views. This is most reasonable. Fashions are magnificent stimulants of progress. They mobilize a large amount of the needed cooperation for the full development of certain approaches. Yet fashions are often not pluralistic enough but are, instead, very constrictive. To stimulate the development of the exciting and rewarding comprehensive systems of the world and experience we urgently need, we must not merely be tolerant of but be actually supportive of the unfashionable approaches. (Fortunately, some of us can afford to work outside the dominant streams of philosophical research of our time.) At each time, all the encompassing theories singing to the same rich data base are voices in one and the same philosophical symphony.[1]

3. Philosphical Data

Because of their maximal generality and pervasiveness, ontic structures can be found anywhere, underlying any claim whatever we make about reality, or even about irreality and fiction. Any experience whatever, any object whatever, any entity whatever is a source of philosophical questions. Consider, for instance, a *comma,* the one after the italicized token of '*comma*' that the read will perceive. By then it will have endured and will have a history. It is an intersubjective entity. Here we have quite a number of pervasive structures that need understanding and clarification: having properties; being a subject of relations; being part of several persons' visual fields; coming into existence; having a history; being a subject of change; having causal connections; being an individual object, rather than a property; etc.

That tiny comma is, furthermore, enveloped by a complicated network of deep structures through which it is a token of a linguistic sign. Patently, that comma is a linguistic token by appearing in the midst of strings of marks that count as English words. Thus, that comma, as a linguistic token, sits at the convergence of phonetic structures that are themselves molded as linguistic units by syntactic and semantic structures. And, of course, semantic structures are such because they represent, and are causally involved with, the more pervasive structures that connect the mental with the physical.

Evidently, any physical object whatever gives rise to one and the same battery of philosophical questions. This has sometimes been misinterpreted as philosophy being an entirely *a priori* discipline in need of no empirical data. The situation as just described belies this conclusion. We *can* start our philosophical questioning with *any* physical object whatever in its empirical context as it is at a given time; but so to start is to start with empirical data. We must distinguish between the pervasiveness of certain data and the nonempirical character of the data. Philosophy needs the *initial empirical and existential assumption* that the universe contains certain particular entities. Basic descriptions of particular entities are at the basis of philosophical investigation.

Yet a fruitful philosophical investigation cannot be based on a short description of a particular entity. The structures we investigate as philosophers span the whole universe, regardless of how vividly and concentrated those structures may be represented at the entity we have selected as a starting point. The universal structures we want to understand may be more tortuous and circuitous than may appear at any particular juncture. To illustrate, the above example of a comma, as well as any other physical object whatever, may initially suggest that perhaps what accounts for the comma's individuality is also what accounts for its being a subject of change, and also for the comma's having causal connections, for its occupying a place and time, for its unity as an entity, for its perceptibility, etc. A careful reflection, comparing the situation of the comma with the situations of other entities, especially the ones to which it is related throughout its career, reveals that those general structural features of the comma cannot be simply accounted for in the same way. The structures are *more complex* than they appear at their intersection at each physical object—or psychic entity, for that matter. Consequently, those structures must be studied *in the context* of many and variegated entities and their relationships.

Philosophical data are, then, each of the entities we find in the universe and each of their properties and relations. Ordinary facts of experience, general facts discovered by observation, and more general facts postulated by science, are all philosophical data. But there is another most (caution: most, *not* more) important type of philosphical datum, namely, the *semantico-syntactical contrasts of ordinary language,* especially in one's own idiolects—as they manifest themselves in large linguistic contexts. Just as we must consider networks of objects to glean the ontic structures involving them, we must consider, *not* mere isolated sentences, let alone words or other single expressions, but networks of sentences and of *discourses* in which significant portions of ontic structure are depicted. The structure of the world we face in experience, and of the experience through which we encounter reality, is precisely the structure of *all* the semantico-syntactic contrasts of the language through which we have that encounter.[2]

4. Our Entry Case: The "Paradox of Reference"

Given that the fundamental structures of the world impinge on and converge at particulars, the nature of our reference to particulars and the nature of the particulars we refer to constitute major problems in phenomenological ontology, in phenomenological linguistics, and in theory of the referring mind. These problems can be found in reasonably complex cases of reference. Consider, for example, the following situation:

(1)   Jocasta, at the beginning of the pestilence, believed that both (a) Oedipus's father was (the same as) Oedipus's father and (b) Oedipus's father was not (the same as) the previous King of Thebes.

(2)   Oedipus's father was (the same as) the previous King of Thebes [or so we believe].

(3)   Jocasta's belief as reported in (1) is self-consistent.

(T1)   For any individuals x and y: if x is (genuinely or strictly) identical with y, then whatever is true of x is true of y, and vice versa.

(T2)   The sentential matrix (like other similar expressions in which 'blanks' *not* mentioned but used in (1)) "Jocasta, at the beginning of the pestilence, believed that: both (a) Oedipus's father was (the same as) Oedipus's father and (b) Oedipus's father was not (the same as) _____" expresses something true of the individual such that an expression used to refer to it put in the blank in the matrix yields a sentence expressing a truth.

(T3)   The expression "was (the same as)" in premise (2) denotes (or expresses) strict or genuine identity, governed by (T1).

By (T2), premise (1) expresses something true of the individual, the previous King of Thebes. By (T1) and (T3) whatever is true of this individual is true of the individual Oedipus's father. Hence, by (T2) and (2), the sentence (4) below should express the same truth that (1) expresses about the previous King of Thebes, except that it should not be a truth about the individual Oedipus's father:

(4)   Jocasta, at the beginning of the pestilence, believed that: both (a) Oedipus's father was (the same as) Oedipus's father, and (b) Oedipus's father was not (the same as) Oedipus's father.

But (4) contradicts (3). This is one case of the "Paradox of Reference." There are other cases.

Patently, when we confront a contradiction, we must give up something. What?

5. Logical and Theoretical Exegesis of the "Paradox of Reference"

Logically, the situation is simply that on the more or less standard logic we have taken for granted, the set of propositions (1), (2),

(3), (T1), (T2), and (T3) imply a contradiction. Hence, logically, we must renounce at least one of these six premises. Of course, we can *also* change our logic. But logic does not tell us which of the premises we must renounce. For this we must make a *theoretical decision*. As far as I can see, we have, therefore, in principle (at least) *six* different types of theory that just within the present datum seem initially plausible. Here is the juncture at which the fashions step in. It is nowadays most fashionable to say that psychological matrices like the one referred to in (T2) do not express properties of objects. This is immaterial; for nothing in the above derivation of the contradiction hinges on the word 'property,' which was deliberately left unused. The point must be that psychological sentences cannot express anything true, or false, of individuals that at all appearances are mentioned in them. Another fashionable thing to say is that Leibniz's law, a name given to (T1), does not apply in psychological contexts, like (1). It is also generally fashionable to accept premises (1)–(3).

My meta-philosophical position here includes two tenets. *First,* it seems to me utterly irresponsible to claim to "solve" the "paradox" by *simply* rejecting (T1) or (T2). The serious rejection of *any* of the six premises of the "paradox" carries with it the commitment to develop a theory that deal with the problems that lurk behind the "paradox." These problems are initially three: (i) What is it to be an individual? (ii) What is it to have properties, or having something true of it? (iii) What is identity? These are the problems of *individuation, predication,* and *identity.* But as already hinted at, the problem of propertyhood is there, too, just as much as the problem of *truth.* Futhermore, since we want the *whole* world and the *whole* of experience to come out as the detailed topic of a master all-encompassing theory, *any* theory that rejects any one of the six premises of the "paradox" has to be embedded in more and more comprehensive theories.

Which approach is better? Who knows? I want *all* the six initially plausible approaches to be pursued as far as they can. Perhaps some of them will conflate; and some of them will branch out into sub-approaches. In my view of philosphy *none* should be spared until it collapses of its own weight. This is my *second* tenet.

One note may not be amiss. The nonfashionable approaches will not be easily pursued. Thus, two interesting programs can be neglected. One program—the one I have spent more time developing under the title *Guise Theory*—takes as departure point premise (T3). According to this approach, the individuals—Oedipus's father and the previous King of Thebes—are the same, as established by premise (2), but they are not strictly identical. Hence, since strict identity is governed by a wholly unrestricted application of (T1), they are the same in a form of sameness not governed by (T1). The other nonfashionable approach rejects premise (3). I would like this approach to be developed with views on identity, individuation, predication, reference, truth, etc.

One important methodological point is worth recording. Many a researcher feels obliged to refute alternative views before he/she develops a new one. This has one advantage, namely, that their research cannot help taking into account the data on which the theories he/she attacks are erected. (It does not guarantee that, of course.) But such proceedings have one defect. Often the researcher forgets that a partial theory cannot be erected upon a refutation of alternative approaches. An approach that seems defeated at a given time, because the theories embodying it are cumbersome, may, in the very aspects that make it cumbersome, contain structures that will be useful for explaining additional data. Later on the approach is revived, perhaps deprived of some old assumptions. And the merry-go-round starts all over again. Given that we only have partial theories to be embedded in more encompassing ones, and we cannot predict that other theories cannot be embedded within larger ones, even if with some revisions, there is *no* need as such to refute the existing, or prospective alternatives. *What is needed is a theorization catering to large collections of rich and complex data:* all the data available at the time of theorization. We need comprehensive theories.

6. The World-Mind Tension at the Core of the "Paradox of Reference"

The preceding determination of (at least) six initially plausible approaches to the "paradox of reference" was mechanical: Six premises, six approaches. This robotlike analysis was tempered by the remark that none of the six approaches is worth considering seriously, unless it is developed to the point of dealing with the structural problems above mentioned (predication, individuation, etc.).

We can obtain a more direct guidance from the "paradox" by asking ourselves: What exactly is the tension, the paradoxical tension depicted in the "paradox"? A little reflection reveals that the crucial tension in the "paradox" is the tension between the *sameness* between Oedipus's father and the previous King of Thebes proclaimed by premise (2), and the *non-sameness,* the difference between these two proclaimed by premise (1). Whereas premise (2) asserts that *somehow* in the real world [or in the beliefs of those persons who believe (1)–(3)] Oedipus's father and the previous King of Thebes are the same, premise (1) reports that, as far as Jocasta's beliefs are concerned, these two individuals are not the same. The solution to the "paradox" cannot simply consist of rejecting one of the premises. It must consist of a theory that resolves the conflict between the *worldly sameness* of premise (2) and the *epistemic sameness,* or lack thereof, involved in premise (1). Patently, this requires a theory as to how the world [or we the speakers] and (Jocasta's) mind connect. Clearly, the tension arises because of the finitude of Jocasta's mind. Her mind is, or has, a representation of the world, but only a cursory representation, a finite one. These are the profound issues underlying the "paradox of reference." The total solution is, consequently, a total theory of the world and of our experience of it. Can we be happy with anything less? At least the largest structures should be included in any significant solution.

7. The Fregean Sense/Referent Solution and Guise Theory

Frege thought seriously and deeply about the "paradox." For that reason it is justified that some philosophers refer to it as "Frege's Paradox." His solution seems to me brilliant. It goes directly to the heart of the issue: the tension between wordly sameness and epistemic sameness. (The expressions are mine, however.) Frege solves the tension by assigning different individuals to the two samenesses in question. The worldly sameness proclaimed by premise (2) is strict identity, governed by Leibniz's law (T1), and it holds in what he calls the (primary) *referents* of the two terms 'Oedipus's father' and 'the previous King of Thebes.' On the other hand, the non-sameness proclaimed by premise (1) is strict non-identity, governed by (T1), but it holds between *two* different (primary) *individual senses,* each functioning as the meaning of one of the two preceding terms. Thus, Frege manages brilliantly to adhere to all six premises, with certain restrictions. For instance, Frege maintains premise (T2), which seems essential to connect world and mind, but in modified form, as expressing a property of senses, not of referents.

Frege's solution lies within the category of *individuals*, but preserves—or so it seems—the other categories. There is, however, a problem about predication, i.e., what it is to have properties: Do senses have properties in the same way, or sense, in which referents do? On the other hand, Frege proposes a *dual semantic connection* between a singular term and its referent (if any) and its sense. Likewise, senses become intermediaries between referents and the mind that thinks of them.

One consequence of Frege's solution is that the following becomes false:

(SH*)   *Thesis of Semantic Homogeneity of Singular Terms:* A singular term *t* has, or may have, exactly the same meaning and referent in both direct-speech and indirect-speech constructions.

For instance, according to (SH*) the terms 'Oedipus's father' and 'the previous King of Thebes' have exactly the same meaning and referent in both premises (1) and (2). This is ruled out by Frege's solution. Shall we say that this automatically shows that Frege's solution is in error? *Not by my lights.* Yet I like (SH*) and am anxious to see *comprehensive* theories that incorporate (SH*). Of course, such theories have to give up Frege's sense/referent duality. Nevertheless, another duality has to be introduced in order to be able to account for the paradoxical tension between worldly sameness and epistemic sameness. This much is clear.

There is a long history—of which Bertrand Russell is simply the latest, most brilliant, and most thorough representative—that conflates identity, sameness, existence, and predication. An early stage of that history was developed around the old medieval slogan that only existents have properties. This slogan conflates existence with having properties. Since identity is a property that everything (that exists) has, the blending of existence with identity and with having properties is a natural projection base for many theories. Thus, the attempts to distinguish between identity and sameness, and between these and predication are (still) not fashionable.

Guise Theory started precisely as the view that, since the paradoxical core of the "paradox" is the tension between the worldly sameness proclaimed by premise (2) and the epistemic difference proclaimed by premise (1), the simplest (though nonfashionable) solution to the "paradox" is recognition that there we must reckon with a sameness that differs from (strict) identity. This solution lies, not at the level of the category of individuals, or even at the category of properties, but at the level of *predication*. The individuals are kept the same, and they have to be those that can be different. Individuation and (strict) identity go hand in hand. Thus, Oedipus's father and the previous King of Thebes are different individuals. These are the individuals denoted by the singular terms 'Oedipus's father' and 'the previous King of Thebes,' whether these occur in direct-speech sentences or in indirect-speech constructions, thus conforming to (SH*). Such individuals, called *individual guises,* are not intermediaries between the thinking mind and the world: they *are* the only referents of the singular terms. They are thinkable individuals. This requires that the world be composed of systems of guises formed through the linkage of guises by the special relation of worldly sameness of premise (2). This sameness turns out to be in Guise Theory a special form of predication called *consubstantiation.* Since Guise Theory is nonfashionable in distinguishing between identity, existence, individuality, and predication, it can easily apply to a comprehensive treatment of fiction and literary language in unison with the language we use to describe perceptual experiences and our beliefs about existents. For this it postulates other forms of predication, which are called consociation, transubstantiation, conflation, and internal predication. Individual guises do not have to exist. One interesting thesis is that persons are consubstantiations of psychological and physical guises. Hence a mind is contingently identical with the body in a way very much the same in which the morning star is the same as the evening star.

One feature of Guise Theory is the vanishment of Frege's (primary) referents from singular reference. All singular reference is to individual guises, like Oedipus's father, the previous King of Thebes, Jocasta's second husband, etc. Because of their infinite nature, Frege's (primary) referents appear as undetermined referents of *general* reference through quantifiers. In this respect individual guises, which are ontically a good deal like Frege's individual senses, do serve as intermediaries between the mind and Frege's primary referents. But the mediation is neither semantic nor psychological: it is *purely doxastic.* The preceding sketches of Frege's Sense/Referent Theory and Guise Theory are very slim. But their contrasts and their common base are important foil for the ensuing discussion of philosophical method. For each of the theories, the reader can go to the relevant literature.[3] The crucial point at this juncture is that in the preceding discussion we have shunned comparative value judgments. We are not here promoting Guise Theory against Frege's Sense/Referent View, nor are we suggesting that the latter is a better view. Both are treated here as *complementary* views of the same reality of reference. In the model of Wittgenstein's remarks, one presents that reality as a "rabbit," the other as a "duck." It is nice and educational to be able to see that reality in two ways, as well as in other ways.

8. Deduction in Philosophy

An immediate consequence of the preceding discussion is that all those philosophers who ask that a theory be the endpoint of a deductive argument are out of order. The same applies to the historical work in which a writer is considering the proofs for their theories that philosphers were supposed to have furnished. It may be the case, e.g., that Descartes thought he had a proof for this or that; but we know better and see that his philosophical hypotheses do not need deductive support: they may, or may not be supported, by the facts of experience, which those hypotheses should illuminate.

Deductions take place in the exegesis of data and in the development of a theory. For instance, the exegesis of the above datum pertaining to the "paradox of reference" involved the deduction that yielded the contradiction. Nothing less than a full deduction can serve the purpose. But the move from the datum, the contradiction, to a theory, whatever theory, is *not* deductive. The theory results from a hypothesizing leap, and the theory is good, or not, if it solves the original contradiction *and* can be extended to a larger theory solving other contradictions, and provides a rearrangement of data that shows a cohesive way of looking at things.

9. How Can a Philosophical Theory Be Refuted?

So, how can one refute a theory? If deductions are not required to connect the theory with the data, how can it be refuted? This is the exciting question. The answer is that perhaps no theory can be refuted, except within the network of assumptions within its own approach. Obviously, a refutation will have to have its premises. Equally obviously, the one who defends a theory through thick and thin can always find in those refutations at least one premise that he can reject. The argument in support of this premise need not help, because it will only show that another premise will have to be rejected. Indeed, a dispute of this sort is most useful to the defender of a theory: through it he/she can find out all the premises his opponent holds and he/she rejects. Philosophical dispute is inherently perennial. Why? Because we are dealing with the most pervasive and general features of the world, and we can always modify our hypotheses in the light of other experiences and cases.

Clearly, then, it is not only a descriptive truth about actual philosophical practice that, as some philosophers have observed, the *modus tollens* of one philosopher is the *modus ponens* of another. This is exactly as it *should* be, if we are ever going to have the many different alternative views—catering to the same data—that we urgently need. I am jettisoning the belief that for the construction of a theory a crushing refutation of alternatives is required. The effort at refutation does, however, sustain morally the constructive work. One often feels that what one is doing is worth doing only if it is the only thing to stand. If only one hypothesis or theory is to be correct, then one feels that one must destroy the existing hypotheses to have the courage to erect a new one. Thus, while the ludic and esthetic sense is not deeply imbued in the philosophical profession, refutation is good for the philosopher's morale.

Philosophical theories, at least the comprehensive ones, cannot be refuted. Thus, a more constructive endeavor should be interchanged for the prevailing polemical zeal. In any case, many of the refutational techniques in standard practice leave much to be desired. This I proceed to show by subjecting some valuable examples to exegesis.

10. Ockham's Razor and the Charge of Complexity

Simplicity is of little importance. Simplicity has to do with our abilities to understand and to do things, or with the time available to do certain things. We prefer simpler theories, not because they are truer, but because we can understand and apply them more easily. For this reason working within *one* approach or program, when we come to a fork in theory development, we should (perhaps) choose the simpler alternative—provided that the rest of the theory already built up remains constant and there is no diminution in the data the theory caters to. Even so the judgment of simplicity is ephemeral and may have to be revised when new data become available.

An often forgotten truth: judgments of simplicity are complex. They are comparative, involving *two theories and exactly the same data base.*

All that is very simple, trivial, and agreed upon by every philosopher. That is so at least when we discuss method in general. However, when we are philosophizing things are not so clear. Sometimes an author simply attacks a theory on the ground that it is too complex, without mentioning the alternative that is supposed to be simpler. Of course, rarely authors investigate whether the theories they claim to be too complex deal with exactly the same data as the alternatives they may have in mind.

Sometimes an author simply argues that *a* theory violates Ockham's Razor—just by itself! He says nothing else. Now, Ockham's Razor is this: Do not multiply entities beyond necessity. Clearly, theories that violate Ockham's razor are, ontologically, too complex. Patently the claim that a theory, or author, violates Ockham's Razor *cannot* be grounded on just the major premise that is Ockham's Razor itself. The major premise may be assumed to be accepted by everybody, including the theorist under attack. The issue, when the charge of a violation of Ockham's Razor is hurled, *is* precisely the minor premise: Does the theory under consideration posit more entities than the ones demanded by the data? Palpably, the minor premise requires a comparison of *two* theories, and the same collection of data, not just the comparison between a collection of data and one theory. Yet the crucial, simpler theory needed to justify the claim is seldom, if ever, brought in for comparison.

Everybody agrees, of course, on the need to adduce a comparison of theories when the claim is made that Ockham's Razor is violated. But here again we must look at what philosophers do, not at what they say. Let us consider one simple, subtle, and intriguing example, which relates directly to the central topic of this paper. Let us take advantage of our discussion of Guise Theory above. As remarked, the theory provides an ontological account of fiction and literary language. This is explained in my "Fiction and Reality: Their Fundamental Connections," which also contains a large collection of relevant data and discusses some alternative theories of fiction and fictional entities. Now, in an appendix to a brilliant study on both theories about and problems of fictional discourse, Robert Howell has attacked my subtheory of fiction.[4] His main argument relevant to our methodological discussion is as follows:

> Castaneda's treatment is embedded in a complex metaphysical system. Both that treatment and this general system appear to require accepting the idea that a distinct individual or object corresponds to each distinct set of (monadic) properties. As I noted in discussing Parsons in Section 1, I find this idea—which seems to multiply individuals beyond necessity—very difficult to grant. (*Op. cit.,* 175.)

This is a rich and very instructive text, deserving of careful scrutiny. We cannot do full justice to it here and must limit ourselves to the following methodological observations.

First, Howell's remark that the theory he is discussing, let us call it the *G-CCC theory* (short for the theory of Guises, Consubstantiation, Consociation, and Conflation) "seems to multiply individuals beyond necessity" is most casual. He does not offer even the slightest hint as to why the G-CCC theory introduces one more individual than is required by the problems of fictional objects that Howell has posed in his essay—let alone the other problems that he does not consider. Yet this minor premise, to the effect that the G-CCC theory postulates *some* individual that is not needed, is both a crucial issue in the assessment of the theory and a matter of great moment in our understanding of the ontological structure of our experience of fiction.

Second, Howell's suggestion that the theory introduces too many objects is an absolute complaint. Presumably he has in mind his own theory as the other member of the comparison. But, *third,* if this is so, then it is of the utmost urgency to establish that the two theories cater to *exactly* the same collection of data. Yet Howell offers no indication that any comparison of the data at the bases of the theories being compared is even relevant to the judgment as to which one is the simpler one in its ontological commitment to individuals.

Fourth, the whole passage of Howell's just quoted contains a very interested *internal* tension. Howell records the fact that "Castaneda's treatment [of fictional objects] is embedded in a complex general metaphysical system." This strongly suggest that the total system, i.e., the G-CCC theory, has been designed with some data in view *other* than the data pertaining to fictional objects. This is precisely the case in the study that Howell cites. Then G-CCC is an extension of my treatment, call it *T*, of fictional objects, and the data base *D* for *T* is a proper subset of the data base *D'* for G-CCC. *Suppose* that Howell's theory of fictional objects, call it *T'*, caters to exactly the same data *D* to which my treatment *T* of fictional objects caters. *Suppose* further that Howell has established conclusively that his theory of fiction *T'* is simpler than my treatment *T* for the same data *D*. These are heavy suppositions. Nevertheless, it is still open that the G-CCC theory may be simpler than any extension *E(T')* of Howell's theory *T'* of fictional objects catering to the total collection of data *D'*. This is the internal tension in Howell's objection: even *if* he had a way of establishing that his theory of fiction is ontologically simpler than my theory of fiction for the same relevant collection of data *D*, the recognition in his very own claim that my theory of fiction is embedded in a more comprehensive theory, for which he has no comparable theory to offer, undermines the claim that my theory of fiction is ontologically more complex than his, that my theory introduces too many individuals.

Comparisons of theories with respect to simplicity, ontological, formal, or whatever, must be explicit. Even then they are very difficult to establish. Perhaps they can be fruitfully made only when we have reached the most comprehensive theories.

Fifth, let us examine what Howell says about Parsons. Howell's full relevant remark is as follows:

[A]t least four troubling difficulties beset Parson's quasi-actualist treatment of fiction. First—a point that will presumably not move Meinongians themselves—it is *very* hard to believe that a distinct, genuine, and well-individuated object is correlated with every distinct set of properties. Yet without this belief, Parsons' treatment loses all its plausibility. Second, . . . (*Op. cit.,* 133. Original italics.)

Here is a judgment about what entities to recognize in the world for which no grounds or reasons are suggested. Notwithstanding, it would be rash to conclude that there are no data at the basis of the judgment. The data consist of some beliefs about ordinary objects like tables, minerals, plants, animals, and planets. What we have here is something like the Coffee-Pot Approach. (See Section 13 below.) The data are pretty much of the same kind, are left implicit, and no other data are collected—much less exegicized. Few scientists would nowadays dare say that it is very hard to believe that there are individuals of such and such a sort without examining the data for which the theories positing such individuals are built. Consider, e.g., the physical claim, unheard of until this century, that some particles have momentum but no position. The same methodology applies in ontology and in metaphysics. One must be prepared to find unsuspected and surprising entities if one is bent on understanding the general structures of reality and experience. Here again we find the unity of the world, which demands the unity of science and philosophy, both in topics and in methods.

I conclude that appeals to Ockham's razor are often incoherent references to the major premise of an argument, with the crucial minor premise left out of consideration; sometimes they are pseudocomparative judgments with a self-destructive internal tension. In short, they can never substitute for a direct comparison of two theories catering to the very *same* collection of data. The *not* catering to the very same data, by not being attended to in the appeals to Ockham's razor, is often the undoing of such appeals.

11. Deduction and the Refutational Policy of Divide-and-Conquer

As we have recorded, the connection between the data for the illumination or elucidation of which a theory is designed is not deductive. Yet a policy of asking for the reasons for a theory can easily arm itself with the implicit weapon that the connection must be deductive. Indeed, the idea that each of the reasons given in support of a view must provide full support for the view is tantamount to a deductive view of the connection between the reasons and the view. Let us discuss a very subtle and powerful example.

In my views on practical reason, a central place is occupied by the thesis that intending and believing differ *both qua* psychological reality (as networks of different dispositions and propensities) *and* intensionally by having different accusatives. What is intended (which, following Sellars, I often called an *intention*) is different from what is believed (which, following traditional terminology, I frequently call a *proposition*). I have argued at length for this distinction in accusatives, and I have gathered large sets of nearly independent pieces of data. Yet I do not claim that the thesis is deductively proved. My claim is that this thesis, together with other theses about ought-judgments, imperatives, rules, etc., yields a comprehensive and well-knit system of theories.[5]

In an excellent critical study of my *Thinking and Doing*, Roderick Chisholm has attacked that double-accusative theory, and offered the attack as a partial support for a simpler, one-accusative view of his own.[6] This study is important, among other things, because it contains Chisholm's first statement of his view that the fundamental accusatives of believing and of intending are attributes (properties). This intriguing view for the case of believing he has expounded more fully in his masterful treatise *The First Person*.[7] With respect to the methodological issue we are considering, Chisholm's attack on my double-accusative is an example of the refutational policy of Divide-and-Conquer. Here is the beginning of the refutation:

> Castaneda . . . offers a *great variety of reasons and it is not possible to do justice to them all*. In what follows, I will consider *some* of the reasons that he offers—the ones that seem to me most important. I shall restrict myself to the contrast between believing and intending, and will suggest how the traditional conception of these intentional phenomena *might be defended* in view of the considerations Castaneda brings forward. (*Op. cit.,* 388; Chisholm's italics in 'some'; the rest are mine.)

This passage might on a first reading be taken to commit three perplexing operations. *First,* it might be thought to suggest that showing how each of the reasons fails to refute the traditional view suffices to show that the alternative view is mistaken. This is the technique of dividing the force of the reasons for a theory *T*. *Second,* if 'refute' is taking as *logically implies the negation of,* which is how Chisholm *seems* to take it in his following discussion, then the passage contains the claim that the data should imply the falsehood of theory $\sim T$, the contradictory of the alternative theory *T*. *Third,* if this failure of the data to imply the falsehood of‽ $\sim T$ is taken to support $\sim T$, then there is the claim that it is not required that theory $\sim T$, be implied by the data, even though this was demanded for theory T. But aside from dividing the reasons I offer for my theory, Chisholm *cannot* be accused of the other two moves. Indeed, he is very careful in the end to compare his theory as a whole with my theory as a whole and claim that his is *simpler* than mine for the same data. This is a perfectly legitimate move and puts the issue where it should be, namely, at the factual question whether the two theories cater to exactly the same data and whether, assuming both to be consistent, one is really simpler than the other. In any case, *the two* theories should be developed to the hilt; perhaps they can provide materials for a dia-philosophical investigation.[8]

Chisholm does divide my reasons. In the preceding quotation he says that he will select some of my many reasons, and he examines each of the four reasons he selects individually, atomistically. He continues:

> One reason for thinking that intendings have objects of a special sort, according to Castaneda, is the fact that this supposition accounts for certain "non-commutative disjunctions". . . . Certainly the distinction is of basic importance to the theory of intending. But does it *require* us, as Castaneda thinks it does, to appeal to complex relations between different types of intentional objects? There are at least two other possibilities. . . . (*Op. cit.,* p. 388. My italics.)

Chisholm concludes the first segment of criticisms:

> So far, then, we do not seem to *have any reason* for going beyond the ontology of individuals, properties, and propositions. (*Op. cit.,* p. 389; my italics.)

Chisholm writes as if each reason had to be logically sufficient for the theoretical thesis. This proedure does not conform to my view that the data do *not* imply the posited tenets of the theory. In fact, when I assessed the very first reason Chisholm considers, I discussed two alternative theories, which I called *local theories* because they are equally good alternatives for the data; but, I said, we must consider a larger collection of data. I wrote:

> An isolated consideration of intentions (1)–(3) is, of course, capable of suggesting different local views. One such view is . . . we will not argue here that such a theory looks too complicated. On the contrary, we urge anybody interested in developing the suggestion

to do so. The *more theories* there are, the better our understanding of the structure and the functions of practical thinking will be. We must emphasize, however, that the local suggestion about unless-disjunction is worthless, unless both it grows into a theory and, by taking into account all of the relevant data (A)–(L), it grows into a *comprehensive* theory. (*Thinking and Doing*, p. 161f; italics added now.)

Chisholm examines the second and third reasons in the same way. The fourth reason, he claims, is closely connected with my theory and is not independent.

Chisholm recognizes that our philosophical methodologies are in part different:

We have considered particular arguments for the thesis that the objects of intending are proposition-like entities which are not themselves propositions, and I have suggested that *the arguments are not conclusive.* But we must not lose sight of the fact that the thesis is a very comprehensive theory which explains a vast amount of data. The author is convinced that the body of data must be considered cumulatively, and he is inclined, therefore, to reply to particular criticisms of particular arguments with a version of the thesis that the truth is the whole. (*Op. cit.*, p. 390. My italics.)

I hope that the initial discussion of method has made clear the sense in which the truth of a philosophical theory is the whole of the theory together with the criteria of adequacy established by the exegesis of the relevant data. Certainly we must stress the holistic way of treating the reasons, all of the reasons, in their support of a theory.

Chisholm remarks in connection with my fourth reason for my proposition-practition theory that "the proper response is to contrast the general system with one or more of its alternatives" (*Ibid.*, p. 390). Then he proceeds to sketch a most fascinating theory of the contents of belief and intending. It deserves careful development and scrutiny.

It is worth observing that the policy of Divide-and-Conquer can be overdone. Suppose that Carl claims that P is true and he offers *two* reasons: (1) if Q, then P; and (2) Q. Clearly, one can truly say: Carl's first reason does not imply P, and Carl's second reason does not imply P. But it would be excessive to conclude that Carl has given no reason for P. Clearly, a set of nonreasons for P, in the sense that no member of the set implies P, may itself be a powerful reason for P. Obviously, then, the deductive relationship between reasons and conclusion is also holistic. There is, therefore, no reason at all for dividing the reasons for a theory and expecting each reason by itself to establish the theory. The reasons must be taken all together, not even in subsets of principal reasons.

The Divide-and-Conquer refutational tactic can also be used to divide the theses of a view and refute them individually, say, as each being too broad, without taking the whole restrictive impact of the theses taken together.

12. The Constructive Embedding-Plea of Counterexamples

Since the Greeks invented philosophy in the West, counterexamples have been central to philosophical activity. In the analytic tradition of philosophy written in English counterexampling is more than three-quarters—or so it seems—of what is published. In some fields, for instance basic epistemology, concerned with "the analysis of 'knows,'" counterexamples probably constitute 95 percent of the product. Counterexampling, though we all do it in varying degrees, is practiced by some colleagues as a special, highly revered art. This emphasis on counterexampling is, perhaps, the most distinctive technical contrast between so-called analytic philosophy and other, especially Continental and Asian, philosophies. To many a nonanalytic philosopher, the passion for counterexamples, and for deduction in general, seems like an Anglo-Saxon and Anglo-American perversity. Here I want neither to support nor to dispute this point. I simply want to engage in a preliminary discussion of the role of counterexamples in genuine, fruitful philosophizing.

As the technique of counterexampling is practiced, a counterexample is assumed to have the substance of a minor premise in a refuting deduction. Some philosopher has propounded a view of the form: "ALL cases of A are cases of B," and the counterexampling critic describes a case of an A that is not a B. All seems straight-forward. (Of course, some proposed counterexamples miss their targets, because often they are not A-cases, and sometimes they turn out on close inspection to be B-cases as well.) Yet things are *seldom* so clear as that. For one thing, in typical analytic activities what is being analyzed is an ordinary concept, the meaning of an ordinary word, e.g., 'ought,' 'good,' 'knows,' and 'did something intentionally.' Given the vagueness, vagaries, and ambiguities of ordinary-language expressions, there are no sharp boundaries containing the correct uses of words., Thus, the seesaw of counterexample and revised analysis can go on and on in an asymptotic process, every step of which refines and deepens our appreciation of the border between correct and incorrect application. Here is a juncture at which philosophy can perennially grow.

Counter-examples often do no clinch the refutation they aim at. The data to which a theory caters might not be precisely demarcated. Thus, it is not always clear whether the counterexample lies outside the data or not. But here the counterexample plays the role, *not* so much of refuting a theory, but of *pressing* the theory for clarification and development. This is precisely the *main* function of counterexamples: *to present cases for a theory to be embedded into a more comprehensive one.* This is, as it could have been expected, an instance of the general methodological principle, insisted upon above, that all the philosophers working at a given time are members of the same team—whether they acknowledge it or not. Whether a counterexampling philosopher is set on refuting a theory or not is not important, nor is the refutation of the particular formulation of the theory. The theory can always be extended, with revisions, to cover the new data contained in the counterexample. This contribution of data is the *value of the counterexample.* And, on the pluralistic methodology being advocated here, the theory being counterexampled *should* be revised and developed further, not thrown away or forgotten. No philosophical approach should be left undeveloped.

For concretion let us exegecize a very subtle counterexample surrounded with a very ingenious discussion in Steven E. Böer and William G. Lycan's brilliant, fruitful, and powerful essay "Who, Me?"[9] This continues the topic of singular reference with which we started our discussion of method.

I have argued in a battery of papers that the first-person pronoun used indexically is not reducible to other mechanisms of reference, and have argued that expressions used to *depict* indexical attributions to others, which I call *quasi-indicators,* are not strictly reducible to nonquasi-indicators. A consequence of those claims is this: sentences with an indexical first-person pronoun express different propositions, different truths, or falsehoods, from those expressed by sentences with third-person expressions. This goes hand in hand with the thesis that the truth (or falsehood) expressed

by the subordinate clause 'he himself is in danger' in (1) below
is different from the truth (or falsehood) expressed by any other
subordinate clause in which the pronoun 'he himself' is replaced
with a coreferring term, as in (2):

(1)   John believes that he himself is in danger.
(2)   John believes that John is in danger.

Now, Böer and Lycan have an argument against my *Irreducibility
Thesis*. But the argument is based on a premise they call A, which
they acknowledge I reject in the way they interpret it. Clearly, any
other *general* argument is bound to have some premise I must
reject. Thus, the demonstrative proof of the error of the irreducibility
thesis is not forthcoming—unless a defender of it is prepared to
give it up rather than one of the premises of the alledged proof.
I am not. But I welcome proposed proofs, because they help me
clear up what other negative commitments I have implicitly made.

Böer and Lycan understand the situation very well. Yet they
adopt a somewhat excessively polemical (or refutational) attitude
after an insightful discussion of underlying issues, when they say:

> We conclude that our view is *not refuted* by Castaneda's argument
> alone (provided that A and B are also acceptable). (*Op. cit.*, 441;
> my italics.)

My argument for the Irreducibility Thesis has its own assumptions
within my approach. The argument is internal, and *cannot* refute
other approaches. I have already noted that I reject assumption
A they adopt. We have no refutations across the theories. I am
particularly anxious to see their theory developed fully, all the way
to all the data for which Guise Theory has been propounded. That
larger theory is the one I want to compare with Guise Theory
(which includes all my views about indexical properties and indexical and quasi-indexical reference). But even then no argument
internal to Guise Theory can refute Böer and Lycan's comprehensive
theory.

So far, then, Böer and Lycan see themselves as preparing the
terrain for the road to their theory. This is a most reasonable
attitude, which I used to hold—before the fact that approaches
cannot be refuted really struck me. Then, very meticulously, they
proceed to offer an important datum, which they claim turns the

tables in their favor. As they see it, that datum clashes with the Irreducibility Thesis; hence they see themselves as breaking up the opposition and as paving the road to their view with the resulting pieces. The datum is a counterexample:

> Now, we may also add positive strength to our case by calling attention to a type of situation different from Castaneda's paradigm, in which intuitions run squarely *against* the Irreducibility Thesis. Here is an example: Perry Mason has just been approached by a murder suspect, Larson E. Whipsnade. . . . The following dialogue ensues.
> *Mason:* Here are the police now. They will arrest you and ask a lot of questions.
> *Whipsnade:* Oh, God!
> *Mason:* Tell them that I am your lawyer. And refuse to answer any questions prior to the hearing.
> (*Police enter*)
> *Lt. Tragg:* Good morning, counsellor.
> (*Turning.*) You're under arrest, Whipsnade!
> *Whipsnade* (*to Tragg*): Mr. Mason here is my lawyer. And I won't answer any questions until the hearing.
> Mason has issued the order:
> (15) Tell them [the police] that I am your lawyer.
> Let us legalistically suppose that 'Tell *X* that *P*' here means 'Say to *X* a sentence which expresses precisely the proposition that *P*.' Now, in his declaration to Tragg, Whipsnade has told the police that Mason (that very person, etc.) is his lawyer. Thus Whipsnade has obeyed the *unuttered* command:
> (16) Tell the police that Mason (here) is your lawyer.
> But if the Irreducibility Thesis is correct, (16) is not equivalent to (15) as uttered by Mason, since Mason "May not know that he himself is Mason," and so on. And, according to Castaneda's view, Whipsnade has not obeyed (15), since the proposition expressed by the first sentence he uttered to Tragg is not the same proposition as that (if any) expressed by (15)'s complement. . . . *But this is absurd: surely* Whipsnade can obey and *has* obeyed Mason's order, in as *strict* a sense of 'obey' as any non-partisan might care to invoke. So much the worse for the Irreducibility Thesis. (*Op. cit.,* pp. 441f; my italics in 'unuttered,' 'strict,' and 'surely.' The others are Böer and Lycan's.)

Evidently the strong language at the end does not add anything to the force of the counterexample. The point is simply this:

B-L's Datum.

(a) There is in ordinary language good usage of the relevant words to say that when Whipsnade tells Tragg:

(15c) Mr. Mason here is my lawyer.

  Whipsnade is *obeying* Mason's command (15).

(b) Furthermore, there is a use of the words 'what—is what . . .' according to which it is correct to say that in such a case, *what* Whipsnade told Tragg *is what* Mason told him to tell Tragg.

(c) *Some persons*—and after checking with native speakers, I have found some who resist the use of the word 'same'—would go on to say:

(15.s) What Whipsnade told Tragg is the *same* as what Mason told him to tell Tragg.

This datum *must* be taken seriously by any theory of reference. I concede this immediately. Obviously, the nuclear force of *B-L's datum* lies in (c). It is the use of the word 'same' that provides them with the sense of crushing victory. Yet I think we should take things slowly, with full equanimity. Here I want to make some methodological counterpoints, setting the substantive issue aside.

First, after Wittgenstein we should be wary of taking the ordinary occurrences of the word 'same' as semantically crystal-clear. Recall Wittgenstein's remark: "When it is 5 o'clock on the earth it is the same time on the sun."

Second, as the initial "Paradox of Reference" was supposed to illustrate above, whenever we have a conceptual tension we can always put it as a *tension between a sameness and a difference.* Recall how Frege's Sense/Reference Theory catered to the difference involved by postulating different senses. The novelty of Guise Theory is to take the sameness and the difference in tension at face value and enthrone them as theoretical kingpins. The Böer-Lycan counterexample is a typical conceptual puzzle: on the one hand, we have the sameness postulated by B-L(c); on the other hand, we have the difference in commands they themselves carefully note: Mason quite definitely uttered command (15), but, as they say, left command (16) unuttered. Well, by Leibniz's law there is a difference between the two commands, so they are distinct, different. We have, therefore, a philosophical puzzle: the tension between a sameness and a difference. Obviously, the puzzle by itself cannot refute *any* theory Hence, the Irreducibility Thesis is *not* worse off because of this puzzle.

Third, the Irreducibility Thesis *for them* is worse-off after their counterexample only because of the assumptions they make about it. They want to press the sameness we find, and some persons assert in ordinary language. Yet the example of its own force exerts no pressure one way or the other.

Fourth, Böer and Lycan are among the most brilliant philosophers now avidly writing, and in spite of the emotive language at the end of the preceding quotation, they can see that the counterexample leaves things as they are—that what we have is our *underlying* clash of presuppositions, but it is open which ones should be given up. They declare:

> [A] So far as we can see, the only option available to the Irreducibility Theorist is to deny that Whipsnade has literally obeyed Mason's order and to swallow the consequence that the order cannot be obeyed, but only somehow approximated. In effect, [B] this latter claim is just a special case of what the Irreducibility Thesis asserts; [C] so perhaps our Perry Mason argument begs the question against Castaneda in an *extended sense* of that term. But [D] we take the argument to show that the Irreducibility Thesis' plausible consequences for Castaneda's amnesiac cases and mirror cases are offset as least to some degree by its *crassly implausible* consequences for othe cases. (*Op. cit.,* m.p. 443; my italics; the bracketed labeling of the main claims is also my own.)

These four claims are very interesting. Let me comment briefly on each one. Claim [A] is true, if we take it at face value, namely, as an autobiographical statement. Obviously, everything depends on what 'same' in B-L (c) means. As noted above, Böer and Lycan have found a "paradox" as significant as the one that led Frege to his Sense/Referent View. Hence, the Irreducibility Theorist has an open field as to what to do with this new paradox. I will say something about it below. Claim [B] is true, or not, depending on the interpretation of the words 'same' and 'literally.' Claim [C] is correct; although it is also correct in a nonextended sense of 'begs the question.' Of course, Böer and Lycan postulate an extended sense of the expression because they think that there is a special force of the example, over and above the denial of the claim of sameness of the order (15) and (16), which the Irreducibility Theories—they think—cannot annihilate. This point is made emphatically in [D]. Palpably, the emphasis and the strong words 'crassly implausible' do not contribute anything to the force of the example. The implausibility is no more crass than the assumptions underlying the interpretation of the example. Let us turn to a discussion of the example, in order to bring out its true significance.

Fifth, we need a little theory that resolves the tension between the sameness established by B-L (c) and the difference between the two commands (15) and (16), the former being uttered, the latter remaining unuttered. Undoubtedly, *one* theory is to take the sameness to be that of one proposition—in the way in which Frege postulated one referent for the expressions 'Oedipus's father' and 'the previous King of Thebes'—and then postulate some other difference between commands (15) and (16). *I* have no objection to such a theory. Indeed, I urge the interested parties to develop it; I want to insist, however, that this is too small a theory to worry about it by itself. We must consider comprehensive theories that embed it and compare them in richness of data catered to with Guise Theory.

Another approach is to use the word 'proposition' in the traditional sense as referring to the accusatives of mental episodes, as the truths, or falsehoods, that appear in person to a thinker, the ones he can represent with his conceptual resources. In this sense, clearly the fact that command (15) was uttered, but (16) wasn't, and the additional facts about Mason perhaps not knowing that he is Mason, being utterly surprised when Whipsnade says to Tragg: "Mr. Mason, here is my lawyer," reveal that we are confronting here the very representational resources at Mason's disposal. But—I repeat—this is a convention as to how to use the word 'proposition.' What counts is to have views that resolve the tension between the sameness and the difference Böer and Lycan have pointed out.

Let us use the word 'proposition' in the preceding sense. Then we can say that just as commands (15) and (16) are different, so are the proposition Mason put forward to Whipsnade by saying "I am your lawyer" and the one Whipsnade presented to Tragg by saying "Mr. Mason here is my lawyer." Then we have a problem: how do we explain the sameness postulated by datum B-L (c)? To resolve this problem let us return to the concept of sameness, and investigate our uses of the word 'same' in other contexts in order to gain a useful perspective to judge B-L (c).

Sixth, here are some useful cases.

(a) John is standing on a chair looking through an upper window, whereas Mary is scrubbing the floor and sometimes looks through a lower window under the one John looks through. A man passes by. John sees a head; Mary sees a pair of shoes and the end of a pair of legs. Yet they see the *same man.* Do they see the same *thing?* Yes, of course: they saw the same man; No, indeed, one saw a head, the other legs.

(b) Christopher and Martin were pushing the *same car;* but one was pushing the right side of the back bumper, the other was pushing the left side. Were they pushing the same thing?

(c) Paul and Charlotte kicked Anthony, the same Anthony, she on his buttocks, he on his shoulders. Was what one kicked the same as what the other kicked?

(d) Mr. Brown pays a debt to the Whites by paying the money to Mrs. White; and Mrs. Black pays a similar debt to the Whites by paying Mr. White. Did they pay the same payee?

To sum up, very frequently X does some action A to an entity Y by doing A to a part of Y, to a representative of Y, to a member of Y, or to some other entity having the appropriate representational relation toward Y. *Synecdoche is a fundamental form of life,* because of its tremendous pragmatic value, thanks to its encompassing information at the convergence of classes of entities.

Seventh, the question we must ask is, therefore, whether, even though commands (15) and (16) are different, there is an entity to which they are related in an intimate way, so that in a broader, typical sense of 'same' performing certain speech acts on (15) is the same as performing the same acts on (16). The answer is ready at hand: for the purposes of action in the world, as contrasted with actions as conceived either in rehearsals of belief or in rehearsals of intention, we generally do not care about intensional distinctions: co-referring expressions, although denoting different individual guises, denote the same unspecified system of guises to which they belong—in an extended sense of 'denote.' Here 'co-referring' means referring to items that are *consubstantiated.* Hence, all those propositions expressed with sentences that differ in having co-referring terms form one system of ultimate equivalent propositions: these systems constitute the targets of the messages we communicate about through the expression of one or anther proposition in the system. Saying the same message is what I have called PROPOSITIONS or STATES OF AFFAIRS (*sic,* with capitals all through).[10]

Eighth, to say it once again, the preceding account does *not* refute Böer and Lycan's account. The main moral of the discussion is to show that counterexamples by themselves refute *nothing.* Counterexamples are *counter*examples only because certain assumptions have been taken for granted. Thus, part of the value of the proposed counterexample is to allow focusing criticism on some of those underlying assumptions.

Ninth, it is most revealing, even ironic, and of course, a crucial *additional* datum, which I will call Böer and Lycan's datum (*d*), that these authors terminate their paper with the only appropriate answer to the dialogical question in the title of their essay:

> But for now it seems to us that the most reasonable answer to the skeptical 'Who, me?' is 'Yes; *you.*' (*Op. cit.,* p. 463; my italics.)

The answer to the skeptical dialogical "Who, me?" is, of course, as they say: "Yes, you." It is *not* "Yes, Mason (Lycan, Böer, Wilfrid Sellars, Frédéric Chopin, the author of *Self-Knowledge and Self-Identity,* or even *that* man)."[11] The representational mechanisms of what is being referred to require the second-person, which, of course, is subject to another thesis I hold: namely, the Irreducibility Thesis for indexical uses of the second-person pronoun.

Of course, in a monologue *the* answer to "Who, me?" is "Yes, *me* (I)," *not* any of the third-person answers. Thus, we have moved full circle: we are exactly where we began. But now, I believe, a bit wiser.

13. The Coffee-Pot Approach

A theorizing maneuver not uncommon in philosophical papers is the deliberate restriction to limited data. I have seen this operate with dramatic effects in the case of the nature of practical reasoning. A very comprehensive theory of practical reason which dissolves all the known "paradoxes" of deontic logic appears in *Thinking and Doing.* Some critics have objected that the theory is too complex—even that it deals with too much data! Alternative theorists have proposed to formulate theories that simply solve this or that "paradox" of deontic logic. The operation is typical of what I have dubbed *The Coffee-Pot Approach.* It is tantamount to the approach adopted by a "physicist" who argued as follows:

For me the old caloric theory of heat is good enough. I really do not care about all those fancy phenomena that other physicists study. All I care is to know how my coffee gets hot. No need to postulate molecules in rapid motion, or whatever. The whole thing is perfectly clear and simple. The caloric fluid goes through the electric wires, then it goes through the coils of the electric burner; then it jumps to the coffee pot, and then it transfers to the water. That's all. *Simple phenomena* require *simple theories!*

Obviously, this "physicist" is right as far as he goes. His error is simply his refusal to embed his data base into larger data bases and to extend his simple theory to more comprehensive theories that must deal with *all* the phenomena of the relevant type, and then embed that theory into more comprehensive theories that deal with other kind of phenomena, and so on until we understand the unitary structure of the whole world. Our target is, of course, the whole world.

There is, therefore, *no* point at all in studying local theories when we have more comprehensive theories. The only fruitful task is to extend the theories we have to make them even more comprehensive. And that's just all there is to it.

14. Conclusion

To refute a philosophical theory is not an easy task. Yet proposed refutations must be encouraged, because they will force the development of the theories attacked. The role of counterexamples is to enrich the data base of a theory and to focus the heat on their own presuppositions. Furthermore, to ask for proof of a theory is to ask for something inappropriate. The urgent need of the times is the development of more and more encompassing theories, catering to all the relevant data already collated by different approaches.

The most illuminating and educational philosophical experience is the comparison of comprehensive and rich and very different philosophical views.

Notes

1. For a complementary defense of philosophical pluralism and a complementary discussion of method with treatment of its foundations and of several examples, see Castaneda 1980.

2. For a detailed illustration of the semantic-syntactic contrasts that constitute the separation of practical reason from contemplative (sometimes called theoretical or pure thinking), see Castaneda 1980, chs. 3 and 4. The discussion includes a critical history of meta-ethical theories.

3. In particular, for Frege, see his *Sense and Reference* of which there are several translations. For Guise Theory, see Plantinga, "Guise Theory," and Clark, "The Theory of Predication: Guised and Undisguised," together with my replies, in Tomberlin 1983).

4. Robert Howell 1979, pp. 129–77; Castaneda 1979, pp. 31–62.

5. See Castaneda 1975.

6. See Chisholm 1979, pp. 385–86.

7. See Chisholm 1981.

8. For a discussion of dia-philosophy as the comparative study of comprehensive theories in order to ascertain their isomorphisms and their shiftings of complexity (provided they cater to the same rich data base), see Castaneda 1980, chs. 1 and 3.

9. Böer and Lycan 1980, pp. 427–66.

10. See Castaneda 1977, pp. 285–351, pt. II, where there is a threefold distinction among: propositions, propositional guises, and PROPOSITIONS, which accounts for a good number of problems, including the "paradox of analysis," the enrichment of perceptual fields through attention, and logical form.

11. My Irreducibility Thesis for the First-person pronoun used indexically includes as a special case the very tempting reduction to third-person *demonstrative* reference to oneself. But an indexical 'I' is not reducible to 'This . . .' even when 'This . . .' is used by the speaker to point to himself. For a discussion of this, see Castaneda 1966, pp. 130–57.

Epilogue

12   The Argument from Ordinary Language

Michael Scriven

1.

The argument from ordinary language has a remarkable status in philosophy in that it is regarded by many philosophers as fallacious or even vicious, and by many others as foundational, indeed unavoidable. Such a disagreement is more notable than, for example, the disagreement over whether intuition has a key place in metaethics or is entirely irrelevant, because it concerns the very foundations of philosophical method, on which depends any approach for the issue in metaethics, or to any other philosophical problem. The situation is reminiscent of that surrounding *argumentum ad hominem*, which has long been regarded as a classical fallacy but has more recently been reclassified by many as including the perfectly legitimate and ubiquitous process of credibility assessment. But the argument from ordinary language (AFOL) is far more central to philosophical discourse than *ad hominem* is to everyday speech.

2.

The aim of this paper is to determine the logical status or propriety of AFOL, but this should not be construed as a treatment of every argument form that has on some occasion been flattened or car-

Special thanks to Michael Tooley for a valuable discussion of an earlier draft.

icatured as "the argument from ordinary language." Opponents often dismiss AFOL as involving the earth-flattening assumption that what everybody says is so must be so. AFOL as conceived here involves no such assumption. Supporters have sometimes defined it as the paradigm case argument, where the paradigm case of linguistic usage is one about which we cannot conceivably be mistaken. But paradigm cases are not the only cases of proper usage and there are circumstances in which the other cases will carry the day. Paradigm cases are indeed special in the sense that one could not be said to understand the meaning of a term if one did not recognize a paradigm case as correct usage *in normal circumstances.* But in special circumstances—the kind with which philosophers are very often concerned—one might have to withdraw that application of the term. What is *prima facie* absurd is not necessarily false.

3.

The crucial question, then, is whether there is some type of AFOL that can avoid the overdefensiveness of the paradigm case argument (as sometimes presented) and the absurdity of *vox populi, vox Dei.* An auxiliary question that turns out to be significant is whether any *useful* conclusions for philosophical inquiry follow from the answer to the first question. Illustrations are used that have some interest in their own right, especially for the analysis of inference and scientific law.

4.

AFOLs do not always wear their colors on their sleeves. They may be dressed in the object language rather than the metalanguage and it is only upon challenge that we discover that an appeal is being made to "what we would ordinarily say." (An example will follow.)

5.

AFOLs may refer to highly technical language as "the ordinary language"; such a language is the ordinary language of the specialist—e.g., a physicist—who uses it regularly. The language becomes "ordinary" as it gets used extensively and in a wide range of applications—"temperature" would be an example. Some technical language never acquires this status and would never be referred to as ordinary language even by those who know what it means—the names of rare and insignificant benzene compounds, for example. The line between ordinary and special language is obviously not sharp, on this account of the two. But it is clear enough to provide a useful distinction, as we shall see.

6.1

A low-profile (object language) AFOL about a semi-technical term: "It's simply not true that a contradiction implies every proposition, or that a tautology is implied by every proposition." This argument might or might not be filled out with other premises, backed up with support for it and them or connected to an explicit conclusion, e.g., "material implication is a fatally flawed rendition of implication." But it is an AFOL if, when challenged, it is defended by appeal to the impropiety of *saying* that a contradiction implies every/any proposition.

6.2

"The first quotation in 6.1, in the appropriate context, is not an enthymeme, it's an argument; that's what many arguments look like. Saying it's not an argument—or that it's an incomplete argument—just because it doesn't fit your ideal model is exactly the kind of move that is rightly called formalist chauvinism." Here the AFOL's nature is revealed by the attack on a standard dismissal of AFOLs.

6.3

"We'd never say 'p implies p' or even 'p and q implies p.' You could say 'p entails p,' if you like, since 'entails' is a logician's invention; but implication is the converse of inference and you can't *infer* a proposition from itself." Paradigm AFOL; note the switch between normative remarks about usage and normative remarks about (in this case) implication.

6.4

"The so-called 'paradoxes of material/formal/strict implication' are not paradoxes at all but simply counterexamples to some crude proposals for analysing the concept of implication." A 'persuasive redefinition' more in the metalanguage that exhibits AFOL loyalties.

7.

The preceding examples, or the line of support for the assertions they contain, are AFOLs; their ultimate appeal is to proper/standard/ordinary usage. In the course of disagreements between two people who *accept* the legitimacy of this kind of argument, there will often occur an exchange, which we might call description-trading or frontier disputes, in which the protagonists offer alternative descriptions (analyses) of the case under discussion. It is this activity—exploring the geography of the terminology—that is the real core of AFOL, not inferences from paradigm cases. The skilled player of this game takes years to become proficient and makes mincemeat of amateaurs; a practice that, not surprisingly, engenders considerable backlash. The same, of course, is true of masters of legalistic or psychoanalytic jargon, the esoteric dialectic between the Paris schoolmen, and other displays of brilliant but slightly shady verbal legerdemain. The problem is whether the skill is empty or not, the trick a mere deceit. Let us take one of our examples a little further.

8.

"Surely *p*'s truth necessarily follows from the truth of '*p* and *q*' and is meaning-connected, which is not the case with '*p* and not *p*' and '*q*.' What else do you need in order to legitimate the move from one line in a proof to the next, which is presumably a paradigm case of inference?"

"Moves from one line in a proof to the next may simply involve simplification or restatement—what we might call formal shuffling rather than inference. It may be useful to have the term 'entails' to cover this. But the key element in the notion of *inference* is the generating of new information. What we infer goes beyond what we previously knew—that's why '*p* implies *p*' is absurd."

"Aren't you assuming that inductive inference is the only legitimate kind? Surely you couldn't deny that the truth of a generalization $((x)F(x))$ contains the truth of each instantiation of it; yet you seem to be denying that $(x)F(x)$ implies $F(x_1)$."

"Not at all—but the formalism has misled you. In most such cases the new information in the conclusion is that x_1 is an x. That may be self-evident in your notation, but there's nothing self-evident about the particular claim that an individual entity, independently identifiable and nameable, is in fact a member of the class F. If the individual is *not* independently identifiable, if it's just *any* member of class F, this is just simplification—entailment but not inference. Even if it's an identifiable individual, this would still not qualify as an inference if the generalization was based on induction by complete enumeration. Induction obviously involves a jump to new epistemic territory; but deductive inference does exactly the same. Pythagoras' Theorem is not epistemically contained in the Euclidean axioms, only logically."

In talking about the mode of discourse here, it seems appropriate to talk of persuasive redefinition or redescription, or of sounding-out of the subsurface topography; and of course this sentence illustrates the same procedure. But might not the hidden topography all be mud, not worth mapping? True, one can get stuck on mudbanks, but that may be an argument for destroying them, or at least for putting channels through them, rather than preserving them.

9.

It is now time to look carefully at the arguments against AFOL. If it is to survive at all, it must be able to cope with these criticisms, either by confrontation or by concession. We will consider four such arguments.

9.1

"Since our language is an artefact, it can, like any artefact, be improved by a process of refinement or extension. AFOL denies the *legitimacy* of such changes, and is thus as unconvincing as any argument from the way things are to the way things ought to be, or have to be, for example the argument that because human embryos have very limited legal rights they cannot properly be given full legal rights. In fact, the legal example is too kind to AFOL because of the powerful argument that can be given for almost any law. Languages, by contrast, are *extremely* arbitrary artefacts; there's far less in common between Mandarin and English as languages than between Chinese and English law. Changes in language are really *just* matters of convenience. Hence the very notion of AFOL is on a par with arguments for the necessity or privileged propriety of Gothic architecture." This complaint against AFOL will be referred to as the complaint that AFOL involves the *denial of linguistic arbitrariness*.

9.2

"This type of argument is today's equivalent of the medieval nonsense arguments about the number of angels that would fit on the head of a pin—trivial, pointless, time-wasting, the worst type of philosophy. What philosophy is about is finding answers to the most profound questions about the universe and our place in it; the absurdity of supposing that you can answer *those* questions by delving into the minutiae of lexicography should be self-evident." This complaint will be referred to as the complaint that AFOL involves the *reduction of philosophy to triviality*.

9.3

"It is a standard procedure in science to introduce new terms for convenience; to redefine prescientific notions like temperature and energy, or even to redefine terms that have already been defined within science, as was done with both temperature and energy because it became clear that one could replace them with a better thought-out substitute. AFOL implicitly rejects the idea that such a procedure can work in philosophy or logic. But the problems of philosphy or logic are at most somewhat more general than the problems of science, not sharply or even topically distinct. It is simply blind prejudice to suggest we should throw away one of our best proved methodologies when we start addressing philo-sophical questions, especially since we often cannot even tell when that moment has occurred—in cosmology, and philosophical psy-chology." This complaint will be referred to as the *rejection of scientific methodology* complaint.

9.4

"If AFOLs are to be taken seriously, then they rest entirely upon certain allegations about patterns of use in ordinary language. They must therefore be supported by extensive empirical research into what the facts really are about the particular point of ordinary usage that is at issue. But philosophers favoring AFOL—with the sole exception of the Oslo Department—never seem interested in doing this. Hence the argument masquerades as an appeal to empirical data; it is just one more in the long and unholy tradition of *a priori* arguments by philosophers about *a posteriori* issues." This complaint will be referred to as the *rejection of scientific empiricism.*

10.

There can be no doubt that AFOLs have been produced of such a nature and/or in such circumstances as to legitimate one or more of the preceding criticisms, and such AFOLs are at least suspect and in fact often invalid.

In addition to such methodological excesses in the name of AFOL, there are innumerable cases where the alleged linguistic data are in fact incorrectly perceived or reported. The denial that one can say "*p* and *q* implies *p*" may strike some in that way. Even John Austin's ear was sometimes at less than absolute pitch; he once spent half-an-hour arguing that the term "prediction" *only* properly applies to statements about the future based on intuitive or extrasensory or magical perception, not to the conclusions of rational inference, a view that few would share.

So we begin by making clear that AFOLs are no exception to the rule that sound arguments need true premises and carefully applied principles of inference. The key question, however, is whether AFOL, properly based and circumscribed, represents a valid *form* or *type* of argument. A second question of considerable importance is whether this form of argument is an *important* one.

11.

Thus the crucial issue is whether anything worthwhile is left after the complaints of 9.1 to 9.4 have been considered. Taking each of these complaints in turn, let us see whether a combination of concession and counterattack can be devised that is not suicidal. In preparing for and then dealing with the first objection to AFOL, we will lay the groundwork for most of the responses; consequently this preparation and treatment will take up much more space than will be accorded to the others.

11.0

The defender of AFOL against these complaints is likely to begin preparing the ground as follows.

How does one ever begin to answer a philosophical question? Usually by trying to get clear about meaning of the often abstract terms in the question—terms like "God" or "free will" or "knowledge" or "ethics." If explicit definitions of such terms are, as has become increasingly clear, no more than partial encapsulations of their meaning, how can we do a serious investigation of that meaning? The answer must lie in the scrutiny of multiple examples of standard usage, both positive and negative; that is, both inclusionary and exclusionary examples. It must lie, in short, in getting the case studies together for an argument from ordinary language. There is no other way.

And, continues the supporter of AFOL, it is that truth that makes AFOL seem as obviously sound to its supporters as the arguments against it seem devastating to those who dismiss it. What can the AFOL supporter say about those arguments?

To begin with, it must immediately be stressed that even the supporter of AFOL does not suppose that there is nothing to philosophical argumentation besides AFOL. There is a great deal more to be done both after and while doing meaning clarification— there are substantive rather than linguistic analyses and implications to be produced and checked against other analyses and empirical evidence, for example. But that is by the way. The AFOL supporter might respond to the complaints previously listed as follows:

11.1

The first complaint was that AFOL denies the essential arbitrariness of language. The response must be that the arbitrariness of the original sign selection is fully conceded. What is called 'red' in English could have been called 'rouge,' as in French or, for that matter, 'green'—if and only if 'green' had not already been used, in English, for the color green or for something else. The choice of linguistic sign, though arbitrary in the preceding sense, is not uncaused. Similarly, it is an arbitrary matter which side of the road a country chooses to legalize as the proper side on which to drive, by contrast with the necessity of picking some one side; though no doubt there is some explanation of the actual choice.

But once the options have been taken up on linguistic signs, they have a no-longer-arbitrary meaning, and this meaning is embedded in *all* their uses. Some of these uses are paradigmatic, others are merely contingent or casual. No one of the uses is immune to refutation, and indeed all of them might—in special circumstances or in the light of deep arguments—be mistaken. Nevertheless, the meaning of the term can be extracted from the uses and cannot be extracted from anything else. The logic of any term is more than denotative.

The AFOL supporter, having made the preceding observations, draws certain conclusions from them about proposed linguistic reform. The first conclusion is that it is virtually never possible to express the full meaning of a term in common use (or deeply embedded in a technical domain of discourse) by means of an explicit definition, though such definitions may provide a useful shorthand, with specific, limited purposes. Hence, attempts to "tidy up" the meaning of terms by precise redefinition (intelligence as IQ, anxiety as the score on the Taylor scale, temperature as the reading of a calibrated hydrogen thermometer, probability as relative frequency, etc.), while they may be useful for certain purposes, are all essentially tentative even for those purposes, because the part of the meaning omitted from the new definition can come back to haunt it even in the demarcated sub-area. This happened with intelligence and led to the redefinition of the IQ scales; with anxiety when the failure of the Taylor scale to discriminate between anxiety and (for example) aggression led to its desuetude; and with temperature on three separate occasions. On each of these occasions, thermodynamicists may have believed they were stipulating the meaning of a term, but that was an error. They were proposing a working definition of an existing concept, which is almost precisely analogous to proposing a working hypothesis to explain an existing phenomenon. It is subject to revision if it doesn't do the job of a good definition, which is *not* (mainly) to simplify a complex concept but to pick out the best meaning-axiom for developing a complex theory. Euclid's fifth postulate does not define "parallel" in the sense of giving all its meaning; it proposes a "working definition" for it, whose validity/utility is open to further test. The same is true of Newton's third law and Peano's postulates for the number system, or for the general gas law as the definition of "ideal gas," etc.

When someone introduces a true neologism, the definition they use only owns the patent for a while. It may be a very long while if it's a simple name for a discrete substance (freon, ytterbium) but even place names are redefined by councils and courts (Greater Los Angeles, Mexico) and general terms take off from their founder's definitions roughly in proportion to their conceptual importance (Skinner's negative reinforcement, Carnap's semantics, Freud's ego).

In view of the above it is a hazardous rather than a trivial enterprise to propose a redefinition of an existing term, especially an important term (implication, temperature), although sometimes a very worthwhile one.

It is on this point that the AFOL protagonist sees the formalist-neopositivist opposition as seriously misinterpreting the scientific examples. The moral from the scientific cases of redefinition is that such efforts are highly fallible, as witness the three redefinitions of the most central concept of thermodynamics. It is not that one can casually pull off redefinitions at will, without the risk of deep criticism or fundamental error. Indeed, the linguistic philosopher, far from thinking that philosophical arguments are merely about words, is the first to completely reject the Korzybskian General Semantics Approach in which the attempt is made to eliminate controversy by defining a number of different senses of the terms at the center of the dispute. Such an approach does a facelift on the real problem, confusing the serious detective for a while but contributing nothing toward a real solution. The formalist penchant for redefinition is seen by the AFOL supporter as only a slightly improved version of General Semantics, not as even half-way toward the enlightenment that occasionally results from the re-definition of a fundamental scientific concept. The thermodynamicists did not redefine temperature without an extremely extensive analysis of the implications of such a move; the formalist tends to produce a redefinition more or less on the basis of a single insight plus a deep conviction about the arbitrariness of language. One insight is not enough and the arbitrariness of language is not the right kind of arbitrariness to justify this move.

All attempts at "solution by definition" eventually run onto the horns of the following dilemma (in the view of the AFOLlower); *either* a new term is used (e.g., "material implication") in which case the big question is why we should bother with *its* properties— the irrelevance horn of the dilemma—*or,* if the proposal is supposed to be an *analysis* of the existing term ("implication") the problem is why we should put up with the inevitable mismatches (the "paradoxes")—the imperfection horn of the dilemma. Why not stay with the original concept, which we can illustrate, explain, clarify, and even refine without any risk of irrelevance or without any question of imperfection?

Perhaps the most seductive type of answer to this question is: because the new analysis is more precise, clearer, or quantitative. On the track record, this answer has some relevance for science but none for philosophy. In the social sciences the redefinitions have nearly always been failures; in the biological sciences, rather frequently failures; and only in the physical sciences do we have a number of clear examples of success. Even these successes have usually been temporary, and in any case the success that has been attained appears to be principally due to the fact that new territory is being mapped. Even if old terms like heat and energy are used, they are used in a new sense to map out vast new areas of physical phenomena. In such a situation it is by no means unlikely that the early cartographers will contribute something of value; it is much less likely that the same efforts at mapping will be successful when the territory has been very carefully charted over a very long time and from many points of view. When we attempt to apply the same approach to the social sciences, where much of the territory has been covered with finely detailed maps from at least some points of view, we run into much more trouble. And the attempt to transfer this approach to philosophy is one stage more unlikely to succeed. Within philosophy, the best bet is surely logic; yet what examples can be given of formal definitions that have clarified a pre-existing logical problem?

It's hard enough to have to sort out the original puzzle, says the AFOLlower, but having to do it by using the tools selected by amateurs simply makes it worse.

So the response from the AFOL camp to the charge that AFOL denies the arbitrariness of language is that sign-arbitrariness is not denied, but is irrelevant to full-blown problems; and that meaning-arbitrariness is false. Full-blown philosophical problems are stated, and the arguments for and against solutions to them are stated, in a mature language, and reflect serious underlying tensions that must at all costs be faced without distorting them. Otherwise the very data for the enquiry is contaminated. The language uses— the things "we are inclined to say" as the AFOLlower puts it— provide a starting point and in the relevant sense are our empirical data. Meddling with them, except for very limited purposes such as for making a temporary clarifying distinction, masks or distorts the problem rather than contributing to its solution.

Even the suggestion, so commonly made, that "we should distinguish two (or more) senses of the term" is hazardous *except* as a convenience for a page or two. Taken more seriously, it usually represents a premature judgment that there is no deeper unitary meaning. Example: Herbert Feigl was fond of distinguishing "ten senses of the term 'cause' "; Carnap is famous, amongst other things, for his "two meanings of probability"; others frequently talk of four or more senses of "explanation," e.g. scientific, historical, meaning, rational. If "senses" is just a *façon de parler* for "types," then this is just a linguistic carelessness that we can tolerate; if it means more than this, it's a claim that needs serious justification and rarely gets it, certainly never in the examples given. Dictionaries often distinguish as different "senses" uses that merely differ in contextual connotations or practical equivalents, not meanings; the same is surely true of the philosophical examples mentioned. What those examples illustrate is one of the pitfalls of *superficial* linguistic analysis; but they are hardly compatible with the view that linguistic analysis is not an appropriate tool in philosophy. As a half-baked approach to it, they can neither reject the entire approach nor withstand criticism for the imperfection with which they apply it. Thus the complaint of the denial of linguistic arbitrariness often turns out to be a smokescreen for linguistic carelessness; and linguistic carelessness guarantees irrelevant solutions. There are not two senses of probability but one, although there are circumstances in which that one can be treated as pragmatically equivalent to relative frequency. But if one carelessly assumes that there *are* two senses, one will not look at the presuppositions of that pragmatic equivalence and will be caught in contradiction in special cases. The strong response to the charge of denying linguistic arbitrariness is in fact the same as another criticism of the AFOL position; it is the claim that linguistic usages are not arbitrary but indeed constitute the factual data on which philosophical analysis must rest.

11.2 The Reduction to Triviality Argument

Einstein said that it was in response to some philosophical questions raised by Ernst Mach that he was led to reanalyse the concept of distant simultaneity and hence to generate the special theory of relativity. Einstein spent much of his working life on conceptual analysis, not mathematical analysis, let alone empirical research. He was interested in the analysis of concepts such as the origin of time, the relation of geometry to space, the idiosyncracy of the moment now, the idea of absolute velocity, the concept of an uncaused event, and so on. It was partly the fact that these happened to be some of the basic concepts of physics that makes us think of him as a theoretical physicist rather than a philosopher, but the mode of his approach, in its early stages, was entirely philosophical. Given the turf on which he worked, it was possible—and he was interested—to carry the analysis on into mathematical formulations and then physical details. But the conceptual insights on which the mathematics and physics were built always began with an examination of the simplest and most fundamental cases of the proper use of the terms "simultaneity," "the event," "time," etc. It is a short step from what he did to the usual turf of the philosopher of science. Similarly, one step beyond the evolutionary theorist in biology brings us to the argument from design; and one step beyond Hoyle's concern about continual creation brings us to the cosmological argument. If this kind of conceptual analysis is at the core of theoretical science and of philosophy, and if AFOL is a key procedure in conceptual analysis (as we have argued on earlier pages), then AFOL can hardly be accused of reducing philosophy to triviality. It is a keystone of philosophical enquiry, as of other conceptual enquiries.

If this is true, then we should find some trace of it in earlier work in philosophy and indeed, with those philosophers whose results are comprehensible without a lifetime of immersion in a special linguistic milieu, we find exactly the footsteps we might expect. Socrates *asks* the slave boy what he would say, Hume starts with and recurs to examples of the standard use of "cause," Russell—who abhorred AFOL—makes clear that it is the standard use of "implies" that he is trying to formalize with the horseshoe, and so on.

And the argument from ordinary language is more than the opening bars of the symphonies these philosophers composed. It is a recurrent theme, the theme that prevents the music from unravelling into random chords.

Despite these historical examples, it can certainly be said that AFOL has only emerged in recent years in its full-blown form; and it is that form to which the objections we have been considering are principally addressed.

The self-conscious form has indeed emerged recently, with its excesses as well as its refinements. In becoming self-conscious, it has improved the precision of the methodology considerably; the fallacies in the simple versions of the paradigm case argument are now generally recognized and the great strength of the basic methodology is equally well accepted by many of the most distinguished philosophers of our time. But the essential argument form is the same today as it was in Socrates's "Would we not say rather. . . ."

What has emerged can be put in one way as the solution to the methodological problem of conceptual analysis given the failure of explicit definition and of the hunt for necessary and sufficient conditions for the application of the important terms. The ambivalence that many of us felt about G. E. Moore's argument for the existence of the external world can now be clarified as we come to understand that the fallibility of the paradigm case is compatible with the impeccability of the argument from ordinary language.

Moore's failure to grasp the refinements that now seem clear enough is evident in his misinterpretation of the consequences of the "naturalistic fallacy." Instead of realizing that any attempt to define a crucial term in a reasonably short explicit definition was necessarily doomed to failure—the reason why any such definition of "good" in naturalistic terms will fail—he drew a conclusion of considerable ontological significance from this relatively simple fact about conceptual analysis. From the point of view of AFOL, "good" is a perfectly tractable term for analysis into naturalistic components, *even though* any attempted explicit definition will fail. It must be analyzed in terms of examples and contrasts, in terms of strands of meaning and relational properties, in terms of context-dependence, speech acts, and performative utterances. There is nothing trivial about the complex methodology of linguistic analysis and its meta theories at this point; nevertheless, they are only conceived of as tools to the deeper end of solving philosophical problems of more-than-linguistic significance. So the charge of reduction to triviality can be met head on and turned aside as confusing a philosophical means with the philosophical ends.

11.3 The Methodology of Redefinition

The use of neologisms in science, and even the redefinition procedure in science is, as has been argued above, much more justifiable and successful in areas where such approaches conflict with no long-established and much-tested linguistic map. And the methodology of redefinition is much less comprehensive, permanent, and successful than is commonly recognized. AFOL in no way excludes the development of new languages and the refinement of existing languages, as one can see from its own literature on speech acts. It merely represents a form of argument that has great respect for the integrity of the natural phenomena that guide us to what we are trying to understand. The switch to a synthetic substitute when the real thing can be managed quite well is usually an unnecessary risk. The gains in simplicity are attractive but the full cost in misrepresentation only gets billed much later, often after much work has been wasted.

So, the argument from ordinary language position (as reconstructed here) does not preclude a well-justified redefinition; it merely regards it as enormously difficult in areas outside the physical sciences and—from the record—almost always unsuccessful. Hence it is committed to a first effort at coping with the language as it stands, to be replaced by redefinition when such an approach obviously becomes unmanageable or confusing. The argument simply becomes an argument about the moment at which this situation emerges. From an AFOL point of view, it occurs rarely, if ever, and always late in the discussion; from the formalist point of view, it occurs much earlier. There is no way to settle the argument except by trying both alternatives. The AFOLlower would argue that ample experience justifies the claim that alternatives to redefinition are almost always better. But in the event, one must consider both approaches on their merits in the particular case. Hence the charge that there is a denial of the legitimacy of a certain approach here is mistaken; there is only a strong warning based on empirical evidence.

11.4 Denial of Scientific Empiricism

There are descriptive sciences and normative sciences, and if grammar were a descriptive science, its rules would have to be extracted from statistical data. It is a normative science, as is structural linguistics, and consequently, to use Chomsky's words, it is the "intuitions of the native speaker" that are the ultimate court of appeal in settling debates about linguistic usage. Contrary to the value-free doctrine about the social sciences, there are a large number of normative sciences; these include such studies as the physics of elastic bodies and ideal gases, as well as the psychology of ideal types. Such sciences are of course based upon empirical phenomena but are not merely aimed to report upon them, but rather to illuminate them by identifying patterns and other underlying regularities. This they do even though the regularities or types only approximate to the phenomena; the trade-off between precise description and economical classification or other representation is as much a feature of the physical sciences as of linguistics. Ideal gases, perfectly elastic bodies, empty space, rectilinear motion, absolute zero—all of these are in one way or another idealizations. And so it is with the "rules of language." They can be inferred from the myriad examples with which native speakers are familiar, and their accuracy or distortion can be discussed without recourse to survey techniques. Normative sciences, in short, do not reject the empirical foundation of science, but they do not treat the description of empirical data as more important than the illumination of such data.

We may conclude, then, that AFOL does not violate the requirement of empirical foundations for discourse about language, and with that conclusion, we have met—in one way or another— each of the objections raised.

12. Conclusion

The argument from ordinary language represents a refinement, in the methological repertoire of philosophy, of a process that has been an essential part of that repertoire since the beginning of philosophy. Although early attempts at stating the principles of AFOL led to erroneous dogmas—the paradigm case argument, as often represented—increased sensitivity to its nature now makes possible a more powerful application of a legitimate technique than ever before, an application that in no way demeans the great challenge of philosophy, the importance of empirical grounding, or the propriety of carefully staged redefinition, nor does it lead to the worship of popular opinion. It marks instead one of those rare events in the long history of philsophy—a significant enrichment of its legitimate methodology.

References

The following bibliography contains only works actually referred to in the text, apart from several additional sources on infinite regress arguments that David Sanford has included. These entries are preceded by an asterisk (*). The editor is grateful to Robert H. Knox for his valuable assistance in the completion of this project.

Ackerman, R., and Stenner, A. 1966. Discussion: A Corrected Model of Explanation. *Philosophy of Science* 33: 168-71.
Åqvist, L. 1971. Revised Foundations for Imperative, Epistemic, and Interrogative Logic. *Theoria* 37: 33-73.
Armstrong, D.M. 1968. *A Materialist Theory of the Mind.* London: Routledge & Kegan Paul.
_____. 1968-69. The Headless Woman the Defence of Materialism. *Analysis* 29: 48-49.
_____. 1974. Infinite Regress Arguments and the Problem of Universals. *Australasian Journal of Philosophy* 52: 191-201.
_____. 1978. *Nominalism and Realism.* Cambridge: Cambridge University Press.
_____. 1980. *The Nature of Mind and Other Essays.* St. Lucia, Queensland: Queensland University Press.
Asquith, P. and Hacking, I., eds. 1981. *PSA 1978,* vol 2. East Lansing, MI: Philosophy of Science Association.
Asquith, P., and Nickles, T. eds. (Forthcoming) *PSA 1982,* vol. 2. East Lansing, MI: Philosophy of Science Association.
Austin, J.L. 1961a. *Philosophical Papers.* Oxford: Oxford University Press.
_____. 1961b. Ifs and Cans. In Austin 1961.
Ayer, A.J. 1946. *Language, Truth and Logic.* New York: Dover Publications.
_____., ed. 1960. *Logical Positivism.* Glencoe, IL: The Free Press.
Baring-Gould, W.S., ed. 1967. *The Annotated Sherlock Holmes,* vols. I-II. New York: Clarkson N. Potter.
Barth, E.M., and Martens, J.L. eds. 1982. *Argumentation: Approaches to Theory Formation.* Amsterdam: John Benjamins.

Barthes, R. 1968. *Elements of Semiology*, translated by A. Lavers and C. Smith. New York: Hill and Wang.
_____. 1972. To Write: An Intransitive Verb. In de George and de George 1972.
Belnap, N.D., and Steele, T.B. 1976. *The Logic of Questions and Answers*. New Haven: Yale University Press.
Berggren, D.C. 1962–63. The Use and Abuse of Metaphor. *The Review of Metaphysics*, Part I, 16(1962): 237–58; Part II, 16(1963): 450–72.
Berlin, I. 1939. Verifiability in Principle. *Proceedings of the Aristotelian Society* 39: 225–228.
Beth, E.W. 1955. Semantic Entailment and Formal Derivability. *Mededelingen van de Koninklijke Nederlandse Akademie van Wetenschappen, Afd. Letterlunder.* N.R. 18: 309–342.
_____. 1964. *The Foundations of Mathematics*. Amsterdam: North-Holland.
Black, M., ed. 1950. *Philosophical Analysis*. Ithaca: Cornell University Press.
Böer, S., and Lycan, W. 1980. Who, Me? *The Philosophical Review* 89: 427–66.
Bogen, J. 1968. Physical Determinism. In Care and Landesman 1968.
Bonjour, L. 1978. Can Empirical Knowledge Have a Foundation? *American Philosophical Quarterly* 15: 1–13.
Braithwaite, R.B. 1953. *Scientific Explanation*. New York: Cambridge University Press.
_____. 1955. *An Empiricist's View of the Nature of Religious Belief.* Darby, PA: Folcroft.
Broad, C.D. 1952a. *Ethics and the History of Philosophy*. London: Routledge & Kegan Paul.
_____. 1952b. Determinism, Indeterminism and Libertarianism. In Broad 1952.
Brown, R., and Zenneberg, E. 1954. A Study in Language and Cognition. *Journal of Abnormal and Social Psychology* 49.
Burks, A. 1977. *Cause, Chance, Reason*. Chicago: University of Chicago Press.
Care, N., and Landesman, C., eds. 1968. *Readings in the Theory of Actions*. Bloomington, IN: Indiana University Press.
Cargile, J. 1979. *Paradoxes*. Cambridge: Cambridge University Press.
Carnap, R. 1956a. *Meaning and Necessity*. Chicago: University of Chicago Press.
_____. 1956b. Empiricism, Semantics and Ontology. In Carnap 1956.
_____. 1960. *The Elimination of Metaphysics*. In Ayer 1960.
Cassirer, E. 1953. *The Philosophy of Symbolic Forms*, vol. I, translated by R. Manheim. New Haven: Yale University Press.
Castaneda, H-N. 1966. 'He': A Study on the Logic of Self-Consciousness. *Ratio* 8: 130–57.
_____. 1975. *Thinking and Doing: The Philosophical Foundations of Institutions*. Dordrecht, Holland: D. Reidel.
_____. 1977. Perception, Belief, and the Structure of Physical Objects and Consciousness. *Synthese* 35: 285–351.
_____. 1979. Fiction and Reality: Their Basic Connections. *Poetics* 8: 31–62.
_____. 1980. *On Philosophical Method*. Bloomington, IN: Nous Publications.
Cheng, C., ed. 1967. *Philosophical Aspects of the Mind-Body Problems*. Honolulu: University of Hawaii Press.
Chisholm, R. 1979. Castaneda's *Thinking and Doing*. *Nous* 13: 385–86.
_____. 1981. *The First Person*. Minneapolis: University of Minnesota Press.
Clark, R. 1983. The Theory of Predication. In Tomberlin 1983.
Clendinnen, F.J. 1982. Rational Expectation and Simplicity. In McLaughlin 1982, pp. 1–25.

Collingwood, R.G. 1940. *An Essay on Metaphysics.* Oxford: Clarendon Press.
_____. 1958. *The Principles of Art.* Oxford: Oxford University Press.
Colodny, R., ed. 1965. *Beyond the Edge of Certainty.* Englewood Cliffs, N.J.: Prentice-Hall.
Croce, B. 1955. *Aesthetic,* translated by D. Ainslie. New York: The Noonday Press.
Davidson, D. 1980. *Actions and Events.* Oxford: Clarendon Press.
de George, R., and de George, F., eds. 1972. *The Structuralists from Marx to Levi-Strauss.* New York: Anchor Books.
Derrida, J. 1976. *Of Grammatology,* translated by G. Spivak. Baltimore: Johns Hopkins Press.
deSantillana, G. 1955. Introduction to Galileo Galilei, *Dialogue on the Great World Systems,* in the Salisbury Translation, Abridged Text Edition. Chicago: University of Chicago Press.
Dewey, J. 1930. *Human Nature and Conduct.* New York: Random House.
Doyle, A.C. 1967a. A Study in Scarlet. In Baring-Gould 1967.
_____. 1967b. Silver Blaze. In Baring-Gould 1967.
Dummett, M. 1978. *Truth and Other Enigmas.* Cambridge: Harvard University Press.
Dunbar, M.H.J. 1980 The Blunting of Occam's Razor, or to Hell with Parsimony. *Canadian Journal of Zoology* 58: 123–28.
Edgar, W.J. 1980. *Evidence.* Lanham, MD: University Press of America.
Essler, W. and Becker, W., eds. 1981. *Konzepte der Dialektik.* Frankfurt a.M.: Vittorio Klostermann.
Feigl, H. 1950. De Principiis Non Disputandum . . . ? in Black 1950, pp. 119–56.
_____. 1958. The 'Mental' and the 'Physical'. In Feigl, et al. 1958, pp. 370–497.
Feigl, H., and Sellars, W., eds. 1949. *Readings in Philosophical Analysis.* New York: Appleton-Century-Crofts, Inc.
Feigl, H., et al., eds. 1958. *Concepts, Theories and the Mind-Body Problem, Minnesota Studies in the Philosophy of Science,* vol. II. Minneapolis: University of Minnesota Press.
Fetzer, J.H. 1981. *Scientific Knowledge.* Dordrecht, Holland: D. Reidel.
Feuer, L.S. 1957. The Principle of Simplicity. *Philosophy of Science* 24: 109–22.
_____. 1959. Rejoinder on the Principle of Simplicity. *Philosophy of Sciences* 26: 43–45.
Feyerabend, P. 1965. Problems of Empiricism. In R. Colodny 1965, pp. 145–260.
Feyerabend, P., and Maxwell, G., eds. 1966. *Mind, Matter and Method: Essays in Honor of Herbert Feigl.* Minneapolis: University of Minnesota Press.
Flew, A., and MacIntyre, A., eds. 1964. *New Essays in Philosophical Theology.* New York: MacMillan.
Foucault, M. 1972. *The Archaeology of Knowledge,* translated by A.M. Sheridan-Smith. New York: Pantheon Books.
_____. 1973. *Madness and Civilization.* New York: Random House.
Gadamer, H.-G. 1975. *Truth and Method.* New York: Continuum.
_____. *Hegel's Dialectic,* translated by P. C. Smith. New Haven: Yale University Press.
_____. 1980. *Dialogue and Dialectic,* translated by P. C. Smith. New Haven: Yale University Press.
*Gardner, M. 1965. The Infinite Regress in Philosophy, Literature, and Mathematical Proof. *Scientific American* 212: 128–35.
Geach, P. 1979. *Truth, Love and Immortality: An Introduction to McTaggart's Philosophy.* Berkeley and Los Angeles: University of California Press.
_____. 1957. *Mental Acts.* London: Routledge & Kegan Paul.

Glymour, C. 1980. *Theory and Evidence.* Princeton: Princeton University Press.
Goldman, A. 1970. *A Theory of Action.* Englewood Cliffs, N.J.: Prentice-Hall.
Goodman, N. 1968. *Language of Art.* Indianapolis: Bobbs-Merril.
——————. 1973. *Fact, Fiction and Forecast.* 3rd ed. Indianapolis: Bobbs Merrill.
——————. 1978. *Ways of Worldmaking.* Brighton: Harvester.
Habermas, J. 1979. *Communication and the Evolution of Society,* translated by T. McCarthy. Boston: Beacon Press.
Hacking, I., ed. 1981. *Scientific Revolutions.* Oxford: Oxford University Press.
Hamilton, W. 1853. *Discussions on Philosophy and Literature.* 2nd ed.
Hanson, N.R. 1958. *Patterns of Discovery: An Inquiry into the Conceptual Foundations of Science.* Cambridge: Cambridge University Press.
Harman, G. 1973. *Thought.* Princeton: Princeton University Press.
Harrah, D. 1963. *Communication: A Logical Model.* Cambridge. MIT Press.
Hart, H.L.A. 1964. Self-Referring Laws. In Lejman 1964.
Hegel, G.W.F. 1967. *The Phenomenology of Mind,* translated by J. B. Baillie. New York: Harper and Row.
Heidegger, M. 1962. *Being and Time,* translated by J. Macquarrie and E. Robinson. New York: Harper and Row.
——————. 1966. *Discourse on Thinking,* translated by J. Anderson and E. H. Freund. New York: Harper and Row.
——————. 1969. *Identity and Difference,* translated by J. Stambaugh. New York: Harper and Row.
Hempel, C.G. 1952. *Fundamentals of Concept Formation in Empirical Science.* Chicago: University of Chicago Press.
——————. 1965a. *Aspects of Scientific Explanation.* New York, The Free Press.
——————. 1965b. Empiricist Criteria of Cognitive Significance: Problems and Changes. In Hempel 1965a.
——————. 1966. *The Philosophy of Natural Science.* Englewood Cliffs, N.J.: Prentice-Hall
——————. 1970. On the 'Standard Conception' of Scientific Theories. In Radner and Winokur 1970, pp. 142–63.
Hempel, C.G., and Oppenheim, P. 1945. Studies in the Logic of Confirmation. *Mind* 54: 1–26 and 97–121. Reprinted in Hempel 1965a.
Hintikka, J. 1955. Form and Content in Quantification Theory. *Acta Philosophica Fennica* 8: 11–55.
——————. 1962. *Knowledge and Belief.* Ithaca: Cornell University Press.
——————. 1969a. *Models for Modalities.* Dordrecht, Holland: D. Reidel.
Hintikka, J. and Suppes, P., eds. 1969. *Information and Inference.* Dordrecht, Holland: D. Reidel.
——————. 1969b. Surface Information vs. Depth Information. In Hintikka and Suppes 1969.
——————., ed. 1969c. *The Philosophy of Mathematics.* Oxford: Oxford University Press.
——————. 1973. *Logic, Language-Games and Information.* Oxford: Clarendon Press.
——————. 1975a. *Knowledge and the Known.* Dordrecht, Holland: D. Reidel.
——————. 1975b. *The Intentions of Intentionality.* Dordrecht, Holland: D. Reidel.
——————. 1975c. Impossible Worlds Vindicated. *Journal of Philosophical Logic* 4: 475–84.
——————. 1976. *The Semantics of Questions and the Questions of Semantics.* Amsterdam: North-Holland.

——————. 1980. C.S. Peirce's 'First Real Discovery' and Its Contemporary Relevance. *The Monist* 63: 304–15.

——————. 1981a. The Logic of Information-Seeking Dialogues: A Model. In Essler and Becker 1981.

——————. 1981b. Intuitions and the Philosophical Method. *Revue Internationale de Philosophie* 35: 127–46.

——————. 1982a. A Dialogical Method of Teaching. *Synthese* 51: 39–59.

——————. 1982b. Questions with Outside Quantifiers. In Schneider et al. 1982, pp. 83–92.

——————. Forthcoming a. The Paradox of Transcendental Knowledge.

——————. Forthcoming b. New Foundations for a Logic of Questions and Answers.

Hintikka, J., and Hintikka, M. 1982. Sherlock Holmes Confronts Modern Logic: Toward a Theory of Information-Seeking Through Questioning. In Barth and Martens 1982, pp. 55–76.

Hintikka, J., and Vaina, L., eds. 1983. *Cognitive Constraints on Communication.* Dordrect, Holland: D. Reidel.

——————. 1983. Rules, Utilities, and Strategies in Dialogical Games. In Hintikka and Vaina 1983.

Holsinger, K. 1981. Comment: The Blunting of Occam's Razor, or to Hell with Parsimony. *Canadian Journal of Zoology* 59: 144–46.

Howell, R. 1979. Fictional Objects: How They Are and How They Aren't. *Poetics* 8: 129–77.

*Hughes, P., and Brecht, G. 1978. *Vicious Circles and Infinity: An Anthology of Paradoxes.* New York: Penguin.

Humphreys, P.W. 1981a. Is 'Physical Randomness' Just Indeterminism in Disguise? In P. Asquith and I. Hacking 1981, pp. 98–113.

——————. 1981b. Aleatory Explanations. *Synthese* 48: 225–32.

——————. 1983. Aleatory Explanations Expanded. In Asquith and Nickles. Forthcoming.

Jeffrey, R. 1967. *Formal Logic.* New York: McGraw-Hill

Kant, I. *The Critique of Pure Reason,* translated by N. K. Smith. London: Macmillan.

Katz, J.J. 1968. The Logic of Questions. In van Rootsellar and Staal 1968.

Kelsen, H., 1946. *General Theory of Law and State.* Cambridge: Harvard University Press.

Kelsik, N.C. 1979. Bibliography. In Pappas 1979.

Kim, J. 1963. Discussion: On the Logical Conditions of Deductive Explanations. *Philosophy of Science* 30: 286–91.

Kojève, A. 1969. *Introduction to the Reading of Hegel,* translated by J. Nichols, Jr. New York: Basic Books.

Kripke, S. 1959. A Completeness Theorem for Modal Logic. *Journal of Symbolic Logic* 24: 1–15.

Kuhn, T.S. 1962. *The Structure of Scientific Revolutions.* Chicago: University of Chicago Press.

——————. 1970a. *The Structure of Scientific Revolutions,* 2nd ed. Chicago: University of Chicago Press.

——————. 1970b. Reflections on My Critics. In Musgrave and Lakatos 1970, pp. 231–78.

Kyburg, H.E., Jr. 1974. *The Logical Foundations of Statistical Inference.* Dordrecht, Holland: D. Reidel.

——————. 1977a. All Acceptable Generalizations are Analytic. *American Philosophical Quarterly* 14: 201–10.

——————. 1977b. A Defense of Conventionalism. *Nous* 11: 75–95.

Lakatos, I. 1970. Falsification and the Methodology of Scientific Research Programmes. In Musgrave and Lakatos 1970, pp. 91–196.

————. 1978a. *Philosophical Papers*, vol I, ed. by J. Worrall and G. Currie. Cambridge: Cambridge University Press.

————. 1978b. The Methodology of Scientific Research Programmes. In Lakatos 1978.

Laudan, L. 1977. *Progress and Its Problems*. Berkeley: University of California Press.

————. 1981a. *Science and Hypothesis*. Dordrecht, Holland: D. Reidel.

————. 1981b. A Problem-Solving Approach to Scientific Progress. In Hacking 1981.

Lejman, F., ed. 1964. *Festkrift Tillagnad Professor Juris Doktor Karl Olivecrona.* Stockholm: Norstedt and Soner.

Levi, I. 1980. *The Enterprise of Knowledge*. Cambridge: MIT Press.

Lovejoy, A. 1960. *The Revolt Against Dualism*. La Salle, Illinois: Open Court.

MacIntyre, A. 1981. *After Virtue*. Notre Dame: University of Notre Dame Press.

MacKay, A.F. 1980a. Impossibility and Infinity. *Ethics* 90: 367–81.

————. 1980b. *Arrow's Theorem: The Paradox of Social Choice*. New Haven: Yale University Press.

Mackie, J.L. 1982. *The Miracle of Theism*. Oxford: Clarendon Press.

McLaughlin, R., ed. 1982. *What? Where? When? Why?* Dordrecht, Holland: D. Reidel.

McTaggart, J. 1908. The Unreality of Time. *Mind* 17: 457–74.

————. 1921. *The Nature of Existence*, vol. 1, ed. by C. D. Broad. Cambridge: Cambridge University Press.

————. 1927. *The Nature of Existence*, vol. 2, ed. by C. D. Broad. Cambridge: Cambridge University Press.

Melden, A.I. 1961. *Free Action*. London: Routledge and Kegan Paul.

Mellor, D.H. 1981. *Real Time*. Cambridge: Cambridge University Press.

Merleau-Ponty, M. 1962. *The Phenomenology of Perception,* translated by C. Smith. London: Routledge & Kegan Paul.

Mill, J.S. 1872. *A System of Logic*. 8th ed. New York: Longman and Green.

————. 1979. *Examination of Sir William Hamilton's Philosophy,* ed. by J. Robson, with an introduction by A. Ryan. London: Routledge & Kegan Paul.

Monod, J. 1972. *Chance and Necessity*. New York: Vintage Books.

Moody, E.A. 1965. *The Logic of William of Ockham*. New York: Russell and Russell.

Moore, G.E. 1962. *Commonplace Book 1919–1953,* ed. by C. Lewy. London: Allen & Unwin.

Morgan, C.G. 1970. Kim on Deductive Explanation. *Philosophy of Science* 37: 434–39.

Musgrave, A., and Lakatos, I., eds. 1970. *Criticism and the Growth of Knowledge.* Cambridge: Cambridge University Press.

Nathan, N.M. 1980. *Evidence and Assurance*. Cambridge: Cambridge University Press.

Norton, B. 1977. *Linguistic Frameworks and Ontology*. The Hague: Mouton.

Nozick, R. 1981. *Philosophical Explanations*. Cambridge: The Belknap Press.

Pappas, G., ed. 1979. *Justification and Knowledge*. Dordrecht, Holland: D. Reidel.

Passmore, J. 1970 *Philosophical Reasoning*. 2nd ed. London: Duckworth.

Peirce, C.S. 1965. *The Collected Papers of Charles Sanders Peirce,* ed. by C. Hartshorne and P. Weiss. Cambridge: Harvard University Press.

284   *References*

Place, U.T. 1956. Is Consciousness a Brain Process? *British Journal for the Philosophy of Science* 47: 44–50.

Plantinga, A. 1967. *God and Other Minds.* Ithaca: Cornell University Press.

————. 1983. Guise Theory. In Tomberlin 1983.

Plato *Meno.*

Plato *Sophist.*

Plato *Theaetetus.*

Polanyi, M. 1966. *The Tacit Dimension.* Garden City, N.Y.: Doubleday & Co.

Pollock, J. 1975. Four Kinds of Conditionals. *American Philosophical Quarterly* 12: 51–59.

Popper, K.R. 1959. *The Logic of Scientific Discovery.* London: Hutchinson and Company.

————. 1972. *Objective Knowledge.* Oxford: Clarendon Press.

————. 1982. *The Open Universe. An Argument for Indeterminism.* Totowa, N.J.: Rowman and Littlefield.

Popper, K.R., and Eccles, J. 1977. *The Self and Its Brain.* London: Springer International.

Presley, C.F., ed. 1967. *The Identity Theory of Mind.* St. Lucia, Queensland: University of Queensland Press.

Putnam, H. 1981. *Reason, Truth, and History.* Cambridge: Cambridge University Press.

Quine, W.V.O. 1969. *Ontological Relativity and Other Essays.* New York: Columbia University Press.

Radner, R., and Winokur, S., eds. 1970. *Minnesota Studies in the Philosophy of Science,* vol. IV. Minneapolis: University of Minnesota Press.

Rantala, V. 1975. Urn Models. *Journal of Philosophical Logic* 4: 455–74.

Reichenbach, H. 1947. *Elements of Symbolic Logic.* New York: Macmillan.

Riley, J. 1982. Arrow's Paradox and Infinite-Regress Arguments. *Ethics* 92: 670–72.

Robinson, R. 1953. *Plato's Earlier Dialectic.* 2nd ed. Oxford: Clarendon Press.

*Rosenberg, J. 1978. *The Practice of Philosophy: A Handbook for Beginners.* Englewood Cliffs: Prentice-Hall.

Routley, R. 1980. *Exploring Meinong's Jungle and Beyond.* Canberra, Department of Philosophy, Research School of Social Science, Australian National University.

Russell, B. 1948. *Human Knowledge: Its Scope and Limits.* New York: Simon and Schuster.

Ryle, G. 1949. *The Concept of Mind.* London: Hutchinson.

Saarinen, E., ed. 1979. *Game-Theoretical Semantics.* Dordrecht, Holland: D. Reidel.

Salmon, W.C., ed. 1979a. *Hans Reichenbach: Logical Empiricist.* Dordrecht, Holland; D. Reidel.

————. 1979b. Why Ask 'Why?' In Salmon 1979, pp. 403–25.

————. 1984. *Scientific Explanation and the Causal Structure of the World.* Princeton: Princeton University Press.

Sanford, D.H. 1968. McTaggart on Time. *Philosophy* 43: 371–78.

————. 1975. Infinity and Vagueness. *Philosophical Review* 84: 520–35.

————. Forthcoming. Review of Mellor 1981. *Philosophical Review.*

Santas, G.X. 1979. *Socrates: Philosophy in Plato's Early Dialogues.* London: Routledge & Kegan Paul.

Sartre, J-P. 1957. *The Transcendence of the Ego.* New York: The Noonday Press.

————. 1966. *Being and Nothingness,* translated by H. Barnes. New York: Washington Square Press.

Saussure, F. de. 1960. *Course on General Linguistics,* translated by W. Baskin and P. Owen. London: Fontana.

Schlesinger, G. 1959. The Principle of Simplicity. *Philosophy of Science* 26: 41–42.
————. 1963. *Method in the Physical Sciences.* London: Routledge & Kegan Paul.
————. 1974. *Confirmation and Confirmability.* Oxford: Clarendon Press.
* ————. 1980. *Aspects of Time.* Indianapolis: Hackett.
Schlick, M. 1936. Meaning and Verification. In Feigl and Sellars 1949.
Schneider, R., et al., eds. 1982. *Papers from the Parasession on Nondeclaratives.* Chicago: Chicago Linguistics Society.
Sellars, W. 1948. Realism and the New Way of Words. In Feigl and Sellars 1949.
Smart, J.J.C. 1959. Sensations and Brain Processes. *Philosophical Review* 68: 141–56.
————. 1963. *Philosophy and Scientific Realism.* London: Routledge & Kegan Paul.
————. 1966. Philosophy and Scientific Plausibility. In Feyerabend and Maxwell 1966, pp. 377–90.
————. 1967. Comments on the Papers. In Presley 1967, pp. 84–93.
————. 1975. "On Some Criticisms of a Physicalist Theory of Colors". In Cheng 1975, pp. 54–63.
Sober, E. 1975. *Simplicity.* Oxford: Clarendon Press.
————. 1981. The Principle of Parsimony. *British Journal for the Philosophy of Science* 32: 145–56.
Stich, S.P., et al. 1973. Entailment and the Verificationist Program. *Ratio* 15: 84–97.
Strawson, P.F. 1966. *The Bounds of Sense.* London: Methuen.
Swinburne, R. 1973. Confirmation and Factual Meaningfulness. *Analysis* 33: 71–76.
————. 1980. *Space and Time.* 2nd ed. London: St. Martin's Press.
Thorburn, W.M. 1918. The Myth of Occam's Razor. *Mind* 27: 345–53.
Timasheff, N. 1939. *An Introduction to the Sociology of Law.* Cambridge: Harvard University Press.
Tomberlin, J., ed. 1983. *Agent, Language, and the Structures of the World.* Indianapolis: Hackett.
Toulmin, S. 1972. *Human Understanding.* Princeton: Princeton University Press.
van Fraassen, B.C. 1980. *The Scientific Image.* Oxford: Clarendon Press.
van Rootsellar, B., and Staal, J.F., eds. 1968. *Logic, Methodology, and Philosophy of Science,* vol. III. Amsterdam: North-Holland.
Vico, G. 1948. *The New Science,* translated by T. G. Bergin and M. H. Fisch. Ithaca: Cornell University Press.
Waismann, F. 1967. *Ludwig Wittgenstein und der Wiener Kreis.* Oxford: Oxford University Press.
————. 1968a. *How I See Philosophy,* ed. by R. Harre. London: Macmillan.
————. 1968b. How I See Philosophy. In Waismann 1968, pp. 1–38.
Whitehead, A.N. 1929. *Process and Reality.* New York: Macmillan.
Williams, J. 1981. Justified Belief and the Infinite Regress Argument. *American Philosophical Quarterly* 18: 85–88.
Wittgenstein, L. 1953. *Philosophical Investigations,* translated by G.E.M. Anscombe. Oxford: Basil Blackwell.
————. 1961. *Tractatus Logico-Philosophicus,* translated by D. F. Pears and B. F. McGuinness. London: Humanities Press.
*Yalden-Thomson, D. 1964. Remarks about Philosophical Refutations. *Monist* 48: 501–12.

Index of Names

Ackermann, R., 153
Adams, J. C., 123
Aquinas, St. T., 10, 100
Aqvist, L., 41
Aristotle, 10, 100, 101, 104, 113, 184, 192, 193, 203, 213
Armstrong, D. M., 116, 126, 128
Arrow, K., 109
Austin, J. L., 215, 226, 267
Ayer, A. J., 9, 74, 77, 86, 189

Bacon, F., 25
Baring-Gould, W. S., 42–43
Barthes, R., 208, 225
Becker, W., 42
Belnap, N., 41
Berggren, D. C., 3, 15, 190, 226
Berlin, I., 74
Beth, E. W., 43
Boer, S., 249, 250, 252, 253, 256, 258
Bogen, J., 226
Bonjour, L., 117
Boscovich, R., 122
Boyle, R., 154, 159
Braithwaite, R. B., 189
Broad, C. D., 216, 226
Brown, R., 225
Burks, A., 132

Campbell, K. K., 128
Cargile, J., 7, 8, 16, 20, 44
Carnap, R., 77, 82, 86, 208, 213, 220, 225, 270, 272
Cassirer, E., 215, 220, 225
Castaneda, H-N., 16, 17, 18, 21, 227, 245, 251, 253, 257, 258
Cezanne, P., 197
Chametzky, R., 42
Chisholm, R., 245, 246, 247, 258
Chomsky, N., 276
Chopin, F., 256
Church, A., 74, 182
Clark, R., 258
Clendinnen, F. J., 122, 123, 128
Collingwood, R. G., 25, 41, 201
Condillac, E. B. de, 119
Copernicus, N., 123, 128
Croce, B., 201, 225

Dali, S., 206
Davidson, D., 214, 226
deSantillana, G., 128
Derrida, J., 15, 217, 219, 220, 226

Descartes, R., 132, 172, 239
Dewey, J., 102, 103
Doyle, A. C., 37, 42, 43
Dummett, M., 188
Dunbar, M. H. J., 124

Eccles, J., 225, 226
Edgar, W. J., 82
Einstein, A., 273
Essler, W., 42
Euclid, 265, 270

Feigl, H., 72–73, 84, 122, 124, 272
Fetzer, J. H., iii–iv, 3, 18, 19, 21, 189
Feuer, L. S., 128
Feyerabend, P., 135
Flew, A., 88
Foucault, M., 201, 204, 208, 225
Frege, G., 51, 236, 237, 238, 239, 252, 253, 254, 258
Freud, S., 270

Gadamer, H-G., 25, 41, 211, 225, 226
Geach, P., 39, 40, 43, 93, 94, 95, 96, 100, 116
Gettier, E., 162
Gewirth, A., 204
Glymour, C., 74, 75
Godel, K., 176
Golding, M., 116
Goldman, A., 214, 226
Goodman, N., 118, 119

Habermas, J., 220, 225
Hacking, I., 41
Hamilton, W., 119
Hare, R. M., 88
Harman, G., 13, 162, 163, 164
Harrah, D., 41
Hart, H. L. A., 116
Hegel, G. W. F., 15, 204, 211, 213, 218, 219, 221, 224, 225, 226
Heidegger, M., 86, 200, 202, 203, 213, 217, 219, 224, 225, 226
Heisenberg, W., 176
Hempel, C. G, v, x, 4, 10, 13, 14, 15, 20, 135, 153, 155, 156, 159, 173, 178, 189
Henkin, L., 46
Heraclitus, 219
Hick, J., 88
Hilbert, D., 176
Hintikka, J., 6, 7, 16, 20, 25, 42, 43
Hintikka, M., 402

Holsinger, K., 123–124
Howell, R., 242, 243, 258
Hoyle, F., 273
Hume, D., 89, 90, 187, 196, 274
Humphreys, P., 13, 14, 172, 189

Jackson, F. C., 128
Jeffrey, R., 43

Kant, I., 15, 25, 26, 33, 41, 42, 52, 176, 192, 196, 204, 216, 217, 224
Katz, J. J., 41
Kelsen, H., 116
Kelsik, N. C., 117
Kepler, J., 123, 154, 159
Kim, J., 155
Knox, R. H., 278
Kojeve, A., 226
Korzybski, J., 270
Kripke, S., 134
Kuhn, T. S., 132, 135, 209, 220, 225
Kyburg, H. E., 11, 12, 131

Lakatos, I., 132
Laudan, L., 25, 41
Leibniz, G. W., 48, 172, 234, 236, 252
Leverrier, J. J., 123
Levi, I., 137, 139, 140, 141, 150
Loemker, L. F., 48
Lovejoy, A., 225
Lycan, W., 249, 250, 252, 253, 256, 258

MacIntyre, A., 88, 226
MacKay, A. F., 109
Mach, E., 273
Mackie, J. L., 188
Marx, K., 222
McTaggart, J., 10, 93, 94, 95, 96, 97, 100, 116, 117, 176
Melden, A. I., 226
Mellor, D. H., 10, 93, 96, 97, 98, 99, 116
Meno, 31, 32
Merleau-Ponty, M., 222, 225, 226
Mill, J. S., 11, 119, 120, 167, 178, 181, 189
Monod, J., 226
Montague, R., 182
Moody, E. A., 123
Moore, G. E., 50, 94, 100, 115, 274
Morgan, C. G., 155
Moseley, J., 3

Nathan, N. M., 117
Newton, I., 121, 123, 154, 159, 183, 270
Newton-Smith, W. H., 91
Nietzsche, F., 208
Norton, B., 225
Nozick, R., 188, 191, 224

Ockham, W., ix, 11, 16, 17, 118–128, 228, 241, 242, 244
Oppenheim, P., 10

Parsons, C., 243
Passmore, J., 93, 94, 95, 96, 100, 116
Pauli, W., 176
Peano, G., 270
Peirce, C. S., 36, 37, 39, 40, 43, 181, 217
Pettit, P. N., 128

Place, U. T., 126
Plantinga, A., 13, 89, 166, 167, 258
Plato, 15, 25, 38, 39, 40, 43, 95, 113, 203, 211, 222, 225, 227
Polanyi, M., 199, 224
Pollock, J., 13, 168, 169, 170, 171
Popper, K. R., 4, 5, 18, 133, 174, 186, 189, 220, 225, 226
Price, H., 128
Putnam, H., 188, 189
Pythagoras, 265

Quine, W. V. D., 61, 188, 220, 225

Rantala, V., 42
Rawls, J., 204
Reichenbach, H., 99, 172
Rescher, N., ii
Riley, J., 109
Robinson, R., 41
Routley, R., 128
Russell, B., 88, 132, 162, 237, 274
Ryle, G., 116, 226

Saarinen, E., 42
Salmon, W. C., 189
Sanford, D., 10, 11, 93, 109, 116, 117, 278
Santas, G. X., 41
Sartre, J. P., 199, 222, 223, 224, 225, 226
Saussure, F. de, 224, 227
Schlesinger, G., ix, 8, 9–10, 13, 20, 71, 122, 123, 128, 151
Schlick, M., 85, 86
Schneider, R., 42
Scriven, M., 18, 20, 261
Sellars, W., 224, 245, 256
Shoemaker, S., 91
Skinner, B. F., 270
Smart, J. J. C., 11, 118, 127
Smillie, D., 3
Sober, E., 120
Socrates, 6, 25, 31, 32, 38, 274
Steele, T. B., 41
Stenner, A., 153
Stich, S., 78
Strawson, P. F., 224, 226
Swinburne, R., 78, 79, 80, 91

Tarski, A., 176, 177
Thend, O., 227
Thorburn, W. M., 118
Timasheff, N., 116
Tomberlin, J., 258
Tooley, M., 261
Toulmin, S., 213, 226
Tuite, K., 42

Vaina, L., 42
vanFraassen, B., 189
Vico, G., 201, 225

Waismann, F., 72
Whitehead, A. N., 213, 223, 226
Williams, J., 117
Wittgenstein, L., 200, 203, 220, 225, 226, 230, 239, 252

Zenneberg, E., 225
Zeno, 176

Index of Subjects

a priori knowledge, 56, 64
a priori truths, 132
A-series, McTaggart's, 96–100, 176
abhanden, 204, 205
absolute spontaneity, Sartre's, 222
abstract entities, 182
accepting a position, 201
acceptance, 135, 136, 137, 143
accidental correlations, 195
accidental regularities, 186–188
actions, 101, 193, 213, 223
ad hoc hypotheses, 122
ad hoc rescues, 13
additive, 6
adequacy of a theory, 229
ampliative, 6
ampliative conclusions, 21
analytic *a priori* knowledge, 81
analytic philosophy, 227–228
analytic sentences, 50, 82
answers, 7
answers (intended full and complete), 26
antecedent probability, 119
archaeological explanations, 15, 193, 206, 209–210, 219
archaeological reduction, 213
archaeological thinking, 193
argument for independent reality, 196–197
argument for objective coherency, 197–198
argument for self-ascription, 196
argument from ordinary language (AFOL), 261–277
argumentum ad hominem, 261
Aristotle's four causes, 192
as the result of, 193, 211
asserting, 67
atomic predicates, 60
atomic sentences, 59
auxiliary hypotheses, 9
Ayer's empiricist criterion, 9, 74

because of, 194, 212
belief, 51, 52, 67
brain processes, 124–126
brain states, 11

category-mistake, 221
causal explanations, 4
causal necessities, 15, 193, 212
certainty, 132, 195
chronologizing predications, 16
chronologizing properties, 16, 56
classical line in philosophical reasoning, 12

classical logic, 7, 44–70
closed loops of desires, 111
Coffee-Pot Approach, 244, 256–257
common cause principle, 14–15, 180–184
Commonplace Book, Moore's, 94
community of philosophers, 21
community of scientists, 21
completeness, 49
complex questions, 29
comprehensive theories, 230, 235
conceptual change, 140
conclusive answers, 27, 28, 40
conclusive confirmation, 9
condition (P), 75–78
confirmability, 73
confirmation, 73, 74
conflation, 238
conjectures and refutations, 17
consciousness, 199
consciousness (of), 199
consistency, 48, 137
consociation, 238
consubstantiation, 238, 255
context of discovery, 4
context of justification, 4
conventional necessities, 15, 194, 213
converse consequence condition, 10
corollarial (synthetic) reasoning, 37
correct, definition of, 8
correlations, 187
correspondence theory of truth, 179
cosmological explanations, 175
cosmology, 123, 266
could have done otherwise, 214
counterexamples, 12, 13, 17, 133, 248–256, 264
counterfactual conditionals, 195
counterfactuals, theory of, 168–171
covering laws, 14
creative-discovery, 221, 223
creativity, 133
credibility, 75
Critique of Pure Reason, Kant's, 33

deception, 126
deduction, 33, 36, 136, 239, 244, 247–248
deductive arguments, 191
deductive inference, 5–6, 11, 42, 131, 265
deductive logic, 7, 36, 80
deductive methodology, 18
deductive principles of inference, 15
deductive reasoning, ix, 6, 37
definitional relevance, 20
demonstrative, 6

denial of linguistic arbitrariness, 266, 272
denial of scientific empiricism, 276–277
descriptive conceptions, 4, 7
deterministic laws of nature, 176–177
dialectical method, 221
dialectical method of elimination, 215
dialectical reasoning, ix, 15
dialectical thinking, 190, 210–226
dictionaries, 272
Dictum de Omni et Nullo, 61
direct inference, 136, 141–142
disciplinary matrix, 132
discourse, 39, 40
distinctively philosophical investigations, 19–21
distribution of error, 138–139
Divide and Conquer, 244–248
Dr. Watson, 33–36
dualism, 124

efficient causes, 192
elegance, 11
elimination of uncertainty, 26
empirical data, 231
empirical foundations, 276
empirical generalizations, 131
empirical meaningfulness, 74
empirical science, 19
empirical significance, 74, 77
enthymemes, 263
epistemic logic, 28
epistemic sameness, 17, 236, 237
epistemic why-questions, 172, 185
errors of measurement, 136
ethical theory, 203
ethics, 148–149
events, 193
evidence, 140
evidential certainty, 141, 142
existential hypotheses, 118
exoneration, 19
experiential difference, 72
experiential findings, 12
experimental psychology, 4
explanation, 13, 98
explanation in philosophy, ix
explanation in science, ix
explanatory arguments, 185
explanatory force, 119
explanatory why-questions, 172, 184
explication, 13, 20, 82, 121, 155, 161, 213
explications, conditions of adequacy for, 20
explicit definitions, 268
extensional language, 98

fallibilism, 165
fiction, 231, 242–243
final causes, 192
first-order logic, 134
first-order predicate calculi, 16
for the sake of, 102, 115
form plus restrictions, 45, 49
formal causes, 192
formal derivability, 48
formal proof, 47
formal validity, 47
forms of inference, 47
Frege's Paradox, 236
Frege's sense–reference theory, 252
Fregean thoughts, 51
fundamental ontology, Heidegger's, 200

G-CCC Theory, 242–243
game of the world, 223
game of the world, Derrida's, 221
general reference, 238
general relativity, 120
geometric notion of form, 45

Gettier problem, 162–165
God and Other Minds, Plantinga's, 168
guessing, 122
guise theory, 16, 235, 238, 242, 250

habitual sedimentation, Merleau-Ponty's, 222
having a position, 199
Henkin completeness proof, 47
hermeneutical method, 25
hypothetico-deductive conception, 9, 75

idealizations, 276
identity, 16–17, 28–32, 55–56, 221–222, 233, 234, 237
identity across time, 16, 56
identity of indiscernibles, 16
imagination and conjecture, 4, 18
impossibility results, 176–177
in order to, 193, 211
inconsistency, 137
incorrigibility, 139, 144, 145
independence, 46, 49
independent reality, 202, 203, 205
indeterminism, 216
indiscernibility of identicals, 16, 55–56
individual guises, 238
individuation, 234, 238
individuation of beliefs, 53
individuation of propositions, 53
individuation of sentences, 53
induction, definition of, 165–167
induction by enumeration, 121, 265
inductive arguments, 121
inductive inference, 5–6, 9, 42, 265
inductive logic, 80
inductive methodology, 18
inductive reasoning, ix, 8
infallibility, 139
inference, 264
inference to the best explanation, 14, 173, 186
inferential principles, 179–180
infinite regress, 66, 188, 216
infinite regress arguments, ix, 93–117
infinite series, 93
infinite sets, 44–45
information, 26, 27, 29, 264
information-gathering, 25
innate ideas, 38
instantiation, 61
instrumental goods, 103
instrumental necessities, 15, 193, 212
instrumentalism, 14, 178, 179
intensional logics, 133
intention, 245
intentionality of actions, 213–214
internal predication, 238
interpreting formulae, 57
intrinsic goods, 103
introspection, 198
intuition, 12, 29, 36, 134, 261, 276
intuitive aproaches, 12
irreality, 231
Irreducibility Thesis, Castaneda's, 250, 251–253

judging, 39
justificatory activities, types of, 19
justificatory arguments, 185

knowledge, conditions for, 162–165
knowledge-expanding, 6
knowledge-seeking, 25, 29, 30

language, 198
language framework, 3, 5
language framework, replacement of, 131
language frameworks, ix
language rules, 64

lawlike regularities, 186–188
laws of classical logic, 44
laws of logic, 8, 44–70
Leibniz' Law, 233–234, 236, 252–253
linguistic change, 140
linguistic contexts, 19
linguistic conventions, 146
linguistic dispositions, 5
linguistic-substitutional approach, 8, 59, 62, 63, 69
linguistic-translational approach, 8, 58, 62, 63, 69
literal meaning, 220–221
local theories, 246–247
logic of discourse, 39
logic of questions, 25, 39
Logical Atomism, 60
Logical Positivism, 160–161
logically proper names, 57
looping desires, 110–113

malpractice, 21
master theory, 17, 229
material causes, 192
material conditionals, 169
matrix of the question, 31, 35
meaning, 72
meaningfulness, 71, 72, 73, 77, 79, 85
meaninglessness, 80, 83, 86
mechanical notion of formal proof, 46
Meno, Plato's, 38
Meno's puzzle, 31–33
mental, 124–128
mental states, 11
metaethics, 261
metalanguage, 262
metaphorical meaning, 221
metaphysical hypotheses, 78
metaphysical laws, 49
metaphysical realism, 186
metaphysical truth, 121
metaphysics, 86, 123
metaphysics, science as, 120
metaphysics of presence, Derrida's, 217, 222
method of counterexample, ix, 151–171
method of deconstruction, Derrida's, 219
method of elimination, 211, 217, 221
method of reduction, 211, 217
method of tensional transformation, 212, 218
methodological inference principles, 14
methodological pluralism, 229
methodology of redefinition, 275–276
mind–body problem, 11, 124–128
miracles, 90
modal logics, 134
modality, 56
model-theoretic approach, 8, 27, 29, 41, 57, 62, 63, 68, 69
modern conceptions of logic, 7, 44–70
modes of philosophical reasoning, 3
modes of reasoning, 3

natural language, 29
natural signs, 123
naturalistic fallacy, 274–275
necessary connections, 195
necessary truth, 50, 64
negative regress arguments, 10, 93, 94–100
negative regresses, viciousness of, 106–109
Nicomachean Ethics, Aristotle's, 100
non-quasi-indicators, 249
non-sameness, 236
nonaccidental regularities, 187–188
nonadditive, 6
nonampliative, 6, 7
nondemonstrative, 6
nonrealism, 188
nontrivial (synthetic) reasoning, 36
normative conceptions, 4, 7, 12, 21, 263
normative sciences, 276

object language, 262
objective reality, 197
objectural interpretation, 60, 61, 62
observation, 33, 42
observation predicates, 135
observation sentence, 74, 75, 77, 78, 79
observation statement, 144
Ockham's (Occam's) Principle, 11
Ockham's Razor, ix, 11, 16, 17, 118–128, 228, 241–244
ontological pluralism, 230
ontology, 228, 229
open loops of desires, 111
ordinary experience, 145
ordinary language, 18, 20, 262–263
ordinary language philosophy, 133
ordinary-language expressions, 248–249

paradigm case argument, 262, 277
paradigm case presupposition, 18
paradigms, 132, 209
paradox of analysis, 18
paradox of reference, 16, 17, 228, 232–239
paradoxes, 104
Paradoxes, Cargile's, 65
partial answers, 30
partial verification, 9
patterns of argument, ix, 3
perceptual inference, 5, 13
personal freedom, 223
persuasive redefinition, 264, 265
phenomenalism, 148
phenomenalistic language, 148
phenomenalistic language framework, 12
phenomenological method, 221
phenomenological ontology, 228–230, 232
phenomenology, 126–127
philosophical argument, 131–150
philosophical content, 14
philosophical data, 232
philosophical explanations, 14, 172–189
philosophical inference, 147
philosophical investigations, 20
philosophical knowledge, 141, 145
philosophical method, 25
philosophical methodology, 41
philosophical patterns of argument, 3
philosophical pluralism, 257
philosophical principles of inference, 3
philosophical reasoning, ix, 3–21, 35
Philosophical Reasoning, Passmore's, 94
philosophical refutations, 17, 21, 128, 227–258
philosophical theories, 17
philosophical thinking, 25
philosophy of science, 19
physical, 124–128
physical reality, 222
physicalism, 124
plausibility, 11, 127–128
Popper's World 1, 186, 220, 223
Popper's World 2, 220
Popper's World 3, 186, 220, 223
positive regress arguments, 10, 93, 100–115
possible worlds, 7, 26, 41, 134
practical certainty, 141, 142–143, 145, 146
pragmatics, 3
predicate calculi, 44–70
predication, 66, 67, 234, 238
predictive conditionals, 169
presuppositions, 30, 31, 32, 35, 132, 177, 253
principle of asymmetry, 109
principle of causal determinism, 175–177
principle of difference, Derrida's, 218–219
principle of economy, 11
principle of excluded middle, 49
principle of existence, 109
principle of existential heredity, 109
principle of finitude, 109
principle of identity, 16–17, 49, 55–56, 218, 222

principle of identity, Derrida's, 218–219
principle of identity, Hegel's, 217–218
principle of identity, Plato's, 217
principle of induction, 11, 122
principle of inertia, 206
principle of negation, 49
principle of noncontradiction, 49, 55
principle of parsimony, 11
principle of permissibility, 208, 212
principle of progress, 207
principle of rarity, 203
principle of redundancy, 50, 65–66
principle of simplicity, 11
principle of sufficient reason, 14, 181
principle of the common cause, 14–15, 180–184
principle of transitivity, 109
principle of universal causation, 14
principle of universal explanation, 181
principle of verifiability, 71–92
principles of identity, 15, 16
principles of inference, ix, 3
probabilistic explanation, 13
probability, 135–143
problem of imperfection, 18
problem of irrelevance, 18
Problems of Philosophy, Russell's, 162
proper, definition of, 8
properties, 55
property, 234
property approach, 8, 62, 65, 69
property interpretation, 57
propositions, 8, 41, 50, 51, 52, 53, 54–55, 56, 67, 245, 254, 255
pseudoproblems, 86
psychology of discovery, 4–5

Q-desires, 104
quantum mechanics, 120, 183
quasi-indicators, 249
question-answer relationship, 26
questioning, 6, 25, 29, 36
questioning as a philosophical method, 25–43
questions and answers, ix, 6, 16, 30, 34, 37

randomness, 144
rational beliefs, 102
rational desires, 101, 102
rational series of desires, 108, 112
rationality, 149–150
realism, 14, 148, 173–174, 177–180
realistic language, 148
realistic language framework, 12
reality, 228, 230–231, 239
reality of time, 10
reasoning, 39
recommendations, 82
reductio ad absurdum, 212
reduction of philosophy to triviality, 266
reduction to triviality argument, 273–275
referents, Frege's, 236
refutations, 17, 21, 128, 133
refutations, philosophical, 17, 21, 128, 227–258
regress, 143
regress arguments, 10
rejection of scientific empiricism, 267
rejection of scientific methodology, 266
research programs, 132
Rules of Reasoning, Newton's, 183

sameness, 16, 236, 237
saying, 39, 40
scientific argument, 131–150
scientific empiricism, 180, 186
scientific explanation, 14, 153–160, 172–189, 191
scientific inference, 146–147
scientific knowledge, 131, 145
scientific method, 25

scientific methodology, ix
scientific realism, 180, 183, 186
scientific reasoning, ix
self-contradiction, 95
self-determinism, 216
Self-Knowledge and Self-Identity, 256
semantic paradoxes, 64, 66, 68
semantical completeness, 46
semantical validity, 50
semantico-syntactical contrasts of ordinary language, 232
semantics, 3, 7, 33, 52, 64
semiological explanations, 15, 195, 204, 206, 209–210, 219
semiological reduction, 212
semiological thinking, 192
sensations, 124–126
sense/referent duality, 237
senses, Frege's, 236
sentential meaningfulness, 9, 78
series of desires, 101, 106, 115
Sherlock Holmes, 33–38
signifiers, 194
simplicity, 120
singular reference, 238
skepticism, 132, 165
social conventions, 204
Socratic method, ix, 25
solutions by definition, 18, 271
Sorites Paradox, 55
sound, definition of, 8
space-time, 121
speaking, 39
special consequence condition, 10
statistical inference, 11, 131, 147
strict identity, 16, 235, 238
subjective appearances, 197
substitutional interpretation, 60
Summa Totius Logicae, Ockham's, 123
Super-Predictor (SP), 82–85
syllogistic logic, 61
symbolic constructs, 202, 204
symmetrical counterparts, 158–160
symmetry of explanation and prediction, 5, 179
synecdoche, 255
syntactical completeness, 46
syntactical determinacy, 20
syntax, 3, 8, 64
synthetic *a posteriori* knowledge, 81

tacit knowledge, 34, 36
taking a position, 200
technical language, 263
teleological explanations, 15, 193, 206, 209–210, 219
teleological reduction, 213
teleological thinking, 192
tensed facts, 10, 96–100
tensional transformation, 221, 223
The First Person, Chisholm's, 245
Theism, 87–90
thematic (synthetic) reasoning, 37
theorems, 46
theoretical and conceptual frameworks, 19, 20
theoretical explanations, 42
theoretical predicates, 135
theoretical reasoning, ix
theoretical significance, 20
Theory and Evidence, Glymour's, 74
Thesis of Semantic Homogeneity of Singular Terms, 237
thinking, 39, 40
Thinking and Doing, Castaneda's, 245, 256
time, 90–92
token, 68
total evidence requirement, 15, 42
Tractatus Logico-Philosophicus, Wittgenstein's, 203
traditional conceptions of logic, 7, 44–70
transcendental argument, Kant's, 216–217

transcendental deductions, 41
transcendental idealism, 215
transcendental reasoning, ix, 15
transcendental thinking, 190–210
transformational grammar, 47
translational notion of form, 46
transubstantiation, 238
trial and error, 17
truth, 64, 65, 67, 68, 69, 72, 79, 177–178, 212, 223, 233, 234, 247, 249–250
truth conditions, 57
truth definition, 58
truth-preserving, 6
Twilight of the Idols, Nietzsche's, 210
two tiered system, Kyburg's, 138
type, 68

unexplained explainers, 15
unintelligibility, 87
unnamed things, 60

valid, definition of, 8

validation, 19, 122
verifiability, 9, 72, 161
verifiability, principle of, 71–92
vicious infinite series, definition of, 94
Vienna Circle, 72, 85
vindication, 19, 122
vorhanden, 202, 205

Ways of Worldmaking, Goodman's, 118
weak verification, 73
well-formed formulae, 47
well-formed sentences, 77
why-necessarily questions, 175
why-questions, 31, 35
why-questions, explanation-seeking, 13
why-questions, reason-seeking, 13
work of art, 222
working definitions, 18, 269
working hypotheses, 18, 269
world of games, 220
worldly sameness, 17, 236, 237

zuhanden, 203, 205

Contributors

JAMES H. FETZER is MacArthur Visiting Professor in the Arts and Sciences at New College of the University of South Florida for 1983-84.

JAAKKO HINTIKKA is Professor of Philosophy at Florida State University.

JAMES CARGILE is Professor of Philosophy at the University of Virginia.

GEORGE SCHLESINGER is Professor of Philosophy at the University of North Carolina at Chapel Hill.

DAVID SANFORD is Professor of Philosophy at Duke University.

J. J. C. SMART is Professor of Philosophy in the Research School of Social Sciences at the Australian National University.

HENRY E. KYBURG, JR., is Burbank Professor of Moral and Intellectual Philosophy at the University of Rochester.

PAUL HUMPHREYS is Assistant Professor of Philosophy at the University of Virginia and Visiting Fellow in the Center for Philosophy of Science at the University of Pittsburgh for 1983-84.

DOUGLAS BERGGREN is Professor of Philosophy at New College of the University of South Florida.

HECTOR-NERI CASTANEDA is Mahlon Powell Professor of Philosophy at Indiana University.

MICHAEL SCRIVEN is University Professor at the University of San Francisco and Professor of Education at the University of Western Australia.